Bruce P. Sanders

The Judgment of History

THE JUDGMENT

OF HISTORY

MARIE COLLINS SWABEY

Associate Professor of Philosophy in New York University

PHILOSOPHICAL LIBRARY   •   NEW YORK

"It is given a man, sir, to attack the rights of others, seize their goods, assault the lives of those who defend their nationality, make of their virtues crimes, and of one's own vices a virtue, but there is one thing beyond the reach of such perversity—the tremendous judgment of history." *Benito Juarez, the Indian, to the Hapsburg Prince Maximilian on his arrival with a French army to make himself emperor of Mexico.*

CONTENTS

FOREWORD

In an age concerned with the redefinition of time and the manufacture of versions of man's past as weapons for shaping his future, there is no need to apologize for another book on history. Today all too many believe that by capturing the arts of representing the past they can control the course of events to come. Since bygone times are said to exist only in men's memories or in mute records and remains, by remoulding or suppressing these, they think they can truly remake the vanished world. While by education and social drill the memories of living generations can be reshaped, the masters of the present can expunge and rewrite the records in line with their future plans. Against this tendency to accept the plasticity of the past and the perversions of myth, this essay is an attempt to state the case for historical truth, the rights of the inviolable past, and for values beyond the flux of temporality.

The following authors and publishers have kindly allowed the use of quotations from the works cited.

Appleton-Century-Crofts, Inc. From *Laura Bridgman* by Laura E. Richards.

Cobbett Press Ltd. From *Decline of the Roman Empire in the West* by F. W. Walbank.

Doubleday and Co. From *The Story of My Life* by Helen Keller.

Dover Publications, Inc. New York 19. From *Language, Truth and Logic* by A. J. Ayer.

E. P. Dutton and Co., Inc. From *On the Writing of History* by Charles Oman.

Henry Holt and Co., Inc. From *The Frontier in American History* by F. J. Turner; from *Human Nature and Conduct* by John Dewey; from *The Ancient Regime* by H. Taine.

Houghton Mifflin Co. From *The Education of Henry Adams* by Henry Adams.

International Publishers. From *The History of the Civil War in the U.S.S.R.* by M. Gorky and others; from *The History of the Communist Party in the Soviet Union* (Little Lenin Library, Vol. XXV); from *Collected Works of V. Lenin,* Vol. XXV; from *Problems of Leninism* by J. Stalin.

A. A. Knopf, Inc. From *The Decline of the West* by Oswald Spengler.

Longmans, Green and Co., Inc. From *The History of England* by G. Trevelyan.

The Macmillan Co. From *Modern Democracies* by James Bryce; from *The Economic Interpretation of the Constitution of the U. S.* and from *The Discussion of Human Affairs* by Charles Beard; from *The Rise of American Civilization* by Charles and Mary Beard; from *The New History* by James Harvey Robinson; from *Science and the Modern World* and *The Adventures of Ideas* by Alfred North Whitehead.

Macmillan and Co. Ltd. From *Comparative Politics* by E. A. Freeman.

W. W. Norton and Co. From *History as the Story of Liberty* by Benedetto Croce.

Oxford University Press. From *History and Historical Problems* by Ernest Scott; from *A Study of History* (abridged by D. C. Somervell) by Arnold Toynbee; from *Civilization on Trial* by Arnold Toynbee.

The Viking Press, Inc. From *The Republic* by Charles Beard.

The Judgment of History

CHAPTER ONE

The Overall Outlook

A COMMON PROPOSAL TODAY is that history should frankly renounce its pretensions to know the past as it was, together
with the claims to omniscience, and impartiality. Uncritical
acceptance of the historian as a kind of overarching spectator
with power to grasp the actual passage of events, to read the
secrets in men's hearts, and to allot to them their just deserts,
is said to have been superseded. Talk of the 'verdict' and 'lessons' of history, of 'niches' and 'places' to be assigned in its
'eternal page' is held to be gone forever. The old notion of it
as a superior court of appeal dispensing decisive praise and
blame, passing sentence on men and movements, deeds and
empires, is dismissed as an outworn delusion. On the contrary,
histories are now said to be always partial, relative, circumscribed, incapable in any respect of finality.

Here as elsewhere scientific knowledge is held to have been
the great enlightener, apprising us that chronicles are written
by specific individuals situationally attached, reflecting their
conditions of life and local factors. Inevitably the account written by a man of one temperament, social class, and political
persuasion will not agree with the presentation of the same
subject offered by a man of different background, period, and
place. History must accordingly, on this view, be rewritten for
every age, if not for every social group as well. From this new
vantage-ground Thucydides, in presuming to make men "know
the exact nature of events that once took place" and in offering

3

his work as "a possession forever," launched a fatal error. For as a so-called father of history he led men to believe that the actual passage of events, regardless of historical perspective, could really be known. Yet all too plainly his own outlook, circumscribed by the views of his age, failed adequately to present to the wider horizons of later times the forces and issues at stake in his subject matter. To understand the Peloponnesian war a modern reader, it is said, would do better to turn to some recent authority who understands as Thucydides did not the complex tendencies at work: class tensions and social needs, the struggle for metals and grains, for colonial and commercial power, of which the military and political events were but a surface indication.

Admittedly in such frank recognition of the historian's thought as existentially determined there is a vein of scepticism and relativism. But many would agree with Carlyle that:

> It is in no case the real historical transaction but only some more or less plausible scheme and theory of the transaction, or the harmonized result of many such schemes, each varying from the other and all varying from the truth, that we can ever hope to behold.[1]

From this angle realists like Ranke who set themselves to describe what 'really happened' without addition or subtraction faced an impossible task. On the contrary, the historian who grasps the inseparability of facts from perspective must repudiate the past as it was; with Charles Beard he must agree that "history as it actually was is not known and cannot be known."[2]

Nevertheless in this conclusion there is something admittedly disappointing. If what occurred cannot be known as it actually occurred, the substance of man's yesterdays seems to resolve into something relative and transitional. To be told that all we can grasp is how things look to our shifting local perspectives gives us, it must be confessed, a certain sense of

---

[1] *Works of Thomas Carlyle* (New York, 1905) Vol. XXVII 'On History,' p. 88.

[2] Charles Beard, *The Discussion of Human Affairs* (New York, 1936) p. 87.

frustration. In place of an absolute past there appears a plasticity in events which enables them to change, as it were, with changes in their description. The old notion of the historian's duty to a sacred, inviolable past becomes suddenly an illusion. Anchored in the living scene, limited to evidence available now, confined to current methods and vistas, this new attitude is functional, utilitarian, in no sense reverential. But if the bygone world as it was is genuinely beyond our reach, what we may ask more specifically is the goal of the historian? To this question many moderns have a ready answer. Just as the satisfaction of man's needs, the improvement of his future course is elsewhere the goal of knowledge, so, they say, the enrichment of his present life is similarly the aim of history. Today no ashes from a bygone world can rule us from their urn, since living is the paramount duty. To use the records of the past to chart men's future good, to find in alternatives tried, experiments made, suggestions for the perplexities of our time, is the historian's vital function.

Fortunately there are those who demur at this outlook and retain respect for traditional historiography. Instead of considering events primarily for their subsequent use, history, they would insist, must study the past for itself as a world we are compelled to accept on the basis of evidence whether it profits us or not. To be sure, present interests often move the historian to inquire and partly determine his work. Nevertheless he distinguishes truth from use, recognizing the truth of his statements to consist in their congruence with the totality of the evidence rather than in their effects upon human fortunes. In historical study as elsewhere the attitude of knowledge is primarily to let the facts speak rather than our interests speak, to view events for their own sake rather than for ours, to exalt the object above the subject. In many fields the great landmarks of human knowledge represent stages in man's escape from self-centeredness, escape from delusion that the world revolves around himself, his culture, his species or his planet. By the long labor of thought his path has led him from circumscribed, utilitarian views to those more theoretical and inclusive. When men turned from practical earth-measuring to the geometrical relations of space, when they linked their development to that of the animal species of earth, when they inquired how planetary motions would appear from the sun, and calculated events in differently moving worlds, they increased their mental stature. By changing places through ideal experiment so to speak, they gained fuller access to reality.

And as the scientist assumes his power to survey men, stars, and atoms in one inclusive scheme without destroying their authenticity, similarly the historian presumes his right to grasp great arcs of human life in a single imaginative experience. Places he has never seen, lives he has never lived, civilizations alien to his own, he takes as open to his scrutiny. Nor is it merely the old fashioned historians who play God as 'omniscient author' in this manner, but the most empirical modern. The latter too in comparing country with country, age with age, other cultures with his own, takes an overall view. In framing hypotheses and performing feats of mental construction impossible to execute literally, he constantly claims to surmount his situational perspective. Taken in good faith, his method implies the freedom of the mind to practice ideal transposition which tacitly belies the premise of his organic imprisonment.

But at this point a naturalist who is strict in his logic may protest. You are going too far, he may object. The historian, being fixed in his life-situation, cannot escape his space-time niche by any trick of fact or theory. The blunt truth is that the historical mind which claims to embrace the long pageantry of the crusades, the rise of kings, their struggle with the church, the growth of parliaments and towns, is matched by no corresponding organism. Actually each man is rooted in his local setting; he cannot see the world with others' eyes or borrowed perspectives. No pretense to the contrary can override his limitations. Being the child of his age, the prisoner of his place, his claims to alien and cosmic views are in the last analysis but fabrications. Actually no modern has shared the medieval's outlook at first hand, lived in ancient Greece, or looked at the world with the eyes of an ancient Egyptian. On a strictly empirical logic such claims to transcendence are patently myths founded on what is physically speaking impossible.

However, for the most part historians like the rest of us do not accept such naturalistic limitations. On the contrary, without hardly giving a thought to the matter the student of the past claims genuine access to other times and cultures. Far from being confined to his natural situation, he roams in knowledge far and wide enjoying a kind of aerial perspective. That human intelligence and imagination should have this power to outreach man's bodily scope seems to him no mystery but the veriest commonplace. Everywhere in speech and action we assume a man's ability to surmount both his organic exclusiveness and his social context. By taking different points of view, by putting himself in others' place, he avoids submergence in his particular existence. Similarly the historian by ideal exchange and hypothetical surveys advances in knowledge. To view other periods as if they were his own, to saturate himself in other times is part of his essential function. Nor does he ordinarily question that such procedure is progressively self-corrective and reliable. To the charge that such exchange of personality and place is the antithesis of naturalism, he would reply that the opposite *insistence on man's situational confinement in a disconnected plurality of frames renders history impossible.* Faced with the naturalistic alternative in this form, it would seem he must either renounce knowledge of the past or frankly acknowledge his assumptions as transcendental. Even to review the events of his own day, the historian must assume that he ideally encompasses the period he is actually encompassed by to gain significance for his judgments.

But in most cases, as was said, the historian is not disturbed by the 'unnatural' and transcendental nature of his assumptions. In his field lack of direct acquaintance is not the exception but the rule. He is accustomed to judge one period from another. Perhaps his deepest assurance is that he can occupy a plurality of frames and move in idea among them in such a way as to preserve their several validities. Just as historical practice assumes that the languages, currencies, calendars, weights and measures of different peoples can be translated into one another, similarly it allows that past purposes and events can with appropriate allowances be rendered in terms intelligible to us today. Though admittedly human attitudes and actions vary from age to age and group to group, it is only by assuming that they alter in some intelligible ratio that the conclusions drawn by men in one period can be understood by those in another.

Nevertheless such relational constancy between perspectives is very different from the static uniformity of empiricists like Hume and Buckle. It escapes the crude monism of assuming nature and human nature identical in all places and times, as controlled by precisely the same unchanging positive laws. To-day many historians would not agree with Hume that "In all nations and ages . . . human nature remains still the same . . . The same motives always produce the same actions."[3] To them his famous advice for the study of classical times would seem naively to oversimplify the issue.

> Would you know the sentiments, inclinations, and course of life of the Greeks and Romans? Study well the temper and actions of the French and English: you cannot be much mistaken in transferring to the former most of the observations which you have made with regard to the latter.

Admittedly study of the tempers and actions of modern men helps us to understand the ancients; admittedly, if not pushed too far, the methods of comparison and analogy are invaluable. Nevertheless your antique Roman is no mere John Bull in a toga speaking Latin prose. To most students of the past the diversities of historical characters and situations seem at least as apparent as their similarities; while accident, individuality, and human purpose go far to override the argument for simple causal determinism. Limits can hardly be set to the variety of human nature and its mutability in action.

[3] David Hume, *An Enquiry Concerning Human Understanding* (Oxford, 1902) Sect. VIII Pt. 1 p. 65.

To support his dogma of man's unalterable sameness everywhere as an empirical fact, Hume is forced to a sweeping environmentalism. Divergence in human characters and affairs are ascribed to external factors, to custom and habit, in the modern phrase to social conditioning. By contrast few writers today are as forthright as he in applying determinism to history by treating the variations of human fortune as no more than an environmental gloss on the 'constant and universal' lineaments of human nature. The reason is plain. Their opponents too pointedly ask: Why, if such principles are satisfactory in explaining the past, do they so signally fail at predicting the future and at controlling the present before our eyes?

In place of supposing original human nature everywhere the same, it would seem wiser, as we have suggested, for the historian frankly to accept its empirical differences and to rely instead on relational common factors. In this way, while allowing for an endless variation in human types and an evolutionary aspect to positive laws, he could still maintain an identity of ordering principles. The basic sameness in history which makes cross-reference possible would seem to be relational, a matter of scale and proportion, rather than of literal sameness of fact. Somewhat as a man with a field glass trusts his deliverances because through changes of focus the patterns of imagery alter proportionately, the student of the past in comparing different peoples and periods draws confidence from a certain relational constancy that persists. Our learned works are filled with statements like the following, accepted as accredited information: "Modern science represents an advance over ancient and medieval science;" "Pithecanthropus possessed essentially human articulate speech;" "Greek sculpture of the fifth century B.C. was superior to that of the third." That such historic cross-reference is possible and is more than a trick of perspective must surely indicate some veritable objective frame which renders phenomena of one period intelligible in terms of another. Were this relational invariance illusory, and were it impossible to compare the diversities of ages and groups, then indeed the historical enterprise would be hopeless. At the same time no pattern of events exactly repeats nor does a particular phenomenon precisely recur. In history as in art each character and scene seems possessed of an inimitable uniqueness, a kind of perpetual youth, each "enjoys," as Croce says, "its own private individuality."[4]

One of the purposes of the present essay is to recall what is in constant danger of being forgotten, namely, that written history is more than a sifting of data and causes in specialized research; that indeed in its reliance on overarching views and a general conception of things it is at bottom philosophical. By penetrating the past with the ideality of thought history claims to grasp the gist of movements, the worth of characters in a wider, fairer way than is usual in the living of actual life. Nevertheless in recent discussions this is by implication all too often denied. The world of the past is held without intrinsic value of its own or total significance. Even if it had such things, it is said, the historian confined to his life situation would be powerless to discover them. For man, on the teaching of naturalism, appears through and through a local creature encompassed by facts. Even his ideas are causal derivatives of the non-ideational matrix, adjuncts of interest and need. Critically interpreted, his judgments of meaning and value are found usually to point the wrong way. That is, they tell us far more of the subjects who hold them than of the objects to which they refer. Moral and political opinions, for instance, express the writer's social habits and bias combined with his organic inclinations. Historical judgments, though appearing to delineate the past, reveal the impact of the present upon the historian enunciating them. The fact is that men turn to the study of the past for means of mastery of present life rather than for genuine understanding. Since by the edict of science logic and values have been put back in their natural frame, history today must forfeit its larger pretensions. The old view of a Great High Court, of an unbiased, omniscient judge dispensing justice from the clouds, is seen as but a legacy from

[4] Benedetto Croce. *History as the Story of Liberty* (trans. by S. Sprigge, New York, 1941) p. 103.

theology. A new orientation is said to be necessary. Since naturalism admits no cosmic mind distinct from limited human mentalities, the historian must give up posturing as divinity. Quite frankly he must admit that there are as many 'histories' of events as there are writers of them, each with its ruling perspective; and since all perspectives are partial and partisan, all histories must be likewise.

Yet, as we have suggested, those who look more deeply into the matter reject this view. In practice few thinkers in the fields employing historical categories (including astronomy, physics, biology, and the other natural sciences) accept historical relativism. By implication they deny that accounts of the past are wholly relative to the proponents of them and their circumstances. Such a position, they realize, makes knowledge untenable. For to the complete relativist, who rejects the *a priori*, all knowledge is historical. Yet if no historical assertion is in any respect unconditionally true, and all assertions are historical, there is no truth in his saying so. His view, being on its own terms but the product of local, changing conditions and circumstances, cannot claim to be binding on others. By confessing itself wholly relative, historical relativism negates its own pretensions to proof and to establish validity. The difficulty is ancient and unanswerable. Psychologically, of course, the historical relativist wishes to suggest the relativity of all views save his own as to the absoluteness of relativity. In labelling other outlooks as partisan, he insinuates his own views as non-partisan, that while other accounts reflect mere local attachment, his has a kind of overarching detachment. Yet this tacit exception in his own favor destroys confidence in him and his rule.[5] If all judgments are biased, his is also; if all outlooks are attached and exclusive, his cannot be detached and inclusive. In the attempt to discredit others, the relativist discredits himself, exposing by the force of his argument the untenability of his assumptions.

---

[5] Nor can he find an 'out' by way of a meta-language, since the rule establishing the distinction that "No language can refer to itself," to be meaningful must include this very language in its negation.

Fortunately belief in the objectivity of values and a universal scheme remains firm in certain quarters. To common sense and the more philosophical historian, neither sceptical relativism nor any materialistic explanations of science can finally supersede reliance on the inspective power of consciousness in its integrity. Presumably the strongest evidence in favor of the objectivity of meanings and values (as being really what they purport to be) is to be found in the study of consciousness, its power to comprehend and certify its own deliverances. That reliance on its authority is widespread is plain to anyone who considers the procedures of practical life in fields like politics, medicine, law, and business. Much is accepted in these fields as objective that is actually beyond physical check. Credence is placed in the awareness, memory, and judgment of witnesses whose testimony is assumed trustworthy and informative till proved to the contrary. Issues of life and death are decided through reliance on the ability of men to report their own motives, to remember past situations aright, to evaluate and reason things out correctly. In all this there is acceptance of the inner agency of men's minds as revealed through the coherent texture of their lives and expressions. Histories written in this vein assert that men may fight for a righteous cause, make war to defend cherished values, and even assume that these values are ingredient in reality. Obviously this view is the reverse of that of relativistic naturalism. To the latter, man being a creature of circumstance must have his conscious deliverances finally checked in alien terms. Being the product of a maze of subliminal processes, human awareness as such cannot be trusted to comprehend itself or to give on its own a reliable account of the world. Hence it is not by accepting men's professed purposes and reports at their face value, but by tracing their underlying determinants that history must be written. A war, for instance, that the combatants themselves honestly depict as being fought for liberty and democracy will almost certainly be described by naturalistic historians in very different and less flattering terms. Because the participants in events rarely comprehend them, their conscious record may be hardly more than a surface accompaniment of underlying mechanisms.

But against such current tendencies of naturalism, writers who hold consciousness the seat of authority must protest. Any account which dissolves human character into environmental factors, they would urge, must in the long run discredit itself. For when history, the study of human affairs made by men for men regarding men as its chief subject matter, denies the point of view of man himself, it tends to absurdity. In refusing to treat conscious personality as self-directive on its own terms, authors destroy faith in their work. Instead of a judge and critic of the historical process, the historian becomes a mere eddy in the stream, a flotsam on the tide of events. Hidden states of affairs control his account of affairs, and when he imagines he sits in judgment of the past direct him to ends he neither knows nor intends. For once he assumes that men's versions of the flux are no more than products of the flux, he must apply the same canon to his own activity with consequent bankruptcy. On the other hand, as we have seen, his failure to do this (by making an exception in his own favor) involves him in self-contradiction. Though eager to regard other men's works as the product of environing forces, it is as the expression of his own free consciousness that he regards his own. He cannot bring himself to deny that his ideas and judgments really mean what they claim to mean, he cannot renounce his inner light. Yet if he distrusts and impugns others' conscious versions of the past, he cannot without inconsistency trust his own. To the degree that he envisions others' laborious, long-meditated researches as but precipitates of social forces, situational bias, and irrelevant conditioning, he must apply the same principles to his own work. But in so doing, histories as history—in one case as in the other—become of slight account. Instead of faithful records of the past, they become but reflections of present influences upon the authors.

The implications of these remarks will become apparent in the ensuing chapters. To begin with, it is interesting to recall that the movement which began with Descartes in modern thought made self-certification by reflective consciousness the supreme test, and so broke with the argument from authority. Today a new authoritarianism rears its head, not in the guise of theology but of science and the so-called 'compulsions of nature.' Today history is experiencing the effects of great advances in other fields. Borrowing their conclusions, emulating their techniques, the student of the past is led to view the world with new eyes. The burden of this shift of emphasis is for him to interpret human lives as far as possible through their physical backgrounds, the conscious through the unconscious, the individual through his social setting. Most revolutionary of all is the effort wholly to naturalize human intelligence. Once mentality is regarded simply as a natural growth, as a late product of organic change with a social office to perform, the inward side of human life undergoes a profound reorientation. Subjective awareness, ideal values, judgments, and goals are no longer taken at their old rating, but are subordinated to alien forces for constitutive and veto power. Consciousness with its running commentary dissolves as a touchstone of life; selves or persons lose their status as first causes, creative agents, explanatory wholes. In being naturalized, as we have seen, the work of the historian forfeits its claim to decisive, embracing knowledge. Being situationally determined, his productions are held to be relative to their source. But to the degree that his background rules his work, admittedly he tends to beg issues in advance. He forces his scheme of valuations upon a bygone world. And through injecting his views into the subject viewed, his 'history' becomes less a description of another age than a projection of his own.

Yet the historian, we shall urge, never really accepts such situational confinement. Just as the scientist is generally allowed to conceive nature or evolution as a whole, so the historian claims power to conceive the total historical process. Usually, of course, he is concerned only with some fragment of it. He considers, for instance, the growth of an institution like feudalism or the Catholic church, something which no medieval pope or baron implanted in the process could fully trace. Yet whether a participant or mere spectator of the events he describes, the historian succeeds to the degree that he not merely penetrates but rises above the scene, surveys it from a wider base, triangulates from a farther horizon. Inevitably the wealth of facts he confronts is incompressible to his scale of representation. The necessity for abridgement compels him to formulate a philosophy. In deciding what to omit and what to include, he is forced to appraise things in their larger relevancy. If his work is to be more than a miscellany, it must handle critical turning-points by relating things to each other in the light of a foreground and background and a general view of the world. Directly or indirectly his account will disclose his conception of life, mind, society, and the forces involved in them; while his ideas on these matters will operate to control the narrative no less than the burden of facts. For instance, in ordering and relating influences decision must be made as to whether material forces always preponderate in shaping the patterns of history, or whether they are but part of the story; in short, whether mind and the values clustering round it are in themselves genuine sources of action and on occasion decisive. However much the author may wish to escape such problems, he cannot do so. Because the relation of man to his world enters into the very stuff of history, the historian must claim knowledge of such issues or admit that he is wandering in blind mazes of encircling ignorance.

CHAPTER TWO

Alternative Perspectives

THE SUSPICION THAT HISTORY proves that anything can be proved by history is unavoidable to anyone seriously concerned with the past. For the record of the world's events is essentially construed by human minds and as such shares the conflicting variety of perspectives that gave them birth. Considering the countless diversity of outlooks possible to man on man, there is nothing surprising in the inexhaustible variety of tales he tells about himself. His histories are themselves products of history, precipitates, it would appear, of obscure webs of conditions in the natural matrix. Ruling notions often dictate his accounts; presuppositions determine his arrangement of the facts; personal preference orders their importance so that they prove what is expected of them.

Today we are coming to realize how largely social circumstance controls men's thinking, how group interests prescribe their outlooks in advance. Planted by nature in some narrow habitat, fed with the influences of his surroundings, a man might seem to outrun his shadow more easily than to free himself from the unconscious localisms coloring his views of life, politics, and the culture of the past. How can he doff the pervasive emotions, transcend the natural determinants, that make him the product of his country and his time? Not merely his physical context, but his wants, needs, occupation guide his reading of the evidence. Just as the view that wars and monarchs shape history appears almost inevitable to writers under strong dynastic governments, so the economic view seems no less so to authors bred in industrialism with its violent periodic shifts. As social pressures alter from age to age, historians vary in their analyses. They veer with the weather. If their versions of causal factors change, it is because they too are subject to the law of social exigency and follow the main chance of fortune and popularity. In this sense the historian's chronicles are often 'inspired,' since the social or political version profitable in one age may well prove fatal in another. So circles abound in accounts of the past; and the impression is hard to resist that a man's findings are largely governed by his conception of things, while his interests govern his conception.

Yet if it is possible to avoid mistaking what is assumed from what is proved in history, notice must be taken of certain broad convictions underlying credible narration. To begin with, no historian doubts that there has been a past, a state of affairs once existent, now non-existent, although its genuineness remains beyond direct empirical check, since he can never make the past recur. However unlikely the hypothesis may appear, it is always possible that what he takes to be the past in any specific case may be only an imperious phantom of present fancy. Access to by-gone events would seem to be by way of memory, inference, and imagination. Only by supposing that previous generations faced a world much like our own and were equipped with related motives, organs, and interests, can we hope to understand their lives. Differences, though admitted, must be construed by tracing orderly modifications backward from present states of affairs. In brief, if we would comprehend these other times, we must do so through analogy with our own experience, assimilating the remote to the near, others to ourselves, by adjustment of scale and perspective.

Again there is the assumption of historical truth. Usually students of the past take for granted that, as opposed to all possible or imaginable ways in which events might have come about, there is a single, definite manner of their occurrence. Disclosure of this actual course of events, though all too often beyond our reach, remains the goal of historical investi-

gation. As such it is held to be antecedent to and distinct from
the multiple opinions or reports in regard to it. Once true that
a given event occurred, it is always true that it did so, even
though the knowledge be lost to posterity.[1] (To this
view, relativism remains an exception.) But to suppose
historical verity possible of attainment involves auxiliary
assumptions: for instance, that human beings are capable of
reliably reconstructing episodes in periods with which they
have had no bodily acquaintance. Thus the claims made by
twentieth century Englishmen to give trustworthy accounts
of events that occurred in the second millennium B.C. in the
Egypt of Tutankhamen or at the Minoan court in Crete seem
to imply the power of the historian's thought to transcend its
local station and to visit scenes with which as a natural man he
could have had no face-to-face acquaintance. Taken at its
face value, as unimpeachably doing what it purports to do,
this pretension of the historian to the role of virtually ubiqui-
tous spectator, able to leap from generation to generation, race
to race, clime to clime, and to penetrate the lives of men long
dead, puts our faith in history to the supreme test.

In supposing such truth capable of attainment, trust is
implied not merely in human veracity and ability to weigh
the probative value of facts, but in the capacity of mute
records and remains to bear witness of them. For the interpretation of signs as indicative of events is essential to history.
In a bodily sense, we repeat, we can neither visit its vanished
world nor can it come to us. Entrance must be had through
the gateway of memory or intuitive faith, through others'
testimony or speechless relics. Shapes seen, fragments found,
manuscript markings are one and all seized upon, and through

---

[1] Truth, we should say, is the logical integration of the totality of evidence
with the referent of which it is evidence. Though knowledge of the truth
(mental integration of the total evidence and its imputed referent) may be
lacking (since most truth is undiscovered or forgotten), nevertheless the
coherent pattern of relevant terms, relations, and evidence remains once true
always true. Truth then, while independent of the belief of existing minds,
depends on logic or on mind as such, so that if men gain a logically comprehensive nexus of evidence supporting an event, they will accept the event as
true.

analogy with present experience construed as indices of events in a dead, lost world. That the periodic laws of nature, the changes of seasons and crops, the life cycles of animals, the drives of men operated then much as now appears a natural supposition. Although the individuality of history centers in the differences of different times, it is nonetheless only through some continuity and identity in the process that we are able to understand what the past was like. Some common ground inevitably serves as our bridge of interpretation. Were discontinuity and dissimilarity the key to the past, history would resolve into myth and superstition. While admitting no duplication, we must yet suppose that yesterday, today, and tomorrow are of a piece, parts of a totality in which current clues may suffice to trace the lineaments of other times. Far from being incongruous with belief in change, this assumption merely recognizes that some background of unchanging conditions is necessary to make the detection of change possible. For instance, through comparing rock implements used by savages today with stone relics found in fossil beds of inferred geologic date, the archeologist claims to penetrate prehistory. By assuming constant relations in change (that things alter in orderly ways according to decipherable laws), he deduces from similar artifacts the activities of our early ancestors. Were this supposition illusory, and were it impossible to infer from conclusions got under certain conditions to conclusions under others, because no functional dependency held between them, then indeed the basis of historical knowledge would be open to question.

So inseparably connected is our knowledge of the past with the survival of relics that it is often said "Without records and remains, no history." Indeed, false currency is sometimes gained for this truism through ambiguous use of the term 'history,' which may be taken to stand either for *events themselves* or for *their record,* either for the *course of affairs* or the *verbal description* of them. In consequence, the saying "No records and remains, no history" is occasionally equivocally construed to suggest "No present clues, no past events" rather

than "No present clues, no knowledge of them." Yet although
records and remains are plainly a necessary condition of our
knowing of past occurrences, few historians would accept the
sophistry that they are the sufficient condition of their happening. To be sure, in the absence of hieroglyphics and cunei-
form tracing we should know little of the dynasties of ancient
Egypt and Mesopotamia; yet this is no equivalent to asserting
that had these sources not survived, the original dynasties
would not have been. Knowledge of the past, the past itself,
and present traces are quite different matters for the historian,
as the existence of many enigmatic ruins and undecipherable
inscriptions show.

Of course, the records of history may be part of the history,
and relics not merely signs of episodes but fragments of them
as well. Yet while the monuments, inscriptions, regalia of
men's lives frequently outlast them, these hardly speak for
themselves, but remain mere cast-off husks, dead trappings,
until assigned their place through the work of historical interpretation. Charlemagne's faded coronation robes in St. Peter's,
Bonaparte's abdication letter at Fontainebleau are but symbols,
trifling hints of the founding of the Holy Roman Empire in
800 or of the collapse of the Napoleonic Empire in 1814. Nor
does critical inquiry suppose that the preservation of relics
from subsequent destruction was essential to the original
events. The occurrences were what they were, regardless of
the eventualities that were to follow. Usually the historian
regards his evidence as a means of knowing about the past,
rarely as a turning-point in the action itself. To the best of our
knowledge it was irrelevant to the issue of the battle of Salamis
that one of the combatants was probably Aeschylus, a writer
of genius, who left to posterity in *The Persians* what appears
to be an eye-witness account of it.

Explicitness on a point so obvious as that the traces left by
events and their preservation, are not essential to the events
themselves is necessary owing to the vogue enjoyed by certain
recent theories. As part of the broader doctrine that things are
reducible to their consequences, the thesis which resolves

history into its eventualities gains equivocal support. By trading on the indispensability of records and remains, the inseparability of the known from the means by which it is known, the absurdity is suggested that the past as we know it is nothing but its effects. No fallacy is more insidious in history than that of confusing inseparability with sameness, of mistaking the evidence conveying the facts for the facts conveyed, the means of knowing with the object known. Too often, through the weakness of human nature, some after-effect that gains emphasis tends to bulk larger and larger in people's minds till it is all but identified with the events it reports. Against such dangers the historical student must be continually on his guard. Just as a few snap-shots taken on a pleasure trip become a substitute for the experiences of the trip or a dramatic tale of adventure may replace the adventure, so elsewhere in dealing with the past views are converted into the objects viewed, the map becomes the terrain, the reports replace the facts reported, and the mind salutes a bastard truth.

One of the most difficult problems of history is to decide what constitutes history, to agree in advance what it aims to disclose. Like science its inquiry seems to embrace a dual function. While the scientist, on the one hand, is concerned with giving a faithful description of facts, on the other, he has the equally important task of construing them in relation to some explanatory conjecture. Similarly the historian has a double duty: both of reporting the past as nearly as possible as it passed or was lived through by men at the time (without doctoring up events to fit later developments or some 'more enlightened' reading of them); and, second, of interpreting their import in the light of a present hypothesis. Here the modern historian, equipped with a fund of comparative and scientific information, is undeniably able to perceive many more factors at work shaping events, and to see them in different relative significance, than did their actual contemporaries. Nevertheless his task is still to rank these influences in order, allowing each its fitting weight, but in so doing to guard against confusing his hypothesis with the data.

To interpret past psychological events in terms of categories foreign to the time, which the participants could not wittingly have used in their decisions, is to be guilty of a kind of anachronism. Yet the temptation is almost irresistible in the light of later knowledge to read a more sophisticated comprehension of situations into the minds of historical characters than they could possibly have had. A twentieth century writer viewing the Napoleonic wars in the light of subsequent social conceptions may be led to portray Napoleon as the Fascist betrayer of the French Revolution or as the voice of capitalist imperialism speaking to rival imperialisms in the economic cockpit of Europe. The fact that Napoleon apparently looked upon his career quite differently as an end carved by personal ambition, while many contemporaries invoked the cult of genius and divine destiny, may to all intents and purposes be disregarded. In errors of this sort lies the hazard of the modernization of history. Current inquiry with the latest social and scientific aids may be able to furnish more varied techniques by which to estimate historical significance. Yet it cannot alter that bygone life as it was lived in a world without comprehension of certain causes apparent only to later enlightenment. To distinguish the description of happenings as they occurred from the import put upon them by later advances in knowledge may seem well-nigh impossible; yet in this consists the dual task of historical writing, a task in which the scrupulous performance of the first may be a condition of success in the second.

Broadly speaking histories reveal men's views of life and the world and the forces involved in them. Their overtones are metaphysical without intending to be so. Accordingly, it is no surprise to find reflected in the major outlooks of such works the chief contrasts of perspective that have influenced mankind. Some of these we shall discuss in the ensuing chapters. As historians of history are fond of pointing out, man's earliest records are largely of a mythical sort: stories of creation, cosmologies, wild and wonderful tales of gods contending with heroes. In them men's powers of logical, factual, and moral discrimination appear as yet rudely developed. A childlike inquisitiveness seems conjoined with an unbounded appetite for marvels and an almost total absence of criticism. Dragons, prodigies, miraculous feats pass unchallenged, while the most ferocious, inhuman acts are casually recounted without apparent indignation.

Yet slowly as the record of experience grows, entries become more factual and annalistic. Stories of the origin of the world, of battles of gods with men, tend to recede into the background in favor of more mundane occurrences. The line between the possible and the impossible begins to be more clearly drawn as reason throws fetters over the imagination. Instead of the great cloudy questions of whence and whither, concern shifts to a more familiar neighboring past and more workaday happenings. Genealogies, lists of kings, battles, eclipses now appear as landmarks and begin to provide a framework for chronology. As the poetry and wonder fades, the common sense attitudes of practical life come increasingly to occupy the foreground. Strings of proverbs, biographies, and episodes connected by 'and' reflect men's lack of a clear-cut overall outlook, their collector's instinct and prosy garrulity. Then imperceptibly the historian's vision suffers a further change. In addition to human incidents and practical lore he develops an interest in dissecting the causes of things, in tracing their roots in their natural setting. More and more events are seen to take their rise from each other as products of involved trains of influences. Concern with causes sharpens his eye for the gradual, the inconspicuous, and the collective, while increasing awareness of social wholes weans him from personal narration to a more analytic approach. Nor is this the end of the matter. Not content with fashioning fables, chronicling events, dramatizing biographies, deciphering causes, historians seek to judge the world. Indeed, it is hard to deny that it is only with the emergence of clear logical connections and valuational judgments that history comes of age. As Charles Oman puts the matter (illustrating from the annals of ancient Palestine and early England):

Real historical perspective comes when among the bald annalistic
record of judges' names we find inserted the hero-stories of Gideon,
Barak, or Jephthah ... 'There was no king in Israel and every man did that
which was right in his own eyes.' Historical perspective has arrived and
deductions are made. The same is the case with the Anglo-Saxon Chronicle, when the compiler, breaking away from his arid yearly entries,
taken from some earlier annalistic screed, bursts out in indignation
against the wickedness of his own days. 'The earth bears no corn . . .
The land is all ruined by evil deeds.' . . . Such commentary in Palestine
or England implies the beginnings of reasoning and judgment on cause
and effect. The chronicler is making himself the exponent of the thought
of his generation and expresses its opinions as to the consequences of a
political tendency or a moral degeneracy which has begun to work itself
out.[2]

In comparing one age or society with another for decline
or improvement, the keeper of the past has set out on the long
road to find a logical structure and frame of values in the flux,
to develop what may be called a philosophic view. However
imperfectly, he is striving to raise himself above the temporal
flood, to reach a generality of outlook proper to the spokesman
of an age or even to a universal judge. With the emergence of
the search for an underlying framework of sanctions and war-
rants, evils and goods, consequents and grounds, we have the
appearance of the philosophic spirit.

Passing over the early legends and myths in which wide-
eyed wonder and license of invention makes almost everything
disputable, we shall consider in the ensuing chapters what may
not improperly be called: the 'common sense,' the 'scientific,'
and 'philosophic' views of history. As already suggested, this
three-fold division is perhaps most naturally treated as an
order of temporal development, since it seems not too difficult
to show how historical thought passed from a naive, untechnical outlook (often called the 'childhood of the race') to tech-
nicality, how analysis and scientific views emerged from
traditional, common sense notions, to be supplemented in turn
by deepening philosophical perspective. Nevertheless it would
be a mistake to suppose that these attitudes are always sharply

2 Charles Oman, *On the Writing of History* (1939, New York) pp. 82-83.

separated or wholly confined to different periods, writers or schools. Perhaps there is a dash of the hero-worshipper and legend-maker, the traditional chronicler and scientific analyst, the sage and Olympian in every great historian. Despite differences of emphasis, the historical impulse seems finally to combine them all, since in addition to telling tales, and sifting facts, men set themselves to judge the world.

Yet the division of possible attitudes in history may be made in another way. Instead of being regarded as historical stages, they may be taken as correlative modes of procedure. Usually the student of history pays little attention to this distinction. Nevertheless in the nature of knowledge there are three orders: an *historical* one of temporal genesis, an *analytic* one from effects to causes, and lastly an order of evidence or *logical dependence* involving relevancies or grounds. In history assertions are found to fall into one of these three patterns: (1) the temporal, as when I say that "Hitler's invasion of Poland was followed by the outbreak of the second world war;" (2) its reverse or the statement of causal analysis that "The outbreak of the second world war was caused by Hitler's invasion of Poland;" or (3) one of logical dependence as in saying "Hitler's aggression in Poland and disregard of treaties was a reason for the war." To associate these three orders with the *common sense*, the *scientific*, and the *philosophic* attitudes in history seems also broadly feasible, since the scientist is essentially concerned with causal analysis, the layman with temporal genesis, and the philosopher with logical relevancies or grounds. But at this point in tracing back his threads to their source, the student of the past becomes aware of intricacies in his assumptions he had little suspected. His historical procedure, he now sees, claims the power to reverse and to transcend the temporal sequence. While the first of these orders is temporal, the others are definitely not. But if the historian assumes the validity of both the temporal and non-temporal orders which he traverses, the question arises as to which of them is basic and tests the rest. The task, for instance, of a student of the recent war is to try to reconstruct from

archives and evidence available now its grounds and precipitating influences. But to analyze its temporal sequence he
finds that he mus' pass over it in reverse. Only by studying
records here and now, and working backward from the given,
can he gain access to the there and then. From materials in
the present he builds his conception of those earlier years
and reconstitutes the historical succession. By picking to pieces
the traces of events, he claims to learn how they came about,
the original manner of their occurrence. Continually, without
realizing it, he concedes his power through the order of analysis
to grasp the genetic order of becoming.

Nevertheless the historian in most cases stops short of
accepting the claims of analysis in their entirety. He cannot
quite believe that in knowledge order makes no difference, and
that backward and forward are one and the same. Can history
really show by its method that Hitler's invasion of Poland was
the cause of the war? Somehow the irreversibility of time
lingers as a feeling in his bones. He hesitates to concede that
the analytic regress can fully recapture the progress of events,
although to this the scientist seemingly finds no objection.
By taking things apart, the scientific mind claims to learn the
secret of their genesis. Synthesis is to it the correlative of
analysis, composition one with reduction, the same process
unfolding in opposite ways. Being concerned with the measurable and repeatable, the scientist can afford to ignore the
many unique, qualitative features that fail to survive his
transformations. To him it makes no difference if in the decom-
position of a chemical compound, the texture, aroma, and
usage characteristic of its combination are lost on the way.
What matter that our table salt, for instance, so white, solid,
and healthful, when reduced to its elements yields a waxy
instable metal and a greenish poisonous gas? Scientifically
regarded the important thing is not this evaporation of characters but that the *experiment is reversible,* and that in the
process the number and weight of components remains
throughout the same.

But against reasoning of this sort applied to history your

traditional common sense historian vigorously protests. The fact that an unchanged residuum persists through change is far from proving, in his eyes, that analysis and synthesis are equivalent. Even in the simplest instance, he would urge, the student of the past cannot perform the inversion of an historical process or recreate its character from isolated bits. Unable to 'looking-glass' time or to retrieve the passing moment, he is helpless to persuade the smallest iota of history to unroll backwards. To build or destroy a city, a great man's life or a culture, equating its construction and destruction for all to see, is patently beyond his scope. Lacking the power to repeat, to experiment, to control, the historian is obliged to content himself for the most part with qualitative appraisals and the descriptive narration of events. Somehow although historical factors seem cumulative, their subtraction by increments in an imaginative reversal fails to reveal a law of the process.

Again the historian, unlike the scientist, is rarely the observer of the things he describes. Usually his persons and situations have disappeared. To summon them he must resort to subjective representation and, aided by fragmentary remains, try to recreate imaginary counterparts of the originals. Things he has never seen (Roman triumphs, Druid rites, famous battles and debates), he yet claims to know by virtue of their likeness to things present or remembered. Perhaps memory more than anything else provides the key to the past, initiating faith in its recovery. Because, it may be said, each has a power of revival in himself, a kind of private register, men find it easy to believe in historical knowledge. By assuming an extension of memory, as it were, in tradition and cultural modes of transmission, they extend their assurance to a wider horizon. Unquestionably in this appeal to inner verification and to the funded recollections of earlier men, history claims the distinction of appeal to an intuitive element. That memory claims a core of authentic reversion, the presence of the absent, can scarcely be gainsaid. Nevertheless the old soldier recalling his campaigns knows that he is not really refighting the battles of his youth. In reviving the past he does not literally fuse with it. A saltation, a gap remains between the subject and object of belief. Union with the past is no bodily face-to-face return to a previous state of affairs. Philosophically speaking, we may revert to it *truly* but not *really*, by an imputation of feeling and cognitive intent. Nevertheless, as the common sense historian would point out, he who remembers a scene participates in it in a way in which the later analyst can never share. Just as the intimacy of one's perceptions is lost to an outsider, so no account by later inquirers can replace the testimony of an experience recalled at first hand. No elaboration of outside views, no scientific hypothesis based on a patchwork of indirect clues can supersede the impressions of eye-witnesses. Despite its shortcomings memory and its transmission have a status in knowledge which external analysis cannot displace. It supplies the sense of familiarity, of living continuity which binds the threads of the present to the past.

Yet while faith in memory inspires the traditional writer and layman, just as faith in analysis inspires the historian of scientific bent, this is not the whole of the matter. In addition to analytic inversion and the flash-back of memory, the student of the past relies on a factor of logical insight, which neither reverses the historical order nor vicariously lives through it, but surveys it in the order of evidence. Instead of backtracking from effects to causes or practicing imaginative revival (aided by original sources), he may seek some larger nexus of meanings and dependencies in events. Historians who emphasize such factors we have called philosophical. In their view it is possible, without exact knowledge of causes, to trace relevancies in the course of affairs and to find reasons to root one action in another. Such writers are more concerned with trying to gain an intelligible explanation why things happened than to register the temporal and proportional sequence of their happening. As Croce puts the matter: "The strength of historiography lies in being able to find the reasons behind every event and in being able to assign a place and office to each event in the drama of the epoch."[3] Though Croce goes too far in his excision of cause altogether from historical inquiry, many would agree with him that its scientific pretensions are largely unjustifiable. Certainly historians have been far more successful, for instance, in presenting the grounds of Rome's fall (by elucidating the implications of wealth, war, slavery, unwieldy size, slackening moral fiber, and corrupt government as applied to it) than they have in establishing any exact weight or temporal sequence of the precipitating factors. For grounds, unlike causes, depend for their confirmation rather on the logical relevancy and inclusiveness of the evidence than on correlations, predictiveness, and empirical test. Indeed, it is only because it is possible to obtain general knowledge of the reasons for events without precise information as to their causes, that from early times in advance of 'scientific' techniques the work of the historian has been credited.

In the ways that men have envisioned the world historically, the lay tradition has predominated. That is to say, in large part writers have framed their work on the conceptions and testimony of laymen. Despite an infiltration of more comprehensive notions, they have viewed the world with common sense eyes: as a succession of actions, incidents, lives, largely connected by 'and' without a clear-cut enveloping frame to link them together. Even great writers like Gibbon and Macaulay remain largely within this tradition: scholarly, cultivated laymen, cosmically nebulous, incipient in their use of scientific and philosophic categories. If asked to describe common sense, one would say that its outlook embodies the ordinary attitudes of everyday business. Its 'spontaneous convictions' bred of familiar use and unaided perception seem to clothe the scene the moment we open our eyes. Unlike science, common sense does not depend on involved analyses, instruments of precision,

---

[3] Benedetto Croce, *ibid.*, p. 184. In declaring (p. 28) that "The concept of cause . . . should remain outside history because it was born in the realm of natural science and its place is there," Croce fails to recognize that the historian, even though unable to determine 'the' cause, may suggest contributing causes with a qualitative probability.

quantitative experiment; unlike philosophy, it does not discern
an overall meaning or the action of logical forces in events.
'Persons' and 'things' are its chief characters: men battling
obstacles, conquering and being conquered, wresting subsistence from surroundings which are the foil to their vital activities. There is a self-centeredness, an earthiness about it; its
ends are near at hand: goods to be seized, had, enjoyed: a
localism and humanism, an obviousness in its perceptions
unlike the far-flung world of science and philosophic
speculation.

But whether common sense can any longer be trusted in the
writing of history is today the question. We do not need to be
told that science claims to have rewritten our cosmology, our
canons of knowledge, even our interpretation of the springs of
human action. In the face of these changes traditional histories
come often to seem strangely naive. The schemes of princes,
the strategy of generals, the politics of legislators are no longer
taken at their old rating. The history of China, for instance,
long written by literary scholars as a tale of emperors and their
favorites, dynasties and wars, with the 'good' and 'bad' times
said to have been induced by them, is today looked at differently. In works written under scientific influence, social and
biological forces are commonly held to have shaped events far
more than these. Inquiry is held necessary into methods of
agriculture, population laws, the effects of diseases, and of a
vegetable diet; nor must the consequences of such things as
the patriarchal family system, the use of ideographs, and the
nemesis latent in unmobilized resources be overlooked. Once
such long-range, hitherto neglected influences be admitted as
critical factors, the historian's interest in wars, rulers, and
politics is greatly reduced. Events are not necessarily as they
seemed to be to those who took part in them, or even to their
immediate successors. An era of apparently peaceful progress
may, in the light of later critical analysis, be shown to have
been an unperceived decline or the preluding stages to disaster. The task of disentangling true from apparent causes,
local disturbances from large scale trends, of distinguishing

hidden springs of action from current creeds and catch-words, is not for the layman but to be left to expert hands.

More and more writers who take science as their mentor tend to withdraw trust in common sense reports. In their eyes, the uninstructed versions of laymen absorbed in obvious issues remain blind to major forces at work. Without proper tools of procedure, their record becomes hardly more than a surface accompaniment of the hidden march of events. The connection between men's lives and the network of influences that shape them remains beyond ordinary detection. No mere statesmen or scholars could grasp the maze of economic forces, the action of genetic crosses and microbes transforming their world. Personalities and their purposes threaten to lose their old primacy in affairs; instead of men's wills and initiative, we have analysis of mass movements, collective causes, scientific laws. Thus old themes give place to new; and the play of social mechanisms tends to supplant the old dramas of conflicting ambitions, of spirit warring with flesh, of vested powers stormed by the forces of outraged justice. Instead of taking the world dualistically with the layman, there is a resurgent belief in the seamless web of the 'natural,' in which material circumstance calls forth and in the last analysis is responsible for the direction of human activities.

Yet despite the scientific and to a lesser degree the philosophic tendencies of the day, there are still those who maintain that written history begins and ends in the interpretation of the past by laymen. Probably the strongest argument in favor of the common sense way of looking at things is neither its ancient origin nor practical use, but our inability not to believe in it. Try as we will we cannot free ourselves from the belief that our naive feelings and perceptions, unspoilt by critical analysis, furnish us with a reliable picture of the world. However purged of 'errors' by science, its outlines persist as before. Trust in the intuitions of daily living, in memory, and tradition is almost irresistibly invasive. Obviously without a microscope in hand, we cannot see a microscopic world; and once our scientific instruments are put by, we lose their fine-grained

discriminations and revert to the layman's categories. By viewing human actions from the inside (dramatically, sympathetically, analogically) and not simply from the outside, it is
urged, we gain true understanding of history. Broadly men are
to be taken as they take themselves and each other in daily
give-and-take: as accountable 'persons' endowed with purposive choice, engaged with 'things' in a substantive setting.
Moreover, the language of everyday life (as opposed to the
symbols of science) is still found adequate for history. Records
are always recorded for an audience. And if you ask for what
audience histories are written, the answer is for laymen. Not
perhaps for quite the plainest man in the street absorbed in
immediate practical affairs, but at any rate for the untechnical
reader interested in the larger panorama of human fortunes.
In the next chapter we shall pursue these contrasts further,
amplifying the common sense perspective in history with illustrations from traditional authors.

CHAPTER THREE

Common Sense History

To the Outlook of Everyday Living, most men seem peculiarly attached. The tenets of common sense, they hold, tell us what the world is really like; and it is on these that traditional history has largely framed its views. Not only is common sense the realm in which we spend the major portion of our waking lives, but its categories claim especial allegiance and authority. History, being knowledge that has suffered least abstraction from daily life, shares many common sense assumptions. Its narratives are compact with 'things' and 'persons,' their uses and actions, characters and worths. For the most part its happenings are endowed with moral and sensory properties as part of themselves, and accepted at their face value. Far from being regarded as mere imputations of the reader or beholder or as effects of organic response, concrete impressions are taken as belonging to the very fabric of events. Things felt, seen, and heard are taken as they appear. Nor does it occur to the traditional historian to push his processes of proof beneath the surface of human action. The reports of unaided perception, the expositions of laymen serve him as adequate accounts of the past. Personal recollections, garrulous chronicles, the literary rehearsals of scholars suffice as materials; while in his own pages he employs graphic narration, moral appraisals, and vivid sensory appeal.

How far this natural historical method diverges from a strictly scientific historiography needs hardly to be pointed

out. For science questions the informational value of most of
our affective and appreciative deliverances regarding the
world. Today conflict with the lay tradition is evident on every
hand,—to the extent that depreciation of traditional, common
sense works passes in certain quarters as the mark of historical
expertness. Weighed by modern standards, older writers tend
to be severely judged: as credulous of their documents, ignorant of many kinds of research (only later perfected), as
prisoners of obsolete dogmas. In their pages the scientific
modern finds that the striving for life-likeness, for the cultivation of popular favor through literary art, often displaces the
pursuit of exact information. Analysis is subordinated to pic-
turesque flights, critical understanding to dramatic interest.
Through stressing personalities, imagery, valuations, the older
historians are held frequently to neglect the requirements of
accurate knowledge in both subject matter and treatment.
They forget that comprehension of the past requires above all
the rigorous testing of facts, to which vivid narration is secondary. If analysis of the evidence fails to yield the elements
of an exciting plot, no invention of the author can fairly provide
one. He must be faithful to the record, soberly constrained by
accredited data, not bent on firing the imagination of the reader.
Too often attempts to vivify the story lead to aberrations of
knowledge. Instead of authenticated research, the work
becomes an art of suggestion, of making men believe without
showing them why they should do so.

Nor is this charge limited to 'romantic' history or to those
works in which biography, plot, and adventure loom large.
At bottom the real divergence of the scientific modern from
popular tradition turns on the common sense categories. In
his eyes, the trouble with popular history is that it borrows the
layman's view of the world, accepting without demur the
matter and manner of its constituents. Personal causes, conscious purposes, the reports of naive observers are continually
allowed without dispute; while the interest of the story centers
in the actions of men as free agents in surroundings uncriti-
cally described in the language of everyday life. To the parti-

san of scientific history, on the contrary, all this is often reversed. In his eyes, as we have seen, collective environmental factors beyond the purview of the layman tend to shape the exigencies of human fate. Complex forces, hidden from the notice of the actors, impersonal causes, physical and social trends more often tip the scale of fortune, with the result that the obvious human story dwindles in importance losing much of its significance to the wider natural setting. Thus stories of the vices and virtues of monarchs, of diplomatic manoeuvres, of military victories and defeats, may have to be rewritten in terms of the effects of a special economy, the havoc of unnoted bacilli, the action of climate and birthrate. For to the scientific outlook it is not so much particular men and their deeds as the march of material circumstance and the influence of social conditions that decides the course of events.

To these charges the believer in the broader, untechnical history has much to reply. And to his response we may well turn in this chapter. Unquestionably the bulk of those generations to whose cultural remains we owe the preservation of the past reflected the world in a naive, spontaneous way free from formal scientific incentive. To them men's immediate experiences were of a piece, alike capable of yielding knowledge. Qualitative and emotional deliverances bore no special burden of distrust; nor was the demand for exact proof a dreaded incubus. Men did not need to wait for science and its techniques to live and understand their world. Nor did they hesitate, in seeking to retain the past, to use most varied means. Through time-honored ceremonies, music, sculpture, the dance, in fields like religion, politics, art, no less than in written chronicles, they sought to reclaim the far-off days. All kinds of expression, practical, homely, artistic, aided by a whole arsenal of imaginative and affective appeal helped to preserve the memory of lessons and achievements. Men of all sorts and conditions added to the store. In the language of everyday life, statesman and busybody, scribe, priest, and soldier reported actions they had heard about or seen. Through these

funded accumulations history came to exist—a source from
which science itself took its rise. Only by accepting all manner
of records made in all manner of ways has an index been kept
of all man has been. Because it has embraced the widest
reflection of human happenings, history has continued close
to the popular heart, as varied in its modes of expression as
human nature itself. That it should remain so is the conviction
of the common sense historian. Only, in his opinion, so long as
history can be shared with the many, only so long as its language is their language, its experiences and thoughts universal,
can it be assured of lasting appeal. To restrict it to the methods
of specialists, on the other hand, would go far to destroy the
subject and impoverish life. Truths, lessons, values precious to
mankind would be subordinated, if not lost, in a narrower
frame of analysis. Imprisoned in the language and outlook of
science, shut out from the participation of laymen, the ancient
tree of human memories would wither at the root.

Usually, as we have said, the lay historian does not forget
that recovery of the past is an imaginative as well as an intellectual process, dependent upon exciting sympathetic impressions in the reader, and not merely on technical 'proof.' Because
for him the core of history is psychic drama, its method centers
in enlisting men's convictions, imaginative revival, and memo-
rial life. Such works often resemble the novel or epic, persuasive to the degree that they omit the show of rigorous
procedure and laborious tests. Though obeying their own
criteria, such authors betray few of the exigencies of science.
"Away with such fruitless compunctions and impossible
checks!" they seem to say. "To be read and to endure, histories
must have vital attractions of concreteness, pace, and spirit.
To pause before the paucity of evidence, the multiplicity of
causes, and unsolved problems, can only paralyze our efforts."
Not that the lay historian lacks method, but his is a method
that conceals itself. To create an impression of reality appears
his prime intent, to excite an interest in the reader so absorbing that for the time being it persuades him such was the

course of life itself.[1] Through the labor of art his end is achieved with bold strokes, passing over in silence the paucity and ambiguities of the documentary material, filling in the gaps with a wealth of circumstantial detail, and clothing the whole in a decisive interpretation. To create the effect of life brought unchanged to the spectator, to induce the feeling that no barriers have intervened, no translating mind has altered the facts, but that upon occasion the motives, thoughts, and action, the very substance of the scene of battle, the secrets of the conference, the dying soliloquy in the bedchamber have been captured in its pages is no small achievement. To be sure, critical doubts may ensue in the reader, but if the impact of the work is strong, and his sympathetic comprehension deeply enlisted, the impression will endure despite subsequent influences.

It is not necessary to recall names like Macaulay, Carlyle, Prescott, to reinforce the point. In many ways Gibbon, though loftier, less graphic in style, remains a monument to the tradition. In his work the spectacle of Rome appears reflected in the mind of the eighteenth century layman, the cultivated gentleman, and man of the world. Though remote from his subject, Gibbon presents us with a living picture, a drama, rather than a scientific hypothesis. Nature is subordinated as background to the burning struggles of men; while over all presides the genius of sceptical common sense, disillusioned of moral enthusiasm, intent to register, without condoning, "the

---

[1] A few lines from Parkman may serve to refresh the reader's mind as to the vividness achieved by masters of the craft. Here Parkman is describing the march of Menendez' forces against Fort Caroline, Florida, in the sixteenth century. He carries the reader to the heart of the desperate adventure by making him almost share the sensations of the toiling men:

"The five hundred pushed their march, now toiling across inundated savannas, waist-deep in bulrushes and mud, now filing through the open forest to the moan and roar of the storm-racked pines; now hacking their way through the palmetto thickets; and now turning their path to shun some pool, quagmire, cypress swamp, or 'hummock' matted with impenetrable bushes, brambles, and vines. As they bent before the tempest, the water trickling from the rusty head-piece crept clammy and cold betwixt the armor and the skin; and when they made their wretched bivouac, their bed was the spongy soil, and the exhaustless clouds their tent." Francis Parkman, *Pioneers of France in the New World* (Boston, 1874) Ch. VIII p. 39.

crimes, follies, and misfortunes of mankind."[2] In his pages
we see the empire at its height; its military triumphs, the
dignity of the imperial throne, the glories of a legal code
involving the tolerant rule of provincials, the whole culminating in the union of varied races and cultures in one
stupendous fabric of civil administration. Then slowly the
structure crumbles before our eyes. Little by little chaos drives
out order; licentiousness triumphs over discipline and thrift.
As the sands of time flow on, an enfeebled senate, corrupt
rulers, brutal mobs, rebellious legions, and class tumult succeed
the ancient virtues. Barbarians beating at the gates find bloody
quarrels within; while an alien religion, triumphant in the
hour of discord, weans men's hearts from their ancient allegiance to the imperial city.

To Gibbon there is no need to delve beneath the surface to
explain all this by hunting for correlations and hidden laws.
The agencies of the process are plain to ordinary eyes: out-
weighing the forces of nature are the vices and virtues of
monarchs, the schemes of soldiers and priests, the tempers of
armies and mobs, all the grossness, heroism, passions that
consume the souls of men. In his 'diligent inquiry' the pageant
of the past becomes an epic of imaginative art, in which the
torrent of events often overwhelms the power of analysis.
Nevertheless while no hypothesis is strictly proved, we sense
beneath the flood the judgment of the moralist. Even though
there be, as he believed, no justice at the root of things, even
though men will not profit from the rehearsal of their crimes,
there still rests upon the historian a sacred duty. While the
keeper of the past cannot, as Tacitus believed,[3] "restrain vice
by the terror of posthumous infamy," he yet to Gibbon occupies a high tribunal. Careless of the lessons of bygone times
men will probably go their ways. Nevertheless in the pages

[2] Edward Gibbon, *Decline and Fall of the Roman Empire* (Everyman ed.
London, 1925) Vol. I Ch. III p. 77. "History, which is, indeed, little more than
the register of the crimes, follies, and misfortunes of mankind."

[3] Tacitus, *Annals*, III 65.

of history justice can be done; there at least the tyrant on his throne, the conqueror in seas of blood can be finally called to account, and the virtuous applauded. To keep the record straight, "to render to posterity a just and perfect delineation of all that may be praised, of all that may be excused, of all that may be censured,"[4] such is Gibbon's conception of his task.

To him the fall of Rome presents a somber tragedy. He cannot view with scientific indifference or philosophic detachment the ruin of that great structure which, to his mind, made possible the widest happiness, prosperity, and order hitherto enjoyed by mankind.[5] Compared to the age of the Antonines, succeeding periods appear to him inferior, betraying signs of unmistakable decline. Hence to this factual standard when "the vast extent of the Roman empire was governed by absolute power under the guidance of virtue and wisdom," he repeatedly recurs. Unlike more philosophical historians who venerate some abstract notion of liberty or progress, he cannot look beyond the successive failures of mankind to the beacon of an ideal theme. Too many facts seem against it. Even though granting that freedom of the mind begets what is rational and generous in human action,[6] he cannot believe that civil liberty makes for the widest human happiness. Certainly the emperors of the Golden Age did not think so; nor does Gibbon question their wisdom. Nerva, Trajan, Hadrian, the Antonines, while insuring their subjects' consent by preserving the 'image of liberty,' wielded an absolute power, well aware that only gov-

---

[4] Edward Gibbon, *Miscellaneous Works* (ed. by J. W. McSpadden, New York, 1907) "A Vindication" etc. p. 596.

[5] *Decline*, Vol. I, Ch. III p. 78. "If a man were called to fix the period in the history of the world during which the condition of the human race was most happy and prosperous, he would without hesitation name that which elapsed from the death of Domitian to the accession of Commodus. The vast extent of the Roman empire was governed by absolute power under the guidance of virtue and wisdom."

[6] D. M. Low, *Edward Gibbon* (London, 1937) p. 330. "Nothing is extolled more often by Gibbon than freedom ... His most insistent lesson—for in the end there is a lesson—is that the freedom of the mind is the source of every generous and rational sentiment (*Decline*, Ch. XXXVII)."

ernment by force could constrain men's turbulent passions and maintain the happiness of their world.[7]

After the great days of the empire, the middle ages seem to Gibbon a sad deterioration; so that his sense of tragic loss obscures his perception of new movements springing from Rome's decay. Lacking a transcendental pivot of history, he can find no consoling substitute in the agelong struggle for freedom or in the idea of social development. Yet living before the triumph of the evolutionary hypothesis, his thought is still free from complete engulfment by scientific causes and belief in the environmental selection of all human traits. For him the assumption of dualism is still possible. To a degree at least man stands apart from nature with resources within himself. Difficulties have not yet arisen against portraying him as a partially free agent, morally accountable, distinct from (though interacting with) the surrounding world. The mechanism has not yet been exposed which will make human history to many minds but a piece and product of its non-human setting.

Gibbon's attitude toward causal relations is indicative of his common sense outlook. Though he once declared the search for causes to be the historian's distinguishing mark, his statement had only the loosest meaning. "History," he says, "is to a philosophic spirit what games of chance were to the Marquis de Dangeau."[8] While it is a game of chance, yet the historian studying the course of man's weal and woe, sudden gains and quick reversals, sees like the gambler behind the play of events "a system, relations, a sequence," where others see only caprices of fortune, tricks of fate. Of course multitudes of facts prove nothing beyond their own existence, yet some appear

[7] *Decline*, Vol. I Ch. III esp. p. 78. Gibbon describes the imperial government instituted by Augustus as "an absolute monarchy disguised by the forms of a commonwealth (p. 68)." "Augustus was sensible that mankind is governed by names; nor was he deceived in his expectation, that the senate and people would submit to slavery, provided they were respectfully assured that they still enjoyed their ancient freedom (p. 71)."

[8] *Miscellaneous Works* (ed. by J. W. McSpadden). "Essay on the Study of Literature" Ch. XLVIII.

as links in a chain, and a few (for those rare minds with power
to glimpse them) light up far vistas. Yet even though the
historian's perception of causal relations resembles the
gambler's, he remains unable to grasp the specific positive
laws of the process and to trace the decisive connections of
events. Certainly in his own work Gibbon offers no complete
explanation, no exact estimate of the causes of Rome's decline,
puts forward no clear-cut hypothesis capable of definitive or
empirical check. Instead he offers alternative accounts of the
causes and (while convinced that no mere series of disconnected accidents was responsible) contents himself with
describing a number of influences and suggesting a variety of
plausible clues. For instance, in his "General Observations on
the Fall" (*Decline,* Vol. IV Ch. XXXVIII) he discusses: the
injuries of nature, hostile attacks of barbarians and Christians,
use and abuse of the materials, and the domestic quarrels of
the Romans. These, moreover, in his final chapter he mentions
as "four principal causes of the ruin of Rome."[9] On the other
hand, in a passage which seems to mark his frankest attempt
at explanation, Gibbon approaches the subject quite differently
ascribing the disaster to the consequence of excessive expansion.

   The decline of Rome (he says) was the natural and inevitable effect
of immoderate greatness. Prosperity ripened the principle of decay; the
causes of destruction multiplied with the extent of conquest; and as soon
as time or accident had removed the critical supports, the stupendous
fabric yielded to the pressure of its own weight.[10]

Here the hint of an organic view of the state as aging like
a living creature (in its 'ripening to decay') merges with an
even stronger suggestion of the classical belief in proportionality and the fatality of excess. Yet obviously causal considerations of this nature are so general and analogical as to be
matters of opinion beyond factual test. That, in any case, it
was not to Gibbon's mind simply the over-expansion of the

[9] *Decline,* Vol. VI Ch. LXXI p. 550.
[10] *Ibid.,* Vol. IV Ch. XXXVIII p. 105.

empire which brought about its ruin is plain from his mention
of sundry other influences. There is the famous closing passage
declaring that his work had described "the triumph of barbarism and religion" coupled with the denial that the assault
of savage tribes was primarily the cause of the fall, but that
"from these innocent barbarians the reproach must be trans-
ferred to the Catholics at Rome."[11] Again he calls the creation
of the praetorian guard, which provided the emperor with a
private army with which to overawe the senate, "the first
symptom and cause of the decline."[12] Still elsewhere inequit-
able taxation favoring the rich at the expense of the poor is
blamed for the political disruption; while the love of luxury
diffused from the court and cities into the army is said to have
hastened the military collapse. Yet if he is lacking in single-
mindedness in listing the definitive causes proximate and
remote, Gibbon makes up for this in the certainty of his denial
that the barbarian invasions (often popularly regarded as the
chief cause) were primarily responsible for the disaster. In a
passage marked by one of those unconfirmable 'ifs' so dear to
historians, he declares that "If all the barbarians had been
annihilated in the same hour, their total destruction would not
have restored the empire in the West."[13] Apparently to him
the very strength of the empire proved in the end its greatest
weakness; and the giant structure reared by the Roman genius
for war and politics crumbled once peace had relaxed the
military government and an untoward growth had drowned
the builders in a sea of less able provincials. Yet it was part of
Gibbon's common sense wisdom to avoid a sharp causal
hypothesis—rather broadly suggesting what appeared to him
the most probable influences without attempting to establish
their exhaustiveness or relative weight. Had he sought inclusiveness or to rate them comparatively, to decide which contributed more to Rome's fall: Christianity or unjust taxation,

11 *Ibid.*, Vol. VI Ch. LXXI pp. 553-554.
12 *Ibid.*, Vol. I Ch. V p. 101.
13 *Ibid.*, Vol. III Ch. XXXV p. 407.

the praetorian bands or immoderate growth, his task would have been far more difficult.

Apparently the further a historian pushes his inquiries the more he becomes aware of the complexity of causes and the host of variables that probably factored in events. Scores of influences, proximate and remote, may have entered into Rome's decline. And in the end whichever factor he chooses for emphasis: whether it be the fatality of a metropolis trying to govern an empire as with Mommsen, the war of classes of the Marxist, or the immoderate greatness of Gibbon, rests largely on the authority of his individual say-so. "Not an inch," cries Henry Adams, "has been gained by Gibbon—or all the historians since towards explaining the Fall."[14] While such impatience may go too far, when we consider for how many centuries Rome has served as the supreme challenge from which men sought to learn the secrets of social-political progress and decay and to gain a yard-stick for measuring the causes, and when against this we consider the variety of divergent answers, it may well seem that decisive verification of causes is beyond the purview of history. Let us not forget how from Augustine to Gibbon the wheel turned full circle, and Christianity once represented as the savior reappeared as the destroyer of human values. During the Enlightenment the issue of popular political liberty (as in Petrarch or Voltaire) tended to provide the key; while today from the spectrum of alternatives we may choose as perhaps most typical this vague, scientific-sounding expression of the *sociological* view:

The cause of the decline of the Roman Empire is not to be sought in any one feature of climate, soil, health of the population, or indeed in any one of those social and political factors which played so important a part in the actual process of decay—but rather in *the whole structure of ancient society*. [Its failure, we are told, like that of Athens, was the failure of the city-state.] Built on a foundation of slave labor, the exploitation of similar groups, including the peasantry, the city-state yielded a brilliant minority civilization. But from the start it was top-

[14] Henry Adams, *The Education of Henry Adams* (New York, 1931) p. 91.

heavy. Through no fault of its citizens, but as a result of the time and place when it arose, it was supported by a woefully low level of technique . . . From the premises from which classical civilization arose, namely, an absolutely low technique and to compensate for this, the institution of slavery, herein lie the real causes of the decline and fall of the Roman Empire.[15]

All in all, Gibbon's wariness of commitment to proof of an exact hypothesis seems justified. Lacking facilities for decisive test, the common sense historian may well rest content to cite patent, fairly widespread influences, while the dramatic appropriateness of the action to time and place may appear to confirm his emphasis on certain factors. When a considerable span of events is involved, causal diagnosis is a difficult matter upon which authorities may not agree. Even when their work is based upon the same sources there are often major points of dispute. In Greek history there is the well-known instance of Mitford and Grote. While the one traced the decline of ancient Greece to the ruinous course of unbridled democracy, the other, using the same materials sixty years later, reached the conclusion that "democracy had worked to their improvement."[16]

In any case there is no lack of great historians whose work illustrates the dominance of the common sense categories. In them the causes, qualities, agents familiar to ordinary life comprise their stock of worldly wisdom. Should an added example be required to reinforce the point, we can hardly pass over Macaulay. With Macaulay in the nineteenth century, as with Gibbon in the eighteenth, the historian's conception of things, far from being scientific or philosophic, is essentially that of the liberal, cultured layman. Less ponderous and more popularly attractive in style than Gibbon, Macaulay is also more strongly marked as a moralist. Being part of the tradition of which he wrote, his judgments are tinged with a certain provincialism, from which Gibbon surveying a different cul-

15 F. W. Walbank, *Decline of the Roman Empire in the West* (London, 1946) pp. 67-69. Italics mine.
16 Ernest Scott, *History and Historical Problems* (New York, 1925) pp. 31-32.

ture and wider span is largely free. Yet this very localism in its imperturbable solidity unvexed by doubts or critical comparisons is all the closer to common sense. In his work Macaulay seeks both to show broadly that moral and religious beliefs are among the strongest agencies in human affairs and to render specific moral judgment on his subject. For what is history but "the late justice of posterity,"[17] the seasoned opinion undeluded by passions and badges, of the moral sentiment of the community? His chosen field of English history turns, in his eyes, on the pivot of three great social revolutions, in all of which ethical and religious issues played the leading role. While the 'Glorious Third,' which overthrew the Stuarts and brought civil and religious liberty to England, is the focus of his writing, the two earlier revolutions, one of which effaced the distinction of Norman and Saxon, and the other of master and slave, are deemed by him no less important.[18]

As a writer of popular narrative history Macaulay scorns the pretense of formal proof. Nevertheless at the outset he supports his thesis that religious and associated moral causes outrank all others with a broad comparative argument. Any impartial observer, he maintains, who fairly contrasts the prosperity and well-being of countries possessed of religious freedom with the condition of countries under an absolute church will have to acknowledge the vindication of the former before his eyes. Cultural and economic evidence plainly shows that fertile lands can do little for a people weighed down by an oppressive religion, whereas liberty of conscience, on the contrary, awakens their energies to surmount the greatest natural obstacles. As subjects of inquiry, he suggests the comparison of Spain with Holland, Italy with Scotland, South with North America, together with the sharp contrasts between the counties of Ireland where sectional divisions mark differences of religious faith. Nevertheless as all too often in history appeal to the argument from difference is effective only among

[17] Thomas Babington Macaulay, *History of England* (London, 1934) Vol. III p. 330.
[18] *Ibid.*, Vol. I p. 25.

those already disposed to accept it. Northern Protestants will
be persuaded by his argument; on the other hand, the effort
to connect religious freedom with social and economic advance
will be indignantly rejected by those who find their pride of
country or religion disparaged by it. At least we may say that
the strength of the disagreement bears witness to the force
of the religious sentiments.

That a work dealing with the storms in England following
the Reformation should stress the importance of religious
beliefs is hardly surprising; nor is it to be wondered at that
Macaulay's personal involvement in the issues led him sometimes to construe morality as the adjunct of a particular creed.
Yet for the most part he saw further, imputing the import of
events to the awakening spirit of liberty and to deeper changes
in the life of the people, rather than to sectarian causes. It was
this sense that the significance of the long contest between
parliament and throne lay in gains to the common lot and to
those simple households that bore the brunt of the struggle,
that gave his history its wide appeal, and made it seem so
perfect an embodiment of common sense. In large measure
the story is spun round the characters of the leaders, through
whose reaction on their followers we catch the issues and the
popular response. The portraits of James II, William I, Marl-
borough, Somers, Seamore, Halifax, though perhaps etched too
strongly in black and white, are absorbing. The lineaments of
veniality, hypocrisy, bigotry are sharply drawn as well as the
rarer strains of nobleness and integrity. Everywhere in Macaulay it is the ferment of the component individuals that makes
his pictures come alive. The England he gives us is Englishmen; while everywhere through the spectacle of parliaments
and courts, the life of country and of towns, of troops in camp
or battle, we sense the common human virtues. Here causes
are treated dramatically as springing in large part from human
action through the free play of character. Fascinated we watch
the high-handed favoritism of the Stuarts slowly alienating the
English parliament and church, forcing them into alliance
with the dissenters. Tension mounts as we follow the long

chain of grievances leading up to the trial of the bishops, culminating finally in the invasion of William. In all the great scenes we have depicted the heroic struggle of Englishmen to combat the worst oppressions of the age. Yet precisely because he invokes no hidden guidance of social forces or dialectic of transcendental good, Macaulay's work is sometimes disparaged. His common sense is dismissed as no more than a simple panegyric of expanding empire and commercialism. Much is lost on such a view. A work like his, undertaking to show how England's greatness sprang from her people's resistance to constraints of conscience, trade, and threats of foreign tyranny is far from lacking depth and a certain nobility. For the struggle against oppression is one form of the struggle for liberty; while the core of the struggle for liberty, outreaching commercial rivalries and sectarian disputes, is a moral theme of unrivalled grandeur.

In Macaulay no apparatus of method, no problems of verification are forced upon the reader. Persuasion is left to the inner movement of the story; while the masterly skill of the telling is enough to convince the average man without supporting documentation. Unlike Gibbon, Macaulay does not hesitate to claim to know the causes of things. Any lingering doubts, if he had them, are concealed along with the marks of his indefatigable scholarship beneath an art that makes history read like fiction. That he was of the lineage of Herodotus, he himself would be the last to deny: a lover of tales, adventure, action, one of those imaginative, colloquial minds possessing a most vivid sense of reality. "Children and servants," he observes admiringly in his essay on *History*,[19] "are remarkably Herodotean. They tell everything dramatically. Their *'says he's'* and *'says she's'* are proverbial." How different from the sophisticated man who—if he chances to tell of a change of prime ministers—can only state the fact baldly and dryly; whereas your porter tells the story "as if he had been hid behind the curtains of the royal bed at Windsor." Character, movement, drama, to make us know the chief persons almost

[19] *Works of Lord Macaulay* (London, 1866) Vol. V p. 124.

as if we had lived with them,—yet at the same time to resist
the temptation to force the facts, to tell things one could not
possibly have known, to improve on actuality—all this is the
historian's supreme challenge. History requires both faithful-
ness to the letter and to the spirit, although fidelity to the
spirit would seem to take precedence in Macaulay's eyes.

Here is a marked difference in the notion of truth from the
scientific historian. Where the latter appears absorbed in
'matching' his statements with facts or checking them against
empirical laws, Macaulay is concerned with the imaginative
vivacity of his presentations. He is impatient with those who
parade their pedestrian labors, who spend their time retrieving
props in the basement and discussing what goes on behind the
scenes. In his eyes, display of method is not history. To sift
the evidence in public, testing hypotheses for all to see, dulls
perception of more vital truth. External checking should be
discarded in the finished work for the more difficult task of
inducing an interior confirmation in the reader. Tools should
be kept out of sight, and the scaffolding of the builder not
allowed to mar the outline of the finished structure.

The greatest historian for Macaulay is the one "in whose
work the character and spirit of an age is exhibited in minia-
ture." While facts as such are "mere dross" (the Bodleian
library could not hold the recorded events of a week), the art
lies in their selection: in preserving the most telling words and
speaking gestures, in choosing those incidents which catch the
gist of far wider situations. Hardly less important is the knack
of knowing when to expand and when to contract, the manage-
ment of scale and perspective. "No picture and no history can
present us with the whole truth, but those are the best pictures
and the best histories which exhibit such parts of truth as most
nearly produce the effect of the whole."[20] Here imaginative
insight grasps many things uncomprehended in scientific categories. In brief, the historian's truth is like the artist's: a matter
of shade and suggestion, of conveying much in little, reducing
the great to the small, compressing into brief compass the

[20] Ibid., p. 129.

lineaments of a time. The effect, while pictorial, combines the depth of a great portrait with the incisiveness of a cartoon from *Punch*. For as a meager pencilled sketch may seize the salient features of a face or situation, may indeed give a clearer idea of it than the details of a richly colored painting, so a great history, though abridging a thousand incidents to one and presenting the temper of the time through a few chosen individuals, may yet convey more essential truth than the fullest chronicle.

But already enough has been said to suggest the case for general common sense history. Whether its mood be somber or hopeful, whether it paints a picture of the decline of empire with Gibbon or of its rise with Macaulay, the text employs the same humanistic and substantial categories. The frame of things familiar to ordinary life provides its outlines. The record of man's memories, feelings, valuations regarding affairs, and their traditional interpretation suffice to account for events. We do not need to wait upon science to discover their significance through search for the hidden relations of man to his natural setting. Against the tendency to submerge 'human' in 'natural' history, the common sense attitude protests. Man is not to be treated as wholly one with his matrix, his actions and values appraised by his success in conforming to its conditions. Instead of construing man in terms of nature, or nature in terms of man, it recognizes a duality of powers: on the one hand, a context of impersonal physical forces, operating for the most part under available mechanical laws, and on the other psychic impulses centering in personalities endowed with free capacities to plan and create. In them appears a source of invention unknown to physical things, a power of origination and fiat begotten by the psyche itself. Thus history represents the interplay of two forces, each irreducible to the other. 'Persons' are never mere 'things speaking,' nor are 'things' mere slumbering psyches.

Yet because the lay tradition assumes the power of consciousness to know itself and to create, it remains outside the scientific fold. To its eyes, on the contrary, scientific writers can never pluck out the heart of the mystery, never capture in their explanations of the past the originative element of personality. Inevitably they must fail, since in refusing to put themselves at the point of view of that which they seek to understand, in viewing subjectivity always in causal and external terms, scientific historians put the core of their subject out of reach. To take man as he takes himself, on the contrary, is to seek his essence in his hopes, plans, memories, feelings, thoughts as he himself entertains them, to admit an inward unity beyond the existential given. Only by taking personality in its own right can the worth of human nature be safe-guarded, its dignity and autonomy preserved. For if a man cannot trust his own consciousness, he can trust nothing else. Although this dynamic view of personalities makes them intui-tive and unique, at least history written about them is not Hamlet without Hamlet, but is truer than their resolution into extraneous elements and laws. Whatever we may say, direct appeal to the authority of awareness, insights, memories marks the starting-point of historical method. Even science despite its cult of the publically observable is bound to admit it. Whenever, in or out of the laboratory, we support our view of an event by an 'I saw,' 'I remember,' 'I felt this to be the case,' we accept the witness of consciousness as a criterion anterior to external check. Each returns to what Croce called 'the living documentation he carries within himself;'[21] and through a symposium of views drawn from inner psychic life men interpret the wider human story.

As is said, common sense history woven on the texture of ordinary life, its ends and explanations, gains the largest hear-ing. For mankind, with the exception of a few experts, is far more interested in a story than in the sifting of conjectures, documents, artifacts. Only where the past touches a person's experience at some point and awakens a sense of kinship does it excite his lively concern. Technical historical writing, in the view of the artist and layman, harbors grave weaknesses. It forgets that impressions are stronger than arguments to authen-

[21] Benedetto Croce, *op. cit.*, p. 19.

ticate the past, and that for the most part men are moved by what they feel, imagine, recall, rather than by an involved train of inferences.

With the growth of the scientific tradition, some complain that the enlightening influence of history has become restricted in scope. Hidden away in archives and technical tomes from the eyes of the public, the annals of the past tend to lose much of their effectiveness. Imprisoned in academic language, contingent upon familiarity with research techniques, such history forfeits its free expression in preoccupation with method and the private warfare of scholars. In the modern world the pervasive influence which it once enjoyed seems more and more sacrificed. It is not simply that bards no longer chant their lays, but that historians of epic grandeur have largely ceased to create. Because the great figures of the past no longer find voices to speak to us, the taste for historical reading as background has begun to decay. However complex the causes of the process, the lover of history in the old sense is convinced that in all this important truths and values are being lost. Life is being made poorer, eviscerated into something cold, hard, meaningless through displacement of concrete interests by the analytic and abstract. The history of our Civil War, for instance, that used to be written around the great issues of slavery and secession as decided by the people's heroic efforts and moral choice, is now presented as the inevitable result of the nation's growth from agriculture to industry with the consequent economic shift in the balance of power. With the change to more technical outlooks in the recovery of the past, the naive reports of laymen become of less and less account. Not what is perceived and related by unsophisticated minds, but what can withstand accurate verification of a peculiar sort is held to be reliably informative. The plain man, the artist, the story-teller and keeper of tradition may well lose heart in a world in which his powers are increasingly challenged and eclipsed.

Nevertheless, to his mind, it is the inward experience, the psychic stigmata beyond external check that generate the strongest belief in events. By exciting some participation in the reader, the author effects a more lasting persuasion than through all the refinements of analysis. Who can doubt that Livy or Tacitus in making us, in Gibbon's phrase, "climb the Alps with Hannibal" and "assist at the councils of Tiberius"[22] conveys a deeper impression than if he had submitted an abstract hypothesis subject to various tests? Filled by turns with horror, indignation, and pity purged by reflection, the reader wins substantiation from the depths. Literally, of course, he cannot grasp the sights and sounds that flashed on men those far-off days, yet by reviving elements in the reader's mind, the author can make their prototypes recur. For "men," as even Buckle noted, "are in imagination constantly changing situations with others."[23] By inducing us to relive in fancy elements from our own lives recombined in some novel, magnified form, the writer enables us to exchange our personal past for a wider arena. "Something like this happened, or might well have happened to me" is the feeling. In these other lives I seem to catch as in a glass an enlarged image of my own, or of some life I might have lived, or was lucky to have escaped. Senator or tribune, cavalier or roundhead, jacobin or *emigré*, frontiersman or redskin,—from them my own existence gains in stature, its outlines reinforced by these parallel ventures, hardships, triumphs or misdeeds,—greater in scale perhaps, yet profoundly akin. Successful resurrection of the past depends more on analogy with concrete experience and empathic art to the layman than on scientific analysis.

Wittingly or unwittingly men have long taken advantage of such means to reclaim the past, using various forms of excitation and appeal, especially the personal and affective. The wider the range of impressions, the more basic the powers enlisted, the more lasting such representations have seemed to be. For most men the major moments of living are predomi-

[22] Edward Gibbon, *Miscellaneous Works*, "Essay on the Study of Literature," LII.

[23] Henry Thomas Buckle, *History of Civilization in England* (New York, 1913) Vol. II, Pt. II p. 345.

nantly emotional rather than intellectual, while what they remember best are scenes of dramatic action or vivid characterization that catch and hold the movement of life. With the aid of memory and emotion, the mind seems effortlessly to revert to the past. By their means the intimate quality, the unforced meaning of the original occurrence appears often better conveyed in the eyes of the many than through the refractive techniques of intellection. Perhaps because these processes present themselves as spontaneous activities touched off by concrete situations, rather than as tools of some extraneous purpose, they seem closer to the initial facts. In utilizing men's memories, feelings, valuations, the traditionalists (as even their opponents must admit) betray a very sound acquaintance with human nature. To grasp the action of other times, they say, we must be roused to share it sympathetically through finding links and kinship between its life and our own. Not that we can go so far as to see ourselves as the saints and heroes, villains and despots of whom we read. Yet much as the student is compelled to depend on his own fund of knowledge to fill in the details when he reads that Richard Coeur de Lion wore chain mail, carried a mace, or used battering rams for siege, so he must borrow from his own experience in part the red blood of Richard's story. At any rate it is only he who has felt the prick of ambition, the lust for power, who has loved, hated, been fired by a cause, or cherished a tradition, who knows what these things are really like. Knowledge of this sort cannot be put bodily into the soul of the reader even by the most scientific language.

The very fact that the historian can have no physical contact with the past obliges him, in the eyes of common sense, to forfeit the scientific method. The situations to which he refers permit no bodily encounter or examination. In history we deal with things beyond our reach in a sense quite different from the nebula or the atom. Victoria's reign or Lincoln's death cannot be retrieved by an ingenious device of electric waves, neuronic pathways or optical reflections. To be sure, the scientist in handling distant events seems sometimes to try

to equate the dimensions of time with each other, by translating the past to terms of present techniques and predictive
activities. For instance, that uranium was imprisoned in the
earth's crust in prehistoric times may be taken to signify that:
If we dig down to a certain depth we shall discover it. Here
the bygone state of affairs may be read in reverse as a methodological hypothesis to be certified prospectively. But common
sense denies this. To common sense, on the contrary, the historian's statements about the past are essentially ontological
not methodological, unconvertible to terms of the future by
any sleight of hand. The historian's assertions are categorical
not hypothetical, factual not instrumental; and to convert their
retrospective reference into predictions or forecasts falsifies
their meaning altogether. Since the past to which he refers is
existent no longer, vanished into incorporeality beyond reach
of bodily tools, the historian has no choice but to rely on the
psychic revival of subjectivity. Of course, some physical traces
are left of the wreck of its world, but they of themselves cannot tell their story. Only through imaginative recreation by a
mind stored with memories and rich in analogical power can
they be woven into graphic patterns of significance. The relics
and documents which serve to evoke the process are but dead
symbols of knowledge. Mind alone has the power to resurrect
their dry bones and to penetrate beyond them to concrete persons and situations. Historical writing therefore requires an art
of awakening intimate recognition, of multiplying threads of
insight by suggestion, an art in which—as the layman reminds
the specialist—one concrete impression may be worth an ell of
theory.

The contentions of common sense history, if we pause to examine them, have undeniable force. If it be true that what
exerts the strongest attraction upon men's minds are not the
laboriously acquired products of learning but personal, affective deliverances, surely historians should take advantage of
these inclinations. Why should they not capitalize to the full
on the use of memories and feelings in their subject matter and
treatment? The fact that these appear deeply involved in man's

nature, associated with the most basic functions on which he relies, surely indicates their importance for knowledge. Out of an infinity of happenings in the course of events, a few have left a deposit strong enough to survive the shiftings of human attention, clear enough to be recognized as turning-points of subsequent lives. By the very fact of being noticed, treasured, recounted, saved from oblivion, such things are declared important. In a sense history is always concerned with the preservation of values, with judging actions as noble or base, achievements or failures, discriminating periods of decline or advance. Everywhere scales of preference and importance are woven into its accounts. To all appearances the races of men by whom histories have been written share a fund of attitudes and appraisals that have almost become second nature. And it is these conceptions used by them in their personal life that are largely employed in traditional works. To such authors the frames of everyday thought seem more natural, reliable, and confirmable than any others. Inevitably they find themselves opposed to those modernists who assert that the day of the 'old school' and 'general historian' of common sense is over. Rather they see in history a subject, in Hume's phrase "suited to every capacity," expressible in ordinary language, close to the common man, committed to the widest appeal. For through familiarity with the past men grow to understand each other, through its common fund of experience the extraordinary becomes appreciable to the ordinary, and the rank and file gains a sense of the salient activities of the race.

At its best the art of traditional history gives a vivid sense of access to other times. To recapture the vitality of events we have to revive their warmth and tone, something which abstract method can never do. Through use of analysis, correlations, intricate causal research, a scientific approach loses the power of emotional comprehension. For instance, I may be enjoying reading of some great event in the past (say the Constitutional Convention of 1787) with a sense of grandeur an appreciation. Yet if, under the guidance of a 'scientific' author, I seek to exhume the causes that brought it about and exhaust the components that entered into it, its significance tends to evaporate. Sceptical doubts ensue; the recital no longer carries conviction. Criticism destroys its values; instead the profitable search for blemishes, for a *succès de scandale* blots out belief in the worth and integrity of the characters. Nevertheless in the pages of common sense writers the heroic still lives as a category; persons are still unique selves earning praise and censure in myriad unpredictable ways. Consciousness carries its authority within itself, and those who recreate the past must reach beyond the public records to more intimate acquaintance. For them reliance upon history depends upon the presence of the absent in an intuitive sense, upon a kind of racial memory as it were through which what is transmitted remains congruent with personal recoverable experience. This means trust in historical writing in the deliverances and explanations of ordinary consciousness, both of oneself and others, something open ultimately only to internal view. But to learn from others their inner experience, something beyond external check, raises the problem of communication, which we pause to examine in the next chapter.

CHAPTER FOUR

Communication in History

HISTORICAL METHOD resembles that used in courts of law in being forced to accept all sorts of evidence, and in not being able (as in the case of science) to restrict its witnesses to those trained in a rigorous technique of observation or to limit the situations considered to those capable of reinstatement and sensory check. Unquestionably history takes for granted without methodological doubt far more than does science. In it *reading* largely supplants observation, while the documents relied on have been compiled by the most diverse persons in diverse ways, in the uncertain language of everyday speech of many periods and countries. Generally the authors of the records which the historian consults take a rough-and-ready view of things, accepting, as we have seen, their sense impressions and valuations indiscriminately with a naive confidence in the absoluteness of their opinions.

Among the basic assumptions of knowledge that of communication is central. Without belief that men can impart awareness of their thoughts and actions to one another there could presumably be no history. Not only does the traditional historian grant without reserve the agency of persons as powerful forces upon their generation, but he accepts the communication of their ideas and influence to other times as well. Throughout the day most of us are reading, writing, conversing, and working with others so constantly that any question as to the reliable transmission of meanings seems purely aca-

demic. Nevertheless when we turn to men and events remote
in period and place, the problem as to how we know them
cannot be so readily ignored. There is something strange, if
one stops to consider it, in the notion of communications from
persons who lived long ago, messages from the dead to subsequent generations. Usually inquiry centers in a story told in a
document purporting to come from and impart the experience
of bygone men. Initially (or until awakened by some discrepancy) the historical reader accepts its veracity on trust, giving
himself up to the account, and assuming that its asserted meanings were in fact to others as they claim to him to have been.
The printed marks on the page serve as symbols—not noticed
on their own account—but primarily taken as informative of
the acts and thoughts of earlier men. Credence in a narrative
involves credence in its author, belief that a mind circum-
stanced in other times can convey by the physical tracing of
symbols to readers at a later date the gist of matters of which
they would otherwise have been ignorant. Through reading the
works of Tacitus, for instance, I seem to gain intimacy with
that gloomy Roman's thought, personality, and times. And certainly common sense allows the claim. Tacitus imparts his
wisdom to me, although my contact with him and his world is
plainly not in space-time terms. Rather it is through a kind of
disembodied voyage of significance, my ascription of the meanings which arise in my mind to a source outside, which I
identify with a man of that name, who lived in Rome in the
first century A. D., who married the daughter of Agricola, was
a lawyer, administrator, and sometime proconsul in Asia. It is
as if in giving myself up to his tale I were looking in a magic
mirror, into life through the mind of another, learning the
terrible secrets of a corrupt age through an incorruptible
master. His convincingness is so great that the demand for
external tests to establish the truth of his claims may appear
to me secondary.

Unquestionably there is an assumption of intuitive knowledge in the writings of traditional historians. On their magic
carpet they claim to transport their readers to other periods

and climes, to reveal the inimitable flavor of events, the secrets of personalities. Without having factually experienced themselves most of the things they report, and without an exact language in which to transmit them, they yet presume to penetrate their very life. At heart the lay historian, like his reader, remains something of a naive realist, who while recognizing the impossibility of physical reversion to the past, still holds to some intuitive compresence or communion with it. While granting that knowing a man by reputation is very different from knowing him by acquaintance, it is nonetheless in this latter sense that he claims a core of historical knowledge. In this vein, for instance, a recent authority on Boswell remarks that he feels that he knows Boswell better than he knows any living man;[1] while Hippolyte Taine depicts himself as "speaking almost aloud with them (the men whose history he is writing) while tracing their hand-writing on the time-stained paper."[2] Motley[3] in Brussels writes similarly: "The dead men of the place are my intimate friends. Any ghost that ever flits by night across the moonlit square is at once hailed by me as a man and a brother. I call him by his Christian name." In like manner, the well-read layman, if asked whether Franklin or Jefferson, Thucydides or Plato communicates with him in their writings would answer almost certainly in the affirmative, albeit admitting that the communication is only one way. Through their works we come in contact with great minds, grasp their thoughts and perspective on the world, still fresh though minted long ago. They and their contents are discoveries, not mere constructions of our own. The news they bring, moreover, is both of essences and existences, of universal meanings as well as of particular personalities and things. In a sense our union with the past turns on an imputation of essences to ulterior sources, not on physical confrontation. Yet were history no more than imputed meanings,

[1] Ralph H. Isham, *T. E. Lawrence by his Friends,* Ed. by A. W. Lawrence (New York, 1937) p. 262.

[2] H. Taine, *Ancient Regime,* trans. by J. Durand (New York, 1931) p. x.

[3] J. S. Bassett, *The Middle Group of American Historians* (New York, 1917) p. 225.

it would not be history, since its ontological status would disappear. As a mere excursion among the essences, historical writing would be indiscriminable from dialectic or art; its objects but emotional and cognitive complexes projected into an intentional domain that might be no more than the product of reverie. But to the run of men the annals of the past grasp *actuality* as well as *significance*, the being of persons and events, not merely a floating, imaginary representation of what they are supposed to be. Unlike the Hamlet of Shakespeare, Plato to the student of history is primarily a discovery not a creation, a unique figure fixed in his space-time niche, communicating fresh insights to us, inexhaustible through the imputations that cluster round his name.

The point is that if communication from persons in the past is possible in history, the imputation of essences is not its whole concern. For intercourse implies the existence of a plurality of selves and the transmission of news from one to another, whereas the projection and reabsorption of essences might occur in a solitary's dream. Personalities, on the contrary, are not mere bundles of essences but are psychic existents, subjects which cannot be predicates, unique beings each forming its own species, not susceptible of exhaustion in general terms. As individuals they are more than universals, and although a temporal stretch enters into their being, they have an aspect which escapes not only physical and temporal but abstract designation. Hence they are not adequately subject to the same canons of knowledge as conceptual or scientific objects, since general uniformities cannot exhaust psychic beings which are in their nature *sui generis*. We ought not therefore to be surprised that acquaintance with historical personalities requires something more than abstract hypothesis or scientific method, which considers particulars only as instances of classes or laws. The fact seems to be that, although glimpses of personalities come *through* the suggestions of essences, they are not grasped *as essences*, but as unique psychic existents by analogy and sympathetic penetration of an intuitive sort. When the historian tries to resolve his characters into lists of traits and activities accountable to certain causes as a scientist might resolve his object into a sum of elements and laws, the effect, the popular historian would maintain, is artificial and unconvincing. Hume's presentation of Luther[4] and of Joan of Arc in his *History of England* are famous cases in point. For all his acute analysis they remain lay figures. His predicates convey no concrete subject; his subtle psychological causes yield no portrait to the life. Illumination is somehow lacking; the spirit of their faith, the fiery contagion emanating from them is wholly lost; so that the reader is left unpersuaded as to the source of their immense influence. Dissection by the keenest intellect fails to penetrate to the heart of their unique force, to acquaint us with the power of their living personalities. Only an enigma remains, and the past seems as distant as ever.

Nonetheless the modern scientific historian, even while criticizing Hume's faulty psychology, accepts a similar view. To him intuition is a myth, and the past irrecoverable in original or living terms. How absurd, he would say, to imagine that we can catch the veritable spirit of men of other days charged with unique force. Luther and Joan are asleep in their graves, nor can their ghosts walk or talk to other times through the pages of history. The layman's faith in such contact springs from his mistaken dualism, which divorces the mind from the body, leading him to believe in the separate commerce of selves, thoughts and values in a realm of ideal being. To the

[4] David Hume, *History of England* (New York, 1850) Vol. II p. 132 (Luther); 344f (Joan). "Martin Luther, an Augustinian friar, Professor in the University of Wittenberg, resenting the affront put upon his order, began to preach against these abuses in the sale of indulgences; and being naturally of a fiery temper and provoked by opposition, he proceeded even to decry indulgences themselves and thence was carried by the heat of dispute, to question the authority of the pope, from which his adversaries derived their chief arguments against him. Still, as he enlarged his reading in order to support these tenets, he discovered some new abuse or error in the church of Rome, and finding his opinions greedily hearkened to, he promulgated them by writing, discourse, sermon, conference; and daily increased the number of his disciples. All Saxony, all Germany, all Europe were in a very little time filled with the voice of this daring innovator; and men, roused from the lethargy in which they had so long slept, began to call in question the most ancient and most received opinions."

scientific historian, traditional writers by hypostatizing dead men and ghostly essences, run counter to naturalistic criteria, a course which he vigorously denies. For him, on the contrary, understanding the past is always hypothetical, causal, involving consequences leading to some sensory test. He allows no romantic flight to other spheres, no participation in others' minds and emotions. To know a man in the past as to know a man in the present, he would say, means to grasp the conditions underlying his actions so as to be able to predict his behavior. To comprehend the intention of a character means to be able to present empirical evidence to substantiate it. Did Hamilton intend to try to kill Burr in the famous duel? If, according to established report, he said just beforehand that he did not mean to, and if a reflex muscular contraction as he fell mortally wounded could account for the late discharge of his pistol, the evidence with a certain probability would seem to establish his negative intent. From present records of the sayings and doings of men in the past, the scientific historian infers their feelings and purposes, assuming the same connections between human action and motive in the past as that now acceptable. Of course, the point of departure of his inquiry remains his own first-hand experience. That the inquirer knows his own experience better than that of others, the present better than the past, and the second by means of the first in both cases, is taken more or less for granted. The event of which he can say "I saw it," "I heard it," "I witnessed it" has for him the highest initial certification. In comparison with such first-hand deliverances, the documentary and oral reports of others' experiences are secondary, less certain. Each, seeing as he does with his own eyes and not with another's, inhabits a private world by reason of the separateness of his organism. In consequence most testimonial and circumstantial evidence comes from the outside through symbols, language, and indirection. Nevertheless, starting with the immediate observation of a small amount of sensory material, the historian of scientific bent infers by trains of hypothetical reflection the experiences of men in the past with a fair degree of assurance. But however much the process gets abridged by habit and custom, there is no psychic penetration or intuitive acquaintance with others.

Yet how, it may be asked, can a view which takes its start from the isolation of the organism explain the social transmission of knowledge? To this the answer is that postulates of physical monism, generic identity, and uniformity are invoked. Your scientific historian assumes a common environment peopled with human beings fundamentally alike and behaving in similar ways. These creatures stimulate each other either directly through contact, or by generating disturbances in a medium which serves to transmit excitations to their neighbors arousing similar responses in them. Communication is not unlike the transmission of radio vibrations between sending and receiving sets attuned in an electric field. Language, written or spoken, is regarded as part of human behavior; and as animal cries in the forest borne from one to other members of a group serve as cues for adaptive reactions, so man's sensori-motor and vocal habits become organized into stable complexes which serve as signals in his speech-community. Similarly men create artifacts and written symbols which through their continuity with vocal, gestural, and other habits are passed on as cultural cues to succeeding generations. Though what is transmitted in history as elsewhere is always a physical impulse, the translating of these impulses into corresponding meaningful terms takes place, on this view, essentially through the action of conditioning. Because the uniformity of nature involves as its corollary a fortunate parallelism, repetition of the same set of initial sensory stimuli can be counted upon to be accompanied by the same set of ideo-motor responses, and advantage taken of this fact in ever widening circles. Thus, as Helen Keller is held to have been released from her psychic imprisonment into the community of speech and knowledge through a process of educative conditioning based upon an original coincidence of kinaesthetic and contact sensations, so every man is held to be liberated from confinement in his organic deliverances into the world of social history by the development of associated ideo-motor habit-patterns in correspondence with environmental stimuli. Furthermore, what is of the greatest importance for history is that such chain reactions serve not only for relations with contemporaries, but for cultural transmission extended indefinitely in time through the continuance of customs through overlapping generations, and through the preservation of linguistic signs which act as stored signals exciting in later generations upon their visual recovery responses very similar to those produced in earlier men.

Yet surely, objects the common sense historian, there is more to learning from the men of the past than this. *Parallelism is not communication;* and this preoccupation with correspondences of behavior, when the problem is one of the transportation of ideas from one mind or generation to another, is hardly more than a gigantic aside. The discovery of certain coincidences and isometric patterns in men's reaction to speech cues is not the same as the transmission of meanings. On the assumptions of positive science nothing passes between persons save what can be observed in a physical sense, hence thoughts are not, properly speaking, transmitted. The whole notion of a separate currency of concepts, values, psychic influences, is as abhorrent to this positivist view as divorcing the mind from the body. Yet it is difficult to see how history as one of the humanities, centering in the cultural transmission of human affairs, can allow such physicalism.

Nevertheless to the scientific historian all talk of 'exchanging ideas' or of communications from men in the past is essentially a figure of speech. The only way to get in touch with men's minds, he would say, is by way of their bodies or by checking the physical traces left by them. Hence all knowledge of minds (including one's own) comes by inference from sense observation. Physically or literally speaking, the notion of a thought leaving the mind of one person and crossing over to that of another (no matter how short the distance in space and time) is sheer nonsense. The only way to know another man's ideas is by observation of his behavior or of some physical marks he has left. From these one constructs a hypothesis as to what his accompanying ideation probably has been. What the historian confronts is always some empirical sign: document or archeological remains, utterance heard or bodily movement seen, which he ascribes to others. These, though unlike the ideas and events to which they refer, may serve to stimulate relevant conjectures. The possibility remains however that the ideas he ascribes to his sources may be nothing but his own. Often historians obviously play tricks upon the dead, reading their own conceptions into the past and rediscovering them by an elaborate circumlocution. Conceivably the thoughts I attribute to Tacitus might be wholly mine, a bedecking of symbols with my private fancies. The only way, say modern empiricists, that we can have reasonable assurance that the meanings attributed to sources are not mere private projections is to employ scientific method. For without the assumption of the empirical unity of the world, of the concomitance of mental with physical behavior, and the accessibility of the one through the other, historical inquiry might well be circular. Only by means of scientific criteria, and only by framing such hypotheses in regard to the past as can be confirmed by consequences in present observation can the student feel confident that his so-called learning from documents comes indeed from the purported historical persons as sources.

But with analysis of this sort no common sense historian can finally agree. While to an extent he allows that interpretation in reading and writing may distort and create its object, yet at some point he draws the line. For common sense never doubts that documents can provide us with more than inferential hypotheses about other men, that in fact they can provide communications from them. As we have said, the layman takes for granted a core of intuitive directness, a genuine meeting of the knowing subject with the subject known. To him historical inquiry is more than external description and stories *about*, more than tentative reconstruction of the mental life of human beings on the basis of psycho-physical parallelism and so-called empirical tests. In his view, knowledge of man's past involves a bridging of the gulf between minds here-and-now and there-and-then through imagery, concepts, intuition. Observing how we are able in memory to revert emotionally and cognitively to vanished persons and situations inspires us with belief in the power of historical inquiry to do something similar on a larger scale. Though the testimony of documents is second-hand as compared with our own recollections and hence less certain, the core of the process seems much the same. As in remembering some red-letter day of one's childhood, one seems to renew old intimacies and to relive vanished scenes, so the student of history by steeping himself in records of the past believes that he gains on occasion genuine acquaintance with bygone men and situations. Though admittedly there may be only a few students who so saturate themselves in the documents as to have a sense of participating in great days like those of the American or the French revolutions, a far larger number appear convinced that they have established acquaintance with certain great men of the past, that they have made friends, for instance, with Franklin, Jefferson, Lincoln, or even Socrates or Confucius, and that these have communicated to them something of their humor, urbanity, and solidity of spirit in a unique and genuine way. To be told by the scientific historian that all this is mere imaginative projection induced by linguistic symbols, mere fabrication on the reader's part, impossible to accept because beyond all empirical check, is exasperating. "One cannot help believing it" the layman replies. To demand proof for assumptions which are themselves the basis of all proof regarding historical experience—namely, the genuineness of mnemonic reversion and of intersubjective acquaintance—seems to him the height of absurdity. Disregarding the sphinx-like enigmas of indirect knowledge, shared perspective, and communion across gulfs of time and space, the layman takes the kernel of intuition in these matters as objective, never doubting but that we are able to gain genuine intimacy with other men in other days.

In accepting shared experience and psychic transmission so unquestioningly, the traditional historian has in him, without knowing it, a touch of the mystic. For him, unlike the naturalist, knowledge is not wholly rooted in bodies and their sense organs, their separateness and situational exclusiveness. The conviction of participation in others' deliverances, of the reception of news from men whose bones are dust is quite natural to the layman, who does not have to explain in strictly physical terms how this communication takes place. Whereas the scientific attitude seems logically committed to an a-social basis of epistemology, since in sense observation each inhabits a private world imprisoned in his own deliverances, common sense, on the contrary, can accept knowledge of others' experience on the simple assurance of sharing as an intuited fact. But for the scientific empiricist the first person singular remains, it would seem, the only point of departure, so long as there exists no *organism in general* and a man can sense with no organs save his own. He at least cannot, by resting his case on the uncritical assumptions of practical life, avoid the theoretical problems of knowledge.

To escape this predicament, naturalists frequently go to great lengths to persuade us that evidence of the social behavior of man is equivalent to proof of the social nature of knowledge. Abetted by sociologists and their lore, they tirelessly repeat accounts of the genesis and utility of social life as evidence of shared experience and its validity. By tracing the prevalence of group life among men from primitive times, by noting how awareness of ego and alter seem to develop concomitantly, they imagine that they have shown both how the transmission of knowledge takes place and demonstrated its reliability. Actually, of course, they have assumed the point to be proved presupposing social knowledge throughout in order to establish it. Among their favorite stipulations are: that just as there are no isolated facts, so there are no independent egos; that, despite his separate embodiment, no man lives to himself but in interaction with others. The individual is an abstraction; for to society, they would say, the individual owes virtually all that he is: nurture, language, learning, the very substance of his being.

But we must be on our guard against suggestions of this sort. We must not be led by our feeling of certainty to mistake a

case built upon an unquestioning assumption of psychic communion and sharing for a scientific verification of the fact.
Mere widespread conviction or initial predication is not
enough to justify a belief. The presumptions, for instance, that
'everything is alive' or that 'one's life will continue forever'
(which makes it necessary to teach each child anew the fact
of death), while seemingly natural to primitive minds, are
negatived by critical test. So similarly even if belief in social
participation in others' deliverances had been one of man's
dogmas from the earliest times, the mere existence of the conviction would not itself prove scientifically the objective fact.
Moreover, as the critic of naturalism would point out, his-
toriographers who stress 'the social' as the fundamental category trade continually on the ambiguity of the term: by dwell-
ing on the notions of associated living and concurrent behavior,
they try to make us believe that a meeting or commingling of
minds takes place in the nature of knowledge. But there is a
vast difference often overlooked between *experience in society
and social or shared experience,* between life in common and a
common life. For men to be associated in a group under the
same conditions, and for them to participate in and communi-
cate to one another the same experiences, are quite different
things. Yet capital is continually made by substituting the one
for the other. That men closely coordinated in action may
remain worlds apart in mental experience is the veriest commonplace. Broken partnerships in business, marriage, politics
too clearly show how persons may live through the same
events, engage in the same tasks, speak the same language, yet
their alienation remain complete.

In brief, naturalism cannot have it both ways. By its initial
acceptance of the senses as the sole fulcrum of knowledge, the
perspectives of men's minds are assumed to reflect the mutual
exclusiveness of their bodies. However experiences may be socially imputed to others, each enjoys and suffers only his own
deliverances. The naturalist rejects as mystical any historian's
pretension to reach out to selves in other spheres and recover
the past in living terms. Despite an inclination to accept gen-

uine participation, he holds cognizance of others' lives comes to him only in terms of and through the intermediary of his own. Were it possible, on the contrary, to share others' experience then the very distinction of 'mine' and 'thine' in perception would disappear, and the whole orientation of historical writing (as the record of individual sources) would be transformed. The difference between naturalism and other views of history thus turns finally on the question whether 'communication' is between bodies or minds. While intuition and the transmission of essences are allowed by the others, naturalists admit only bodily action between corresponding but mutually exclusive systems. So long as there is no communal sensing, for naturalism there can be properly speaking no shared or mutual experience. Since mind is organic to the body, and since no one escapes his body, no one escapes himself. To each bounded center, others' experience remains finally an imputed hypothesis to be checked or confirmed by one's own empirical deliverance. However, though no one experiences another's experience, it is only by assuming a thorough-going sameness throughout nature, its constituents and laws, with a consequent parallelism between overt and internal human behavior, that the concurrence of private experiences commonly called 'communication' takes place.

But to the opponents of naturalism, as already said, correspondence is not enough. Even if naturalism be permitted the assumption that similar creatures in a similar setting will react to similar stimuli in similar ways, such concurrence does not account for the fact of the transmission of knowledge. Traditional and philosophical history, on the contrary, cut the gordian knot by allowing a commerce of concepts and a core of intuitive insight into the minds of other men. As in sense perception, according to common belief, the observer grasps something which is at once a component of his individual experience and of an over-individual setting, similarly the student of documents may receive, as he might in a letter from a friend, messages from distant personalities. At any rate in the transactions of daily life, religion, history, ordinary men believe that they enjoy from time to time a meeting of minds, a parting of the veil as it were, not to be adequately described as scientific hypothesis or the imaginative projection of one's own experience. Perhaps the most extreme instance of this is the widespread conviction of acquaintance with the spirits of great religious founders with whom communion is claimed by the devout. But aside from this there are many more, possibly a majority, who would affirm that men like Paul, Washington, or Napoleon speak to us in their letters and speeches no less genuinely in principle than do contemporary correspondents. Great characters and their ideas may be known less fully in history yet no less truly than monuments and ruins. When Pascal says that "It is not in Montaigne but in myself that I find all that I see in him,"[5] he overlooks that it is only because he presupposes here the utterance of a kindred soul that the meanings and values of the text speak to him with such force.

In so far as men are intelligent beings they grasp concepts as well as percepts, and are able to take sensory particulars not simply as circumscribed existents but as bearers of universal meanings, immaterial essences or ideas. To the degree that they come to suffuse their memories, feelings, and sense experience with insights of a conceptual order, they free themselves from the prison house of their exclusiveness for a wider world of ideal and communicable significance. Through these insights new knowledge flows in and communication, historical or contemporary, takes place. The whole story of communication as the transfiguration of experience through the awakening of awareness to conceptual meanings is well illustrated by an incident in the autobiography of Helen Keller.[6] This incident,

[5] Blaise Pascal, *Pensées* (Trans. by W. Trotter, New York, 1941) p. 20.

[6] Helen Keller, *The Story of My Life* (New York, 1903) p. 23. "We walked down the path to the well-house ... Someone was drawing water and my teacher placed my hand under the spout. As the cool stream gushed over one hand she spelled into the other the word water; at first slowly, then rapidly. I stood still, my whole attention fixed upon the motion of her fingers. Suddenly I felt a misty consciousness of a something forgotten—a thrill of returning thought, and somehow the mystery of language was revealed to me. I knew that 'w-a-t-e-r' meant the wonderful cool something that was flowing over my hand. That living word awakened my soul, gave it light, hope, joy, set it free."

the most momentous in her life, occurred one day in childhood when standing with her teacher (Miss Sullivan) at the garden pump with the water flowing over her hand, and feeling her teacher's fingers tapping the same persistent pattern, she suddenly grasped 'w-a-t-e-r' as the 'meaning' of the action in relation to the situation. It was not merely that she grasped that 'this' (the pressure of the fingers) was associated as a sign for 'that' (the feeling of the water) as a mere tag or correlated signal in experience. Signals regarding her wants already existed between herself and those around her. But here was a symbol in a language indicating an essence or ideal referent; here was a way of detaching things from their experienced locus, of introducing them into novel combinations, a new world of ideal forms, and a way of sending messages to and fro about them. Here was converse with other selves, freedom to express whatever one wanted to, liberation into a new dimension. To interpret the incident, as some psychologists might, as a mere speed-up in the learning of tactual-kinaesthetic correlations induced by the realization that everything had a name, would be to miss the point of the solitary soul's escape from the prison of the body and its senses to membership in a world of selves, universals, and ideal corporate knowledge. In terms similar to Miss Keller's account. Dr. Samuel G. Howe, the teacher of the still earlier Laura Bridgman, describes his efforts to reach the blind, deaf child "alone and helpless in a deep, dark, still pit" and the unforgettable moment when he "saw the light in the child's face and knew that spirit had touched spirit." Up to that point, he remarks, "the processes had been mechanical."

The poor child had sat in mute amazement, and patiently imitated everything her teacher did; but the truth began to flash upon her—her intellect began to work—she perceived that here was a way in which she could herself make a sign for anything that was in her own mind, and to show it to another mind; and at once her countenance lighted up with a human expression; it was no longer a dog or a parrot, it was an immortal spirit, eagerly seizing upon a new link of union with other spirits.[7]

[7] Laura E. Richards, *Laura Bridgman* (New York, 1928) p. 24. Copyrighted by Appleton-Century-Crofts, Inc.

Similar feelings must have been awakened in the breasts of students of history struggling with garbled documents, with an unintelligible patchwork of evidence, or with students like Champollion of unknown languages at the moment when suddenly the bewildering pattern of marks with which they were dealing 'made sense' and a message came through. To be sure, for the historian dealing with documents instead of living persons the process may not be reciprocal, yet the process is much the same. That the heart of the matter involves conception more than perception, that is, makes use of concrete insight as well as universal relations and inferential significance, and not merely the associative tagging of particulars in correspondence, is hard to deny.

While at the outset linguistic marks are taken in fixed association with specific sensa or images, in time through intelligent insight they acquire transference and mobility so that they can be applied through abstraction to a whole group of relationally similar, though empirically dissimilar, objects and situations. To be able to take the sensuous mark, the 'this' as standing for a conceptual 'any' as an index of a universal meaning, a distilled essence, in short, to grasp it as a common denominator standing for many instances, is essential to belief that many minds can comprehend the same notions and that through them minds can receive messages from other psyches even though they have not been visited by the same sensa. Thus a sign-language by means of reflective insight provides a bridge of ideas or essences by which men escape submergence in the solitude of their particular existence and private peculiarities. With its aid, the gulf is spanned, a structure of knowledge raised, and understanding achieved of persons, processes, events beyond the compass of the individual's experience. As indicating concepts, linguistic symbols become for the historian bearers of significance from men of former times, authentic currency circulating through many minds, the medium of exchange of knowledge from age to age. Their contents apprise him of discoveries and tidings about events beyond any possible invention of his own. Indeed his documents in-form him not only of 'whats' but of 'thats,' conveying news not simply of essences but of the blunt actuality of vanished facts. To be sure, the student of history is largely dependent upon his personal fund of experience to fill in with concrete parallels the conceptual outline of the documentary account. As may happen with a radio listener, his power to distinguish an S. O. S. from static, the Morse code signal from a mere meaningless splutter, may depend upon his having the key to its decoding (intuitive and conceptual power and a fund of memories) within himself. Nevertheless what *comes through* convinces him by its pattern that he is in contact with an independent, authentic, personal source. Similarly with the historian. By drawing on his stock of experience in his study of documents, sparks may be struck in the reader that kindle a blaze of comprehension beyond reach of mere ordinary conceptual analysis. In reading the Platonic life of Socrates, for instance, he may assemble from the resources of his memory the picture of a snub-nosed, broad browed, barefoot Greek in a chiton, yet when he comes upon certain of Socrates' words (*e.g.*, that it is better to suffer injustice than commit it) and feels the impact of his teaching, the integral force of his life and death, he can hardly doubt he encounters in these pages a unique, genuine and authentic character. So it is with certain other great characters of history which serve as dynamos of meaning to such an extent that the historian cannot seriously believe that their vital power comes from other than the imputed persons themselves. In short, the convincing historical personage is a psychic complex involving at once intentional meanings of its own and eliciting memories and images in others, yet remaining withal a whole that is *sui generis*.

Hardly anything is more familiar than our use of analogical inference. Many times a day in reading a letter, sizing up a task, listening to the news, or conversing with others about their affairs, we catch ourselves using analogies, interpreting impressions received through weaving fresh complexes from bits of old recollections, familiar feelings, and conceptual similarities. By drawing on the stock of our own experiences,

finding suggestions, parallels, kindred elements in our own
nature, we gain knowledge of others. Have similar happenings
ever befallen me? Do I share motives of this sort? In reading
history this is a man's most natural question; so that, if the
purported events run directly counter to his own observations
of life, they leave him cold and he tends to presume them false.
Why indeed should he accept conclusions for which his deliverances afford no warrant, that go against the witness of his
own consciousness? If, on the contrary, trains of impressions
similar in kind if not in degree to his own are attributed to men
of different times, appeal to his own deliverances serves analogically to bear them out along with their encompassing situations. To check the unfamiliar by the more familiar, the less
known by the better known, seems but sound sense. In squar-
ing accounts against the standard of his own experience, the
historian inevitably interprets the sensory materials of other
lives through the intermediary of his own. While the use of
sympathetic echoes may appear entirely too superficial at the
outset as a method for history, years of research coupled with
a sharp eye to the teachings of experience may in time afford
penetration not unlike personal acquaintance. "The historian,"
as one of them has said, "who 'lives' in a period, who saturates
himself in its literature . . . acquires a kind of intimacy which
exists between close personal friends."[8] At its best, where its
main figures become like living characters we have known,
history passes beyond narration and becomes in Michelet's
word 'resurrection.'

Nevertheless historical analogy, unlike the method of hypothesis, does not resolve the subjects compared into instances of
a universal law. For it the detection of certain resemblances
between particulars taken as particulars suffices; hence objects
retain in its eyes their unannullable distinctions of individuality, inexhaustible by conceptual generalization. Because history, despite its secondary use of hypothesis and empirical
tests from the sciences, depends finally on memory, analogy,
conception, and intuitive insight to link characters, author, and

[8] Ernest Scott, *History and Historical Problems* (New York, 1925) pp. 26-27.

reader, the inner verification of consciousness can never be effaced. Appraisal of the moral bearing of actions, motives, the imponderables of character are beyond the reach of scientific validations by sense. 'Truth is subjectivity,' albeit the subjectivity is subject to the demands of mental coherence, inclusiveness, and other logical tests. The judgment to which it appeals is that of both writer and public, their insight into persons, ideas, values, and clues from the past, assuming a world with an invariant pattern of variables, and their use of the analogies of experience as to the probabilities of life. Just as only the presupposition of a common relational structure makes possible the translation of ancient calendars and coins, codes and penalties to terms of those we use today, so only by assuming an enveloping, transcultural pattern of values can we explain how judgments of praise and censure from ancient Egypt or Rome can be veridically comprehended by our contemporaries. In all such appraisals consciousness must find its witness finally in itself rather than in empirical techniques under dominance of the scientific principle of externality.

Despite the pitfalls of analogy, history has its roots in it. Admittedly cosmic inhuman analogues (like the machine or the organism) when they dominate the background may be, as we shall later show, peculiarly disastrous. Similarly, sweeping parallels that tempt the historian to 'prove' that Socrates was to Greece what Confucius was to China, or to represent Christ as the apogee of all the demi-gods of mythology, are hardly less so. Conclusions drawn from such comparisons in purportedly factual works tend to be more misleading than informing. For once such parallels are set up, there is no way of curbing the reader's labyrinthine associations, no clear-cut check by which to separate actual from imaginary likenesses in interpretation. Since no scientific law is proved (in the absence of measurement and control), the resemblances remain figurative, elusive, incapable of precise formulation. Nevertheless since all knowledge proceeds through the detection of resemblances, in dealing with objects largely beyond empirical check, analogy must be appealed to. Especially in history, where unique individual characters and events are dealt with, this would seem to be the case. For other men's history cannot be viewed save through a frame of common concepts and one's personal history; and the psyche rejected by science becomes the instrument of insight for the detection of kinships between character and reader through which events in other men's lives are vividly disclosed. Because this personal background serves always as the analogical medium, the psychic suscepti- bilities of the reader as well as the peculiar slant of the author enter into and profoundly affect the interpretation of the his- torical record.

Thus, in the end a philosophical outlook on communication from persons in the past, while allowing that we cannot sur- mount the barriers of individual awareness perceptually, holds that intuitively and conceptually we are not so bound. The element of genuine insight achieved is largely through the conveyance of concepts drawn from a common world of es- sences and through sympathetic analogy. Admittedly our separate embodiments mean that, organically speaking, we enjoy and suffer only our own deliverances. At the same time, we cannot accept an account of knowledge which would deny all transmission from person to person and reduce it to mere imputed correspondence and an empirical verification of hy- potheses. The gulf between us and the past is spanned, it would seem, through our reception of concepts, whose source we attribute to minds resident in other times, and to the analogical thinking induced thereby extrapolating from ma- terials of our own experience. Through these constellations of distinctive, interrelated meanings only to be accounted for by transmission from some other mental source, we acquire what can only be described as an intuitive conviction of acquaint- ance with other selves, psychic subjects as substantive wholes, each in its nature *sui generis*. Just how strong this conviction is in a particular case depends apparently on the richness, novelty, relevancy of the meanings coming to us from that particular quarter. Yet our acquaintance with these historical selves is not really mystical, since we are not absorbed in them, nor do we experience them as one does himself. Nonetheless we retain a core of intuitive insight that we know such persons as individuals truly, a conviction transcending the conceptual and analogical intermediaries of the process.

But already we have arrived at the point for a broader discussion of the nature of scientific history, which seems to diverge in its assumptions in various ways from the traditional and philosophical interpretations.

CHAPTER FIVE

Scientific History

I.

ADMITTEDLY WITH THE ADVANCE of technology the layman and the lay tradition are undergoing a slow diminuendo and eclipse. As the functions of life are increasingly borne by inhuman forces and mechanisms, man's center of gravity shifts from untechnical to technical experience. Reliance on everyday ways of looking at things is being more and more superseded through the revolutionary discoveries of science. And with this loss of prestige by common sense goes a decline in the authority of those histories that are written in laymen's categories. To what degree scientific influence may in the long run recast the historian's activity, modify his function, alter the very foundations of his subject, we are only beginning to suspect. But that great changes in man's outlook must result from his awakening to the discrepancy between his naive deliverances and the course of the world as revealed through new techniques is a foregone conclusion. The growing suspicion that the immediate picture in men's minds bears little resemblance to the working of processes outside weakens confidence in the old common sense reports and shifts persuasion to more involved, inhuman methods.

Looked at in this way, the difference between the views of scientific and traditional history turns on the answer to the question whether unaided perception can tell us what the world of events is really like. Hitherto, as we have seen, historians have tended to take men's memories and perceptions for what they gave themselves to be, narrations and descriptions as more or less adequate counterparts of their source. In their eyes, men's stream of forthright impressions, their running commentary on events passed muster as knowledge. Causes, actions, powers accepted in everyday life served as their frame of explanation. But the scientific attitude by contrast is stricter, more sceptical in its course, challenging both the direct realism and representative perception of laymen. In its view, reliable knowledge of events is obtained not by taking impressions at their face value, but by inferences drawn from them in highly indirect ways. Although we are continually engaged in seeing objects, hearing sounds, imagining or remembering situations, to understand and report their significance requires much intermediary interpretation. Effects are rarely like their causes, or responses faithful copies of their stimuli in any obvious pictorial sense. Analysis is necessary both to relate our deliverances to their sources and to construe the character of the latter. In short, to rely on common sense in history seems as absurd as consulting the loungers in the market-place to find out the causes of a war, or palace gossip to learn the origins of a social revolution. Men, being among the most conditionable of animals, rarely report their experiences aright. Irrational promptings and preconceptions, transfer and bias continually distort their accounts.

So science, as we have said, tends to discount common sense reporting of the past which in its eyes often singles out trifling accessories as important, while remaining blind to major underlying factors. But since these often leave slight record in immediate awareness, the layman cannot be blamed for failing to do them justice in his naive, uninstructed categories. Just as common sense offers no hint that the bodies of our world are composed of electric charges, so the 'plain tale' of traditional history affords few clues as to the role played by such things as bacteria, diet, heredity, or even technology in shaping the patterns of human life. Only scientific method, which is prepared to pursue problems beyond the level of ordinary perception and to recognize that the actual course of affairs may bear slight resemblance to the reports of untrained observers, can discover the significant relations. Its bent is, on the one hand, toward what might be called a high-powered microscopic or telescopic outlook and, on the other, toward a statistical and comparative view. In contrast to the popular narrator who emphasizes what is human, individual, and striking, the scientific inquirer is often concerned with a mass of impersonal, inobvious facts. Instead of stressing particular men and their deeds, institutional changes are likely to hold his attention.

Easy though it is to point out a general shift of emphasis of this sort, it is difficult to state with precision the essentials of scientific history. Sometimes the adoption of a vague evolutionary cosmology, with the verbal reduction of final to efficient causes, seems all that is meant. Little effort is made to introduce any recognizable scientific procedure, such as careful induction, proportionate frequencies, methods of agreement or difference into the historical subject matter. Instead sweeping analogies from physics or evolutionary biology are applied to human affairs, without justification of the transfer. Nevertheless to most leaders of the movement 'scientific history' has stood for more than the appropriation of a borrowed language and an extraneous explanatory scheme. Obeisance to the new cosmology they see, if unaccompanied by an adaptation of history to the actual procedures of science, remains but a sham, a makeshift, an empty disguise.

Among early attempts in the field is Buckle's notable, and in many ways typical, effort to discover the causal laws of civilization. Convinced that "the old road is worn out and useless"[1] and that historical movements like other movements in nature are "solely determined by their antecedents," Buckle turns to the 'objective' study of men in society. Instead of peering into his memories, feelings, and imaginings to grasp the world as a panorama of inward reflection, the new historian, according to Buckle, looks outward at the mass behavior of human beings.

[1] Henry Thomas Buckle, *History of Civilization in England*, Vol. II, Pt. II p. 257.

By classifying and comparing the activities of large groups, and by noting correlations with environmental factors, he seeks to bring to light important causal laws. Of course, history written at this level of generality and concerned with societies in relation to their physical setting is very different from the common sense kind, which tries to grasp the dramatic conflicts of persons, the popular temper in crises, the inimitable flavor of characters and events. Here the action of the single man is lost in the collectivity; by implication Buckle agrees with Montesquieu that "In the great march of human affairs, individual peculiarities count for nothing."[2]

Although Buckle did not live to complete his work (published in 1857-61), in it the outlines of the positivist approach are boldly drawn. Cultural developments are studied in relation to their physical setting and historical method is assimilated to science through comparative and quasi-statistical means. By collecting facts from the social, cultural, and political life of different peoples and times, and by noting the presence, absence, and concomitant variations of cognate phenomena in Baconian fashion, Buckle sought through a comprehensive survey to uncover the causes of human progress. Even though not strictly numerical, such comparative procedure, in his opinion, revealed the regulation of human actions by law. In essence it resembled the statistical method, which though still in its infancy, according to Buckle, has already thrown more light on the operations of human nature than the whole of preceding historical inquiry. Thus government statistics by proving that the actions of men are predictable have clearly shown that history can be subject to the same treatment as science. For instance, the proportion of crimes in a society (an important index of its morality) is found to have a uniformity capable of foreknowledge like that of the tides and the planets; while the annual number of marriages, once believed to be wholly a matter of personal inclination, is proved to be "completely controlled by the price of food and the rate of

2 *Ibid.*, Vol. I Pt. II p. 593.

wages."[3] Records gathered in different countries plainly show that events which taken individually appear to be matters of personal choice are actually, when collectively examined, products of social conditions and physical causes. From such studies the historian is led to conclude that the moral actions of men are the result of their antecedents and to accept 'the great social law' that human nature, even in its volitional life, is subject to the same causal regularity as the material world.

On the basis of his acceptance of the universal reign of causality, the new scientific historian pursues his search for the agencies by means of which different societies have gained their ascendency in the world. Among non-mental agencies affecting human history the chief, according to Buckle, are those of physical geography. Everywhere climate, soil, food supply, and what he calls 'the general aspect of nature' determine the course of a people's development. By this 'general aspect' is meant the total impression made on the inhabitants by the geography of a region, an impression which for the best cultural effects must be neither so formidable as to discourage their efforts, nor so mild as to enervate their powers. But above all a favorable climate and soil are indispensable for the growth of a civilization. As Buckle summarizes the matter, "*It requires but a hasty glance* to prove the immense power of these two great physical conditions. For there is no instance in history of any country being civilized by its own efforts, unless it has possessed one of these conditions in very favorable form."[4] On the other hand, there are many instances of barbarian tribes like the Mongols, Tartars, and Arabs, who having left their deserts for more genial lands, have been able to found great cultural empires.

On the basis of his wide reading and discernment of parallels, Buckle alleges discovery of various historical laws. By arguing as above that no nation that has lacked a favorable climate or soil has ever been civilized, and by citing instances of peoples previously uncultivated who on migrating to better

3 *Ibid.*, Vol. I Pt. I p. 24.
4 *Ibid.*, Vol. I Pt. I p. 33. Italics mine.

lands became civilized, he thinks that he proves a 'law' of the dependence of progress on these factors; while another 'vast law' purports to show that only countries spared the dread, overexciting spectacle of earthquakes, hurricanes, very high mountains, and frequent pestilence are capable of great scientific and artistic achievement. In addition to employing agreement and difference in this cavalier fashion, Buckle is sanguine about introducing the experimental method into history. The plan of his work, which he did not live to complete, included a detailed account of the rise of the British people. As in science, so in history he believed that a single well-chosen experiment was sufficient to establish a law. By focusing his treatment upon England (the nation whose development, in his opinion, had been freest from outside interference), he hoped to show the operation of social laws in relative isolation under conditions approximating a 'ready-made experiment.'[5]

So, in Buckle's view, civilization develops where (as in Europe) the climate is moderate, the land not too barren, the topography on a small scale, and the spectacle of nature not too overpowering. Only in such circumstances are men able to mobilize their energies and gain sufficient confidence in themselves to master their world. Obviously without favorable physical conditions, the lash of necessity permits them no leisure for the accumulation of wealth; while in the absence of leisure and wealth, there can be no acquisition of knowledge. Only where the forces of nature are temperate enough to free men from unceasing struggle can they find time to ask questions and to understand the nature of things. Without critical questioning there can be no serious inquiry, and without inquiry no ordered intellectual advance. Invariably man's awakening confidence in his mental powers is marked by sceptical challenge of the past, by revolt against the conservative or 'protective spirit,' and against traditional authority. Thus the same physical conditions which make possible human advance encourage social revolt as well as scientific inquiry. Here

[5] *Ibid.*, Vol. I, Pt. I p. 168.

Buckle is at particular pains to point out the connection which he discerns between the spirit of scientific search and that of political liberty. Like Mill he finds increase in knowledge the predominant force for human progress. Though made by nature, man 'remakes his maker' and though the product of geography recreates by his intellectual ingenuity to an indefinite extent the global scene.

Yet even to those who favor his cause Buckle's approach is disquieting. A victory won so easily makes the triumph of science seem too cheap. Surely it is not enough for the scientific historian to invoke 'hasty glances,' broad parallels, loose citations of positive and negative instances. In any case such devices are far removed from the experimental method of difference, feeble imitations of statistical induction. Despite his professed reverence for inductive methods, the fact remains that Buckle's procedure is largely deductive. Loose generalizations are quickly converted into premises for arguments, and the mere plausibility of conjectures is taken for their substantiation. Faced with the difficulty of tracing historical causes, the scientific student understandably has a natural desire for a short-cut. In these circumstances, it is a temptation to substitute vague generalities regarding physical geography, the influence of unspecified 'moral and intellectual laws,' and the ruling notion of progress for more painstaking labor. But in the long run these things fail to satisfy the criteria which he himself has set up. No talk of 'ready-made experiments' in history, no verbal weighing of likenesses and differences can compensate for the lack of observation, analysis, and control to be found in the true generalizations of science.

To this, of course, Buckle might reply that his history, precisely because it is based on science, finds at the start much of its spade-work done, its labors already abridged. For science has already mapped the lands, registered the climates, analysed the social and economic systems, and traced in large part their specialized effects on human life. Appropriating these conclusions, the task of the historian is simply by combining them into a whole to show their total effect on the progress of civilization. Because his subject entails the entire range of knowledge, however, the scientific historian is forced by borrowing from many fields to attempt the highest generalization. Yet in so doing, in relating the internal to the external, man's mental life to the physical world, he is undeniably subject to the most crucial and severest test. For even though physical laws have already been formulated with immense success by the sciences, the laws of the mind and their relation to the environment are still, as Buckle is forced to admit, largely unknown. Faced with this impasse of scientific ignorance, Buckle tries to ignore it. Mental laws, he boldly declares, are the great source of human advance. Indeed, it is the 'intellectual laws' (those used in creating scientific techniques) as opposed to the 'moral' laws that deserve all the credit for the progress of civilization. Nothing to him is more striking than man's failure in ethical improvement (despite endless preaching) through thousands of years as compared with his immense gains in scientific knowledge. "As the progress of civilization is marked by the triumph of the mental laws over the physical, just so is it marked by the triumph of the intellectual laws over the moral ones."[6]

His argument on this score is interesting. Our modern industrial civilization, for instance, being according to Buckle more peaceful than earlier times can claim in the matter of war an unquestioned advance. Nor is this progress to be credited to the ethical teachings of religion but rather "the warlike spirit of the ancient world has been weakened by the progress of European knowledge."[7] Three causes he finds upon analysis have brought about this change: first, the invention of gunpowder, which through requiring a trained professional army weaned the masses from war; second, the discovery by political economy of the great advantages of free trade, which converted the commercial spirit 'formerly often warlike' into something 'invariably pacific'; and, third, the invention of the steam-engine, which by revolutionizing transportation and in-

[6] *Ibid.*, Vol. I Pt. I p. 164.
[7] *Ibid.*, Vol. I Pt. I p. 146.

creasing travel largely destroyed the ignorant dislike of nations for each other.

Needless to say, almost every point in this reasoning in regard to the decline of war and the connection of industry and invention with pacifism would be challenged by a historian of different assumptions. Buckle's method resembles that of a lawyer pleading a case. Both the evidence he selects and his arguments tend to a foregone conclusion. Such schematic contentions couched in ill-defined terms (like 'moral and intellectual laws' and 'the general aspect of nature') bear little resemblance to scientific proof. And his hiatus in causes, which neglects the specific and proximate for the remote and the general, robs history of its differentia as concrete.

Even his geographical argument upon inspection appears much less decisive than he supposed it to be. Granting that without a bracing climate, rugged soil, and so on, there might have been no glory that was Greece, this by no means establishes the sufficiency of geographical causes to explain Greek culture. To try to argue that, since where a (geographical advantages) are absent, b (high cultural development) is absent, therefore that: where a (geographical advantages) are present, b (high cultural development) will be found, involves the familiar logical fallacy of mistaking a necessary for the sufficient condition, of which Buckle seems unaware. The fact remains that, while a good many countries have enjoyed geographical advantages comparable to Greece, few have produced comparable cultural achievements. Hence it would seem wiser to admit that in history we are dealing with a multiplicity of causes, with many interwoven variables by no means simply determinable from one another. Although geography played a part, probably the flowering of Hellas owed something to its peculiarly gifted stock, something to acquaintance with Minoan and Egyptian civilizations, to its maritime supremacy won from Crete, and to a fortunate juncture of these with other influences in a conflux that seems not likely to recur. In any case, so long as plausible alternative hypotheses are left standing, Buckle's theory of progress remains partly suspended in air. That serious contenders are in the field is hardly open to doubt. Among the rivals of the geographical historians, for instance, are those who emphasize race. Without delving into the biological complexities of the subject, many students find it hard to deny kith or race as a genuine *historical fact* bearing some relations to the cultural advances of groups. To Buckle, on the other hand, original distinctions of stock are "altogether hypothetical";[8] he passes over in contemptuous silence both the issue and the evidence as without historical effect. But in this failure to take account of factors and considerations unfavorable to his views, even though they admit of as much Baconian treatment as his own, Buckle plainly falls short of the scientific spirit.

Later scientific historians find more to agree with in Buckle's ruling assumptions than in his lordly generalities of procedure. His naturalism, collectivism, and futurism still hold sway, although there has been a retreat from his confident intellectualism. Accumulated evidence revealing the strength of irrational and unconscious forces in human nature has weakened faith in the future perfectibility of the world to be obtained, in Buckle's words, through "the totality of human actions being governed by the totality of knowledge."[9] Today historians feel less assured of the inevitability of universal progress through science, and are more on guard against speculative dogmas pretending to prove its necessity in any scientific culture. The mere fact that science affords control over nature, they now see, by no means insures that its techniques will be devoted to the ends of human betterment. While ridding the world of wants, superstitions, diseases that plagued an earlier time, the march of scientific civilization may have merely transformed these evils and brought new ones in its train. While the ravages of pestilence have been checked, the

[8] *Ibid.*, Vol. I Pt. I p. 29. Yet to many qualified inquirers, it need hardly be said, groups claiming blood relationship betray distinctive traits, preserved despite the wide scattering of their members for long periods of time; while, on the other hand, groups of different stocks sometimes retain their racial peculiarities despite close environmental association with each other.

[9] *Ibid.*, Vol. I Pt. I p. 166.

tensions of modern life have vastly increased the incidence of
mental derangement and nervous disorders. And though
benighted religious superstitions may be largely a thing of
the past, political fanaticisms, operating in the name of science, have taken their place, which are even more deadly. Far
from insuring the end of wars and economic stringency, science
by creating the efficient horrors of the atomic age, seems to
have brought man to the edge of a new, more terrible abyss.
Despite loss of their old assurance that science renders progress
inevitable, positivist historians remain incurably sceptical of
spiritual sanctions and energies. Having included man in
nature, the movement is led to reject all principles beyond the
test of science: with the result that confidence is reserved for
essentially amoral,—that is, social, psychological, economic,
and physical factors,—while the power of conscience and
spirit in their own right are denied.

Nevertheless the comparative method so strongly defended
by Buckle has found distinguished supporters. In England men
like Freeman, Frazer, Bryce, even Toynbee, though less concerned with its pretensions as science, have accepted its
assumption of monism. Being part of the natural process,
man's life in its history would seem subject to the same uniformity as the rest of the world. Nor would this uniformity
underlying human diversity appear merely hypothetical. By
the comparative method the historian does not merely suppose
that: if men were alike in different places and times, they
would react similarly. On the contrary, he assumes categorically that human nature, despite differing environmental factors and novelties of response, is everywhere the same, just as
he assumes the basic similarity of the members of a species in
the vegetable or animal kingdom. Indeed, to him it would
seem that it is only because man is always everywhere the
same that we can speak meaningfully of his history as a unity.
As James Bryce said in explaining the comparative method:

There is in the phenomena of human society . . . one element or
factor which is practically always the same and therefore the basis of all
the so-called sciences . . . This is human nature itself. All fairly normal

men have like passions and desires. They are stirred by like motives and they think along similar lines when they have reached the stage of civilization in which arts, sciences, letters have developed, political institutions have grown up, and reason has become so far a guide of conduct that sequences in their action can be under given conditions foretold.[10]

Because of this constancy of human nature, he goes on to say, its laws are open to discovery, and predictions may be made as to the average behavior of men from careful study of their social groups. Even if the conduct of a man taken singly is open to doubt, that of a hundred or a thousand is foretold more readily, since in the treatment of large numbers individual peculiarities tend to be weeded out. Behind institutions and events the comparative method traces everywhere the fundamentals of human nature as modified by race, climate, economy, and historical antecedents; and by allowing for disturbing influences present in one country and absent in another, it arrives at general conclusions through what it takes to be a scientific method approaching agreement and difference.

Even its severest critics must concede that by applying the method to the life of various peoples and by noting similarities and dissimilarities in their languages, myths, technologies, customs, and social arts, interesting analogies can be drawn. Often the discovery of resemblances between linguistic roots, legends, tools, and forms of social organization in periods and countries remote from each other is held to indicate a common source,—with the probability of identical origin increasing proportionately to the amount of similarity. As to the nature of this source there would seem to be two possibilities. It may be supposed with the diffusionists,[11] that these similarities

[10] James Bryce, *Modern Democracies* (New York, 1921) Vol. I p. 14. The comparative method is said to be (p. 18) "scientific in that it reaches general conclusions by tracing similar results to similar causes, eliminating those disturbing influences which . . . make the results in the examined cases different in some points while similar in others." "The fundamentals of human nature, present everywhere, are in each country modified by the influences of race, of external conditions" and "historical antecedents" (p. 17).

[11] G. Elliot Smith, *In The Beginning* (London, 1946), *Human History* (1934). W. J. Perry, *The Growth of Civilization* (London, 1937).

point back to a single original civilization, from which a dispersion of peoples occurred carrying with them a common tongue, common myths, a common store of political and social arts. Or, as is more common, these likenesses may be held to indicate simply the basic identity of human nature, which called forth similar inventions under similar conditions in a plurality of originally separate and independent groups. But whether cultural similarities indicate a *single* or a *multiple* origin of civilization with subsequent interaction and borrowing, it is noteworthy that neither diffusionists nor pluralists seem inclined to deny uniformity. As with Mill, Comte, and Buckle, the comparative method continues to assume the identity of human nature and its laws. Throughout history like causes have had like effects; and discounting counteracting influences men betray the same basic passions and desires, the same motives and modes of thinking at the same levels of culture. Thus, however characters may differ, for the *formation of character* there is the same human stuff and universal positive laws. Indeed, this alone, on this view, makes possible the prediction and explanation of human behavior. But once given a common framework of laws and materials, it is hardly surprising that like evils suggest like remedies, similar needs evoke similar satisfactions, and the same problems broadly call forth the same answers. On the basis of empirical uniformity, the historian can readily explain how so many of the essential tools of civilization have been hit on independently at various places and times: the invention of the bow and the wheel, the taming of the horse, the hollowing out of the canoe; while similarities of mythology and folklore may be accounted for in the same fashion. If human nature is fundamentally the same, there should follow from its standard experiences relatively only a few easily imagined plots and combinations of character; so behind a hundred solar and resurrection myths we find the same spectacle of the heavens, the same mystery of birth and death, of fertility and revival.

Nevertheless while social subjects like history have come more and more to treat their data comparatively, as instances of a class under principles of regularity, the physical sciences in recent years have witnessed a certain recession of belief in individual empirical uniformity. For them the old argument that conformity to the law of averages and predictive probability establishes causal determinism has been thrown open to question. The very line of reasoning used by Buckle as the strongest argument for determinism is now held consonant with indeterminacy. What appears as regularity may be a consequence of the statistical method rather than characteristic of the individual originating phenomena. Faced with the new ultra-microscopic quantum world of almost inexhaustible complexity, physical science seems no longer prepared to assert the old mechanism and exact predictability of nature. As a result historians who patterned their determinism after the example of the physical sciences find their supports suddenly failing them. Moreover, not only does mounting evidence bear witness to the almost endless diversity of the social process, but the very strength of rival schools in history, archeology, anthropology make it increasingly hard to believe that societies always follow the same stages and lines of development. Sooner or later retreat seems inevitable from empirical recurrence to relational common factors. It cannot be simply because men belong to the same natural kind and are determined by the same empirical context and positive laws that we find parallels in their history. These things might conceivably vary and there might still remain an underlying constancy of ordering principles. Rather it is because the world involves a unity of logical structure, a formal invariancy through its varying content, that knowledge has power to survey and to connect the different domains of history. However much the world of men of the Old Stone Age may have differed from that of the Twentieth Century American, a constant functional relationship makes their significant comparison possible.

Even when not concerned with different periods and countries, scientific history is always implicitly comparative in regarding its objects as specimens of a class or as cognate instances under a law, rather than as individuals. Dealing with all manner of data, it may range in practice from specialization to inclusiveness; but always by the canons of science it must approach its subject rigorously, factually, dispassionately, with an attitude relatively value-free. If the subject is political, we must, as Freeman somewhat extravagantly puts it:

> throw ourselves into a state of mind to which political constitutions seem as absolutely colorless as grammatical forms, a state of mind to which the change from monarchy to democracy or from democracy to monarchy seems as little a matter of moral praise or blame as the process by which the Latin language changed into the French.[12]

Coupled with this 'objective' attitude, scientific history has great zest for original sources: for archives, archeological remains, documentation, and the dissection of parallel texts. Wherever possible it seeks for eye-witness accounts and first-hand information; at the same time regarding them most critically and rejecting the authority of many hitherto accepted sources as spurious, prejudiced, exaggerated, or infected with supernatural assumptions. Possessed of a new sense of the importance of background and context, as against the incidents in the foreground, it shifts attention to the massive, inconspicuous features of the scene away from the striking and romantic.[13]

Since its inception about a century ago, scientific history has passed through various phases of emphasis, at one time stressing constitutional history and the collection of archive material, at another the study of institutions, especially the social

12 E. A. Freeman, *Comparative Politics* (London, 1872) p. 23.
13 James Harvey Robinson, *The New History* (New York, 1922) p. 75. "About sixty years ago a new era opened in historical investigation . . . marked by four obvious achievements, *all owing to the example and influence of natural science*. The gist of these advances was: (1) to test and examine sources of information far more critically and to reject partially or wholly many authorities on which predecessors had relied implicitly; (2) to tell the truth like a man regardless of whose feelings might be hurt; (3) to realize the overwhelming importance of the inconspicuous, common, homely, everyday, often obscure, over the rare, spectacular, and romantic; (4) to spurn supernatural thought and anthropocentric explanations which have been the stock in trade of philosophies of history."

and the economic. At the same time, the recognition of further and further subdivisions (*e.g.*, the analysis of the economic field into labor, agriculture, manufacture, trade, currency, *etc.*) has meant increased specialization. Today we are faced with a subject so vast, with techniques requiring such varied skills, that few students scrupulous of scientific restrictions of procedure have the boldness for general history. Fashion turns instead to cooperative works, in which different aspects and periods of a subject are assigned to different writers. (The Cambridge Ancient and Modern Histories are, of course, monuments in this line.) While the results tend to a series of monographs more than to comprehensive synthesis, nevertheless if the proponents of analysis are right (which we cannot believe!) and if the claim to total or overall views is but a false legacy from theology, then such segmented, limited inquiries are the worthiest products of the historian.

However, the outstanding men in scientific history have not been those who themselves engaged in extreme specialization. Their work, on the contrary, has been more ambitious in scope and they have sought to widen its implications by claiming affiliation with some special science or group of sciences as a model. In the ensuing pages we shall try to illustrate some of these tendencies to enlarge the import of human actions by analogy with the physical, the biological or the social sciences. Unquestionably there is a sharp divergence between historians who, like Henry Adams, find the laws of physics supreme in human life, and those who construe events predominantly through the findings of economics or of organic evolution. Since Herbert Spencer there has been increased piecemeal borrowing of biological categories and parallels with an occasional more sweeping effort to fit the course of human events into a full-scale interpretation in terms of some particular science.

Certainly there is nothing strange in the pervasiveness of scientific models in historical writing. The immense success of the sciences has made mechanistic and biological analogies almost as widespread in expression as the veiled personifications of an earlier time. The machine, natural warfare, the organism are today favorite comparisons that shape our thinking. In the subtlest ways they color our presuppositions. The comparison of society to an organism, of its growth to evolution, of life to a battle, or of the processes of nature to the running of clock-work, is traceable through complex ramifications of man's speech and thought. Small wonder that histories written under scientific influence should borrow heavily from such notions to lend light and unity to the maze of events.

That life is a battle, that nature is like a giant power-house stored with generators and transformers, or some juggernaut engine with grinding gears, that social development resembles organic evolution,—how many historical writings are tinged with assumptions of this sort. Under the influence of the sciences, in such works inhuman parallels more and more supplant those of personality. Yet the danger inherent in such metaphorical transfer of categories is not always perceived, and the mistake is made of imagining that the best way to bridge a gap is to ignore it. The result, as we see it, is to introduce a kind of creeping automatism into human action through its control by outside forces, so that a lessening of the role of will and purpose is more and more evident. Human life comes to be regarded as an episode in the doing and undoing of the material flux. Men, societies, cultures follow a generic natural course. As individuals, men are born, age, reproduce, and die; collectively their civilizations arise, mature, decline, and are replaced by others in an uninterrupted interplay of laws and materials. Whatever ensues was rooted in the environmental context; and though events are often difficult to comprehend, the sequence is inviolable. To discover causal chains (that is, to separate out the conditions through whose presence or absence a definite set of events occurred or failed to occur) is held to be the business of history. Only by the disclosure of such tendencies is man thought able to achieve retrospective, and predictive understanding of affairs. Such are the assumptions of what may be called 'mechanomorphism' in history. The logic of the thinking seems the reverse of that of primitive animism. In place of the 'pathetic' we have here what Toynbee called the 'apathetic fallacy.' Instead of endowing everything with something like purposive feeling and life, the living is basically dealt with as though non-living, the human as inhuman, the conscious as though unconscious. Yet surely, it would seem to us, only confusion can result from borrowing from the impersonal, non-human world the models by which to interpret human happenings.

II.

The tendency to invoke a blind cosmic frame is basic to scientific history. Nevertheless the analogues adopted are not always from the organic and social sciences, but sometimes, which is far more surprising, from the physical. One of the most influential figures in establishing scientific historiography in America was Henry Adams. And though Adams lived through the great ferment of Darwinism, he turned away from the evolutionary theory to find the patterns of the human historical sequence finally in entropy and the laws of mechanics. These conclusions he did not arrive at easily but by a long process. In his early extended work, *The History of the United States* (1801-1817), Adams adopted what he then regarded as a generally scientific procedure. Yet despite his zeal in analyzing documents, his use of statistics, and his coverage after a fashion of physical and economic factors in addition to diplomatic, social, and political life, Adams came in the end to a consciousness of defeat. Historical connections had eluded him. In a famous passage he admitted that he had 'toiled in vain' to uncover causal relations.

Historians undertake to arrange sequences, called stories or histories— assuming in silence a relation of cause and effect. These assumptions, hidden in the depths of dusty libraries, have been astounding, but commonly unconscious and childlike; so much so, that if any captious critic were to drag them to light, historians would probably reply, with one voice, they never supposed themselves required to know what they were talking about. Adams, for one, had toiled in vain to find out what he meant. He had even published a dozen volumes in American history for no other purpose than to satisfy himself whether, by the severest process of stating with the least possible comment, such facts as seemed sure in such order as seemed rigorously consequent, he could fix for a familiar moment a necessary sequence of human movement.[14]

But his experiments in writing history had led only to deep disappointment. "Where he saw sequence," he says, "other men saw something quite different, and no one saw the same unit of measure."

Undaunted, however, Adams resolved to apply in turn to human events the procedures of the different sciences. Failing in his efforts to find causal relations analogous to those in the organic and social worlds, unable to present history as "a catalogue, a record, a romance, or an evolution," he turned finally to the sequence of force.[15] Here at last he found his answer. To him the laws of physics appeared in the last analysis dominant in the universe, and the processes of life, thought, and human history essentially just cases of them. Thus the great acceleration in knowledge commonly called the growth of civilization became to Adams a historical movement akin to gravitation in physics. Only in the case of civilization the 'masses' involved are man and nature deployed in time instead of, as in gravitation, the earth-sun system deployed in space. While admitting that the formulation of the law has not yet found its Newton, Adams felt that he had himself glimpsed the action of a universal attraction between thought and matter, increasing in the ratio of the square of the times.[16] Under the spell of this idea he imagines in his later essays that, once the dynamical law is found, history will be able to chart man's past and future after the same fashion as astronomy predicts the movements of the planets. In order to interpret the historical process as the action and reaction of forces, he defines *force* broadly to mean "anything that does or helps to do work"—

[14] *The Education of Henry Adams,* p. 382.

[15] *Ibid.,* p. 382. "Satisfied that the sequence of men led to nothing and that the sequence of their society could lead no further, while the mere sequence of time was artificial, and the sequence of thought was chaos, he turned at last to the sequence of force."

[16] *Ibid.,* p. 492.

so that the sun, coal, waterpower, the dynamo, man, thought, even the gods are all forces, mechanical, occult, or otherwise—; while progress is defined similarly as "the development and economy of forces."[17]

Contrary to the general assumption, human history is not so much the story of man's conquest of nature, as the capture of the lesser mass by the greater, nature's conquest of man. Though man labors to master the forces of nature, they being vastly more powerful finally ensnare and dominate him. Yet uncomprehending, he continues the vain and unequal struggle. What is called man's 'love of power' expresses in one form or another his craving to 'assimilate forces.' From the earliest recorded times he has sought by means of bow and sling, fire and fetish, to enlarge his range of control. Nature, however, has been slow to unlock her secrets. For ages human progress turned mainly on man's ability to economize forces, without much increase in the number known or in means to their development. Although the experience of three thousand years (from the pyramids to the Roman Empire) taught men many things: the use of writing and metals, the building of roads and ships, the production of civil law, geometry, and engineering, such knowledge centered chiefly in the elaboration of forces already known rather than in the discovery of new ones. For all its roads, aqueducts, laws, and free institutions, Rome depended finally on brute manpower, the energy of slaves. Nevertheless Adams finds one of the pinnacles of human civilization in the Roman Empire, although he dates its summit more than a century later than Gibbon.[18] To the inevitable question as to what caused the failure of civilization at the moment of its 'complete success,' Adams, being a man of two minds, has two answers. In his sceptical moods he declares the hopelessness of attempting to establish historical causation

[17] *Ibid.*, p. 474.
[18] *Ibid.*, p. 477. "In the year 305 the Empire had solved the problems of Europe more completely than they have ever been solved since." Yet this was followed by "the scandalous failure of civilization at the moment it had achieved complete success" (the year of Diocletian's abdication). Gibbon, however, places the high point of the Empire not in 305 A.D. but from the death of Domitian (96 A.D.) to the accession of Commodus (180 A.D.).

(we have already quoted his judgment that "Not an inch has been gained by . . . all the historians since—towards explaining the Fall."). On the other hand, as a prophet of the new scientism he has another quite different answer. Looked at *as a problem in mechanics,*" he finds the fatal weakness of the Empire to have been that it "developed too much energy and too fast," so that in striving to make its economy keep pace with its rapid political expansion it was *"torn to pieces by acceleration."* In other words, Rome, having her economy based on manpower, was compelled in the course of her rapid growth immensely to enlarge her slave population, which spread of slavery in turn debased and destroyed the Empire. "The result," says Adams, "might have been stated in a mathematical formula as early as the time of Archimedes, six hundred years before Rome fell."[19]

Like Auguste Comte, Adams accepts the presence of a phase-rule in history together with the implicit assumption that society passes through three stages: the religious, the metaphysical, and the scientific. Unlike Comte, however, he makes the metaphysical (or abstract supersensible) rather than the scientific the final stage. This is because, according to Adams, science through its ever-increasing complexity must soon surpass man's powers of comprehension with the result that physics will be transformed into metaphysics (matter being converted into a supersensuous realm of mathematical objects and invisible radiation)—at which stage man's conquest by the incomprehensible forces of nature will be complete. Moreover, history far from being an organic process of evolution, as Comte held, is a physical process of entropy, a curve in which each stage is accelerated in time over the preceding by a ratio of the square.

While men lived from remote ages under the dominance of 'occult forces' (*i.e.,* in the religious phase), the first great turning-point in human history came with their mastery of mechanical power. This transition is broadly marked by such events as the discovery of gunpowder, coal-power, the invention of the

[19] *Ibid.,* pp. 478-480. Italics mine,

steam-engine and other machines. But once in the scientific or 'mechanical phase' man is propelled with increasing speed along an inevitable path, dragged by the compulsion of nature (in Adams' metaphors) like a fish on a hook or a comet pulled by the sun. While the mechanical phase of the scientific era lasts roughly from 1600-1900 (and in the latter part measures its progress by the doubling of coal-power every decade), with the twentieth century there opens a swifter 'electric' phase. Still greater, undreamt-of forces are released with the invention of the dynamo, turning men's thoughts from mechanical to electrical models, and bringing in the airplane, the automobile, and the motorized age. But by this time the pace has become so killing that within some seventeen years society has raced through the implications of these discoveries, and entered upon the end of the scientific, and the beginning of the metaphysical stage. This new revolution Adams names the 'ether phase.' It is introduced by the discovery of radium and the tremendous forces of invisible radiation by which 'power leaps from every atom.'[20] Scientific thought no longer deals with things perceptible to the senses or ventures to explain causes,[21] but has passed over into a realm of metaphysical and mathematical notions which he calls 'occult mechanism.' Yet if science goes on doubling and quadrupling its complexities every few years (as it must by the phase-rule), its developments will soon outdistance our mathematics and the very possibilities of the human mind. Before his death in 1918 Adams saw the intricacies of scientific events as far beyond the grasp of the average man; and within a few years, he foresaw, the difficulties of comprehension would be far more severe. If civilization is to maintain its rate of progress in controlling the energies of nature, he declares:

The new American—the child of incalculable coal-power, chemical power, electric power, and radiating energy, as well as of new forces yet undetermined—must be a sort of God compared with any former creation of nature. At the rate of progress since 1800, every American

[20] *Ibid.*, p. 494.
[21] *Ibid.*, p. 497.

who lived into the year 2000 would know how to control unlimited power. He would think in complexities unimaginable to an earlier mind.[22]

Nevertheless to Adams it seems unlikely that civilization will be able to continue this accelerated pace. To him it appears probable that by the year 2000 society will be on the road to a long regression. This decline, plainly perceptible, he predicts, around the year 1950, will constitute a melancholy verification of his historical theory.

Adams' reasons for anticipating this retrograde movement of civilization, like his predictions of the atomic age, are curious and interesting. When in his calculations the history of the acceleration of human thought was superposed on the path of a perfect comet, the result clearly showed, he said, that "man's evolution has passed perihelion, and that his movement was already retrograde."[23] Caught in the violent attraction of nature's forces, man, having reached his limits of expansion, must either be extinguished in a violent explosion or else (like a comet) turn and depart by the path by which he has come. In any case the evidence does not point to man's indefinite future advance. With leaders in physics Adams holds that the law of entropy occupies a supreme position among the laws of nature. For him any belief in persistent historical evolution is nullified by science's admission of the universal degradation of energy and the tendency of systems to wear themselves out. It was absurd, held Adams, for social science to teach progress while physical science was committed to destruction.[24] Nor can the life of the mind by any legerdemain be excluded from this tendency, since thought itself functioning as a catalytic agent and mysterious energy-transformer "must obey the laws of force."[25] The great mistake of evolutionary thinkers is to fail to see that the sequence of phases by which societies pass from one way of life to another resembles

[22] *Ibid.*, p. 496.
[23] Henry Adams, *The Tendency of History* (New York, 1928) p. 167.
[24] Henry Adams, "A Letter to American Teachers of History" (1910).
[25] *Tendency of History*, pp. 70-71.

changes like those from ice to water, and water to steam, studied by physicists like Willard Gibbs. Notions of expansion, contraction, acceleration, volume, transformations of energy from higher to lower potential are more applicable to history than ideas of evolution with their inevitable suggestions of elevation and improvement. Far from providing science with any real unity of direction or unit of measure, evolution has actually meant only "roads [that] ran about in every direction overrunning, dividing, subdividing, stopping abruptly, vanishing slowly, with side-paths that led nowhere and sequences that could not be proved."[26] No historian whose thought is in accord with the physical sciences can claim the persistence of progress in human events; instead, for all writers who grasp a dynamic view:

> History would become a record of successive phases of contraction, divided by periods of explosion, tending toward an ultimate equilibrium in the form of a volume of human molecules of equal intensity, without coordination.[27]

Having struggled all his life in the teeth of chaos and multiplicity to find some unity of pattern or general scheme, Adams is driven back upon the generalizations of physics. Here at last he feels that he has a formula almost on the tip of his pen to cover both mind and nature, a hypothesis equally applicable to the sequence of thought, the motion of the planets, and the development of society. Yet the price of discovery comes high. It entails renunciation both of the hope of continuing evolutionary advance and of belief in an intelligible world with inherent moral purpose. He must discard the notion of history as involving a scale of values of ideal significance, and accept it instead as "a sort of Chinese play without end and without lesson,"[28] as "in essence incoherent and immoral."[29] For a universal physics yields essentially a

26 *Education*, p. 400.
27 *Tendency of History*, p. 79.
28 Henry Adams, Letter to Dr. Jameson, quoted by Michael Kraus, *The History of American History* (New York, 1937) p. 322.
29 *Education*, p. 301.

scale of energy levels, a random equilibrium of forces tending
to degradation to their lowest terms, assurance of the bankruptcy of human powers. No wonder that Adams, glimpsing
the scientific future, should be plunged into pessimism and
rue the lost heaven of the ideal.

From his pages the buoyant intellectualism of Buckle has
fled. Far from triumphing over nature, nature triumphs over
human mentality and man. Dragged along 'like a fish on a
hook' in the historical process, "man created nothing."[30] The
mental machinery of his thought only registers the movements
of matter. As complexities increase, science no longer ventures
to explain causes, but merely records the extraordinary mani-
festations of nature's powers. New energies appear that deny
the 'truths' of previous science, so that its later terms are
untranslatable into the earlier; mathematics becomes hypermathematics; conceptions of 'force' grow self-contradictory;
while the notion of the electromagnetic ether is frankly unintelligible. Advancing scientific thought is plunged into a world
of 'occult mechanism,' the world of the future,—in Adams'
telling phrase a world of *"physics stark mad in metaphysics."*[31]

In many ways Adams is the most daring spokesman of the
new scientism. Yet historians, while admitting the competence
of his factual work, have shied away from his predictions and
the speculative reaches of his theory. Nevertheless the presci-
ence of some of his guesses cannot but seem today quite
extraordinary. To us living in the new age of radioactivity,
nuclear fission, and 'power leaping from every atom,' Adams
is seen to be right: nature's energies have indeed passed
beyond the models of the senses; causality, force, the ether
are unintelligible in earlier terms; mathematics has become
hypermathematics, and physics appears in truth stark mad
with metaphysics. Since Hiroshima and Nagasaki, moreover,
Adams' gloomiest forebodings are no longer remote fantasies
but threats of imminent disaster troubling the world. What if,

[30] *Ibid.,* p. 484. Mind merely registers forces. As Bacon saw, thought did
not evolve nature but nature evolved thought; and a revolution in thought was
"as mechanical as the fall of a feather."
[31] *Ibid.,* p. 382.

instead of our conquering nature as we had all along supposed, nature should finally overwhelm man? What if, instead of marking the age of men like gods, the summit of human glory, the new era of atomic power should prove cataclysmic, the downfall of civilization? Undeniably Adams' dating of the explosion around 1950 fits in surprisingly well with the timing of those physicists who warn of the dangers of an atomic war (once the world has the requisite knowledge and technology) as the start of a long regression.

Needless to say, Adams' views are highly distasteful to those who commit to science their basic hopes for continuous social progress. They wave aside his prognostics as chance hits or credit them to means less spectacular than his theory. History, they protest, becomes scientific by employing the method of deductive hypothesis, not by vain attempts to make itself physics. Only grave distortion results from trying to compress the subject into the concepts of a particular science. By using the proper procedure, the historian becomes a scientist even though he handles no apparatus, performs no controlled experiments, discovers no measurable laws. For 'scientific method' is essentially a type of logical inquiry which solves problems by devising hypotheses, elaborating their implications, and subjecting the latter to some sort of empirical test. Successful applications and predictions are the usual means of discriminating true hypotheses from the false.

However, to Adams this does not suffice. He cannot admit the historian as a scientist *sans* experiment, *sans* physical instrumentation, *sans* quantitative measurement simply on the strength of his using an approved form of logical inquiry.[32]

[32] Were the employment of hypothetical method all that was requisite for scientific history, Adams' own argument in his *Education* should be enough in his opinion to convince his opponents of physicalism and his other conclusions. For in that book he sets out *to solve a problem* (viz., to find the cause of progress or man's increasing control over nature) *by considering alternative hypotheses.* He runs through the apparently relevant possibilities: considering whether the favor of Providence, an inherent evolutionary process, or the power of reason may account for the acceleration of knowledge and civilization; and as a final alternative he weighs the chance that human history may operate on a physical principle like entropy or gravitation. From a lifetime of *checking the implications of these alternatives* against the facts, Adams con-

To be scientific, in his eyes, history must have a law with measurable phases and must align itself closely with a specific, positive science. Even those who reject Adams' claim to discern a phase-rule in history, and who ridicule his talk of 'human meteorites' and his pretension to chart the curve of events as an acceleration by squares, must admire his forthrightness. At least, unlike his vaguer, more elusive colleagues he does not claim for history the privileges of a science while wholly evading its strictures. He sees that scientific method involves measurements, laws, mathematical rules; and that historians who refuse to commit themselves to the specific techniques of the positive disciplines remain scientific merely in name. At the same time one must admit that Adams' very honesty in exposing to his readers the requirements of the subject goes far toward dissuading them from accepting 'scientific' history. For the upshot of his argument is that they come to perceive that, if his view is true, the method of scientific intelligence is fatal to mankind in its consequences; while if his view is false, presumably the method is untrustworthy. In his hands, the exercise of intelligence destroys trust in intelligence, and the invitation to scientific history is self-stultifying.

However successful the physical categories may be in the non-human sphere, man in their strait-jacket is reduced to absurdity. Physicalism ends in caricature, in emptying events of significance, in draining away their integrity. To be sure, anything in history can be viewed as a problem in physics. To a Maxwellian demon the barbarian invasions of Rome might appear as an influx of molecules into an already crowded region of space, its wars but explosions incident to

---

cludes that all but the last have been eliminated. On the one hand, the facts of physical science as well as those of human history have nullified the hypothesis of a continuously ascending social evolution, while, on the other, science has negated belief in theism and the sovereignty of reason by exposing the predominance of irrational forces in nature and man. All that remains is the physical hypothesis. By fitting both man's acceleration in knowledge and his release of energy to the algebraic formula of a dynamic law, Adams concludes that human history is but an application of physics. By *hazarding predictions,* which appear to have been subsequently *partly verified,* he further supports his theory.

the collision of myriad particles. But this would be an extravagance of analogy. While historians are never free of analogy, the degree and type of their use of it differ widely. With some the part played by an analogical frame is far more dominant, dogmatic, and far-fetched than with others. By seizing on some tenuous likeness, exploiting some far-flung comparison, by the sudden transfer of concepts from one field to another, they may try to gain possession of some new field of inquiry. When, as in Adams' work, sweeping comparison is made assimilating men to molecules, the animate to the inanimate, history to physics, the effect is truly bewildering.

Works dominated by biological parallels, however, are more common than those invoking physical metaphors. Particularly since Darwin this has become the favorite analogical device in scientific history. By finding the clue to man in his animal nature, by treating him as part of the organic process, they shift the burden of explaining his life to non-purposive and inhuman forces. What can be said, when Taine assures us in the preface of his *L'ancien régime*, that he takes his subject as "the metamorphosis of an insect," and writes this volume on the history of his country as a chapter in organic pathology?[33] As a naturalist he finds the aptest similitude between the transformations undergone by France in her revolutionary disorders and the convulsions of an insect in shedding its coat and entering a new stage. Faced with such parallels shall we seem to consent by our silence or shall we protest such resemblances as forced, fugitive, strained, incapable of exact formulation? To protest is plainly our duty, to point out that the whole notion of societies being organisms subject to metamorphosis, disease, health, age, and death is radically metaphorical. For uncritical analogies are the peculiar plague of the historian; and all too often insinuate themselves as ruling assumptions without the author's being aware of their dominance,—hovering in the background of language beyond clear-cut intellectual or empirical check.

In referring to the organic view of history the cyclic evolu-

[33] Hippolyte Taine, *Ancient Regime*, p. viii.

tion of Spengler comes readily to mind. In his work the 'spirit of analogy' is frankly adopted as the historical method. History is presented as a train of cultures in 'organic succession,' each arising, ripening to fruition, and declining to its death as a 'civilization.' Not only are many devious analogies traced between different aspects of the same culture (*e.g.*, between a society's music and its economic system, or its mathematics and form of government), but far more remote and extravagant ones are discerned between different societies and epochs. For instance, a close parallel is discovered between the history of Graeco-Roman culture and that of modern Western Europe, so that there is said to be "a development which is the complete counterpart of our own Western development, differing ... on the surface but entirely similar as regards the inward power driving the great organism toward its end." As a result historians could long ago have succeeded in

establishing the correspondence item by item from the Trojan War and the Crusades, Homer and the Nibelungenlied, through Doric and Gothic, Dionysian movement and Renaissance, Polycletus and John Sebastian Bach, Athens and Paris, Aristotle and Kant, Alexander and Napoleon, to the world-city and imperialism common to both cultures.[34]

On the strength of this conviction that cultural similarities indicate parallel stages of development in fixed life-cycles, Spengler is ready with sweeping predictions. Using the analogous pattern of decline of the Roman Empire (not to mention that of the Egyptians, Aztecs, Chinese), he foresees the decline of Western civilization following a disastrous outcropping of Caesarism within the next two hundred years.

As a rule professional historians are not respectful of Spengler's analogies. They dismiss his prophecies as melodrama, his organic parallels and unilateral patterns of development as hazy and unfounded. His fixed life-cycles of cultures involving a fatalistic determinism they find to be scientifically unaccredited. Nevertheless the same students will often give

[34] Oswald Spengler, *Decline of the West* (trans. by C. F. Atkinson, New York, 1936) Vol. I pp. 26-27.

a serious hearing to writers whose organic assumptions are less loudly proclaimed, and who are content to sprinkle their pages with evolutionary analogies without bringing them to a sharp focus where the issue of their substantiation must be squarely faced. Thus, while repudiating Spengler, academic historians often find it possible to accept the work of men like F. J. Turner, whose well-known study of the American frontier takes this period in United States history as illustrating a moment in an organic evolutionary development. "Line by line," says Turner, "as we read this continental page from West to East we find the record of social evolution."[35] Growth from simpler to more complex patterns of living, continued differentiation of the organs and functions of the society, and the recurrence of similar stages in its advance seem to be for him the marks of social evolution. For instance, describing the development along the Atlantic coast Turner says:

We have the familiar phenomenon of the evolution of institutions in a limited area, such as the rise of representative government, the differentiation of simple colonial governments into complex organs, the progress from primitive industrial society without division of labor up to a manufacturing civilization (P.2).

Not merely is American history as a whole tacitly regarded as a phase in a universal development, but in the conquest of the frontier the stages of social evolution recur successively in each local area in the westward expansion. Here is history written as evolutionary environmentalism. While individuals are allowed some free play, this is essentially a study of the 'variations' and 'adaptations' effective in American life through the economic and social influences of the new continent,—especially through the free land of the frontier. Without pausing to consider the difficulties of fitting the details of American history into the pattern of social evolution, we may point out that Turner, like Spengler, although more modest in

[35] Frederick J. Turner, *The Frontier in American History* (New York, 1920) p. 11.

not taking the entire world for his province, is similarly under the sway of unsubstantiated organic and Darwinian analogies.

III.

The harm done by such ruling metaphors in history is not often traced, nor the logic examined by which principles of interpretation are transposed from one region to another—from nature to man, from an inhuman, senseless process to the activity of human intelligence, or vice versa—without justification of the transfer. On every side there is talk of social organisms, but few notice the impossibility of specifying precisely how social institutions parallel the structure and functions of living plants and animals. What, for instance, in a society corresponds to the heart, lungs, brain, or intestines of an organic body? Much is said of civilizations and peoples 'maturing' and 'aging' but historians would find it hard to determine by any adequate test where to place China today in her life-span, whether its current social experiments are signs of youth or senescence. Terms like adaptation, variations, the struggle for existence, and notions of recurrent evolutionary stages are employed in such contexts without suspicion of the need for verification.

Again, in comparing man and the universe to a machine, as in the analogy of mechanism, the very extravagance of the leap and the simplicity of the image distracts the reader's attention from the logical somersault by which it is reached. The reader does not pause to ask by what right the idea of the machine—a humanly devised tool manufactured and operated by human intelligence to its ends—is at a stroke converted into the notion of an inhuman, unplanned, aimless process which is identified with the original structure of the world. Actually the machines we know are all invented, made, and operated to men's conscious plan; and the notion of natural 'machines' that just grew and ran of themselves apart from man's conscious construction, is pure analogical metaphor. In a not dissimilar fashion, we have urged, the Darwinian hypothesis suitably disguised inspires a cosmic biomorphism. Here too, if one watches closely, one may detect the scientist's metaphorical sleight-of-hand. By a trick of analogy a conscious human device known as 'artificial selection,' familiar to farmers in the domestic breeding of crops and cattle, is transformed into its opposite and ascribed to the world as a whole—as a blind, fortuitous process called 'natural selection.' Conscious purpose is tacitly replaced by chance variations, while the rise and fall of peoples (like the modification of species) is attributed to a blind fight for life, in which those less suited to changing conditions go to the wall.

At the root of the warfare versions of history so popular today, envisaging the course of human events as an unceasing clash of races, classes, nations for power and wealth, stands a distorted Darwinian analogy. Communist, fascist, imperialist versions—all the Hobbesian realists who, despite differences of ideological gloss, read history as an age-long contest for mastery through force—adopt the biological pattern of *la guerre naturelle*. There is an implicit identification of social with natural selection; the confused assumption just below the surface that the automatic evolutionary process of the struggle for existence is the same as man's conscious art of organized slaughter called war. But to transpose meanings from field to field in this uncritical way only invites deception, if not outright social disaster. By its very assumption of natural inevitability this identification of human military campaigns with a biological process exterminating the unfit destroys man's hopes of peace and harmony. To assume that human life and warfare are essentially the same, that one is the other, and that the plot of history is therefore an unending strife, battle, bloodletting seems by all odds the most dangerous use of analogy.

Against such sweeping parallels both the common sense and the philosophic historian must protest. Who ever heard, they may ask, of a mechanism without any consciously invented machinery? Of selection without purposive choice? Of warfare without cognizance or intent? Discredit is brought upon history by such wholesale borrowing from the blind, inhuman world for the interpretation of human happenings. Would it not be truer to the spirit of science to declare frankly that the ingenuity of the human mind is the storehouse from which these ruling metaphors have come, and that it finds patterns within itself against which to square the world? The layman laughs at the elaborate circumlocution by which the so-called scientific author, having borrowed from human mental activities his notions of the machine, warfare, and selection for use, seeks to obliterate all traces of his borrowing. But why metamorphose these conceptions beyond all recognition of their source and then deny the connection? How much better, says common sense, for historians to choose their analogues from human life rather than from inhuman, impersonal worlds, thus avoiding far-fetched comparisons. Artificial prototypes like man a machine, history as warfare, society as an organism are beyond our concrete deliverances, whereas the comparison of others to ourselves, past to present lives, other countries to our own is something readily confirmable by all of us. Because the subject matter of history is human experience, and because human experience to be known must be not merely conceived but lived through or imaginatively recreated, the best parallels are drawn from the psyche.

But explicit hypotheses explicitly arrived at are not very frequent in historical inquiry. It is far easier for a writer tacitly to assume some reigning conception of things without admitting its conjectural character and without the troublesome effort to substantiate. Views of causal relations, social dynamics, and of the springs of human action tend to linger in the background unaccredited and unannounced, while operating to control the narrative. To be sure, men are always using parallels and comparisons to try to comprehend puzzling facts through others less puzzling. Often too the similarities between things are conceived in an imaginative, figurative way beyond experimental check or exact definition. To assume that because certain events are alike in certain respects they are probably alike in others may be all that is possible in certain

fields, and in this sense analogy may well be the basic procedure in history. In those professing scientific method, we have
sought to show, there is constant analogical borrowing. At the
least, biological phrases and physical parallels are scattered
through the historical text to heighten its authoritative tone.
Nevertheless the effect of talk about 'social statics' and
'dynamics,' 'diseases of the body politic,' or the 'adaptations'
of 'cultural organisms,' instead of clarifying the subject, is
often to insinuate a whole flock of misleading conceptions.
Even more serious is the case in which an analogy like 'social
evolution' or dominion by the 'laws of force' is incorporated
into the general pattern of the work as a basic assumption.
Accepted as a presupposition without critical safeguards, it
may enter as a principle of selection, emphasis, and interpretation into every phase of the treatment with a question-begging
effect upon the whole inquiry.

Associated with this is frequently the method of comparative history, which brings analogical procedure to its full
development. The gist of analogy, as already said, lies in
multiplying the qualitative resemblances detected through
imaginative insight between one specific whole and another.
It deals, in short, with unique individuals and qualitative likenesses between these as particulars. But error arises in its use
when the historian comes to believe that the fluid parallels he
has noted between individual cultures yield a functional
dependence of universal generality or a scientific law. The
efforts of Buckle and Toynbee, for example, to explain the
incidence of civilization through their discernment of certain
environmental resemblances in historical situations, is a case
in point. In both the argument moves in the half-light of ill-
defined wholes: 'societies,' 'peoples,' 'civilizations,' 'favorable'
or 'adverse' environments. Their notions of a favorable environment or (in Toynbee's case) one producing an 'optimum challenge' are so vaguely conceived that, far from providing the
basis of a law they border on the tautologous. That those
peoples possessed of the 'optimum' conditions for achieving a

civilization achieved it, we may be said to know only by
definition or knowledge after the fact. But no clear-cut requirements are set forth by which a historical situation can be
diagnosed in advance as possessing the conditions for the rise
of a civilization. Even empirical instances do little to strengthen
the argument where they are classified to fit the preconceptions of the author. Ancient Greece, for example, is cited by
Buckle as enjoying a favorable environment (access to the sea,
temperate climate, moderate soil), whereas for Toynbee
(believing in the 'virtues of adversity') it was the stimulus of
hard country, internal and external obstacles of all sorts, that
roused Greece to high cultural achievement. Thus these comparative historians are led to the discovery of opposing laws:
in Buckle's case, one making geographical advantages and aids
responsible for the birth of civilizations, while in Toynbee's
case their rise is due to man's response to the challenge of
obstructions, severities, hardships in their geographical or social
situation. What such failure of agreement shows is plainly
failure to rise above the particulars of analogical comparison.

Through converting supposed parallels into hypothetical
deductions, the value of history as history on its own account
(*i.e.*, its narrative uniqueness) is sacrificed to the striving to be
science. The cases compared (*e.g.*, Egypt, Greece, China) lose
their interest as concrete individuals, and become primarily
instances of an imaginary class or still more imaginary law.
Thus the historian is launched on the vain pursuit of the
modus ponens of the scientist without the latter's implementa-
tion either for framing his premises or for testing his conclusions. When one considers the many variables in the field
(including that prime indeterminate, man), and the extent to
which measurement and reinstatement are impossible, small
wonder that in history there is a dearth of widely accepted
generalizations. A striking evidence of this lack is that when
enlightened statesmen take counsel from the 'lessons of the
past' to bolster up their previous policies or for guidance in
action, they appeal to the 'analogies of history.' That is, they
consult individual parallels which they or any layman can find

out for themselves, rather than defer to scientific historians as experts to learn the supposed historical laws.

Because history, for all its subordinate scientific testing of documents and remains, relies ultimately on intuitive acquaintance, concepts, and analogical penetration unresolvable into cases of laws, its relationship to personal consciousness is ineradicable. The judgment to which it appeals is the insight of the writer and his public, the fund of memories, traditions, evaluations, and reflections regarding what seem to them to be the probabilities of life. For these consciousness finds its witness in itself, and not merely in the techniques of knowledge under the dominance of the principle of externality. Historical writing, to repeat, depends upon the art of psychological persuasion, upon enlisting our feelings, attitudes, thoughts to agree with certain concrete parallels in the past beyond the generalities of science. Everywhere the tendency to note kinships and resemblances is a central function of knowledge. Events in the past, things we do not observe, we know by virtue of their resemblance to those in the present we do; others' experience we link with our own (social corroboration being largely based on analogy),[36] and even physical 'force' (if the concept of inertia is derived from our sense of muscular strain) may conceivably be likewise. Everywhere perception of qualitative likenesses and differences in the experiences of persons and societies serves our turn. Nevertheless in recognizing the uniqueness of its subject matter and in failing to reduce it to instances of a law, the procedure of history differs from that of science. In contrast to those who employ biological and physical analogies, the historical method is closer to what its critics are pleased to call anthropomorphism. For in the end, since its evidence involves the imagery, insight, conception of a vanished reality, it has to revert to personal consciousness as its sanction. Though it deals with the whole

[36] That our knowledge of others' experience is essentially analogical is maintained by such philosophers as J. S. Mill, *Examination of Sir William Hamilton's Philosophy*, Ch. XII and Bertrand Russell, *Scientific Method of Philosophy*, Lect. IV. *Cf.* W. Wylie Spencer, *Our Knowledge of Other Minds* (New Haven, 1930) Ch. III.

panorama of life, it does not classify its objects, clock, enumerate or manipulate them, but leaves them as in the experience of the mind unique, irreplaceable, each standing on its own feet in unimpeachable subjectivity.

CHAPTER SIX

The Contrast
with Philosophic History

So Far We Have Contrasted popular traditional history, viewing the world largely as common sense takes it to be, with the history strongly influenced by the methods and conclusions of science. Between them one finds broadly the difference between narration and explanatory hypothesis, between the personal and the impersonal, the dramatic and the causal approach. Often, of course, the distinction is chiefly a matter of emphasis, as is sometimes the case with a third type of history, which we have chosen to call 'philosophical.' This last or philosophical outlook tries to reach beyond personal episodes and the causal analysis of affairs to lay hold of their basis in patterns of essence or ideality. But to find the deepest movements of events in the unfolding and application of ideal principles is an attitude at particular odds with the scientific approach, with its tendency to deny the *a priori* beyond the space-time order, and its commitment to naturalism. In its eyes scientific method is the sole key to knowledge, and the discoveries of natural science the sole arbiters of cosmology. Your scientific historian cannot allow the possibility that there may be ideal patterns beyond empirical confirmation, logical and moral principles regulative of matters of fact but themselves beyond the matters of fact tested. Minds and the values they discover are in his eyes outgrowths and instruments of the natural process which enjoys complete priority.

The issue is clear cut. On one side stands the writer of scientific bent, who sees in history man's age-long efforts at survival in a world whose limits are set by inorganic nature and its potentials of development. Man's worth is measured by his adaptation to it, his success in environmental adjustment. Everything to be taken account of lies within the existent space-time world, in things open to empirical investigation. On the other or philosophic side, stands a line of great historians stretching into the past who have interpreted matters of fact in ideal perspective. The view of history, for instance, as the struggle for liberty and growth in the consciousness of it finds the great turning-points in human affairs, not in moments of practical success, but in man's efforts to rally his spirit from the encroachments of the material world. Though a creature of the natural order, man rises to take part in another. Through his valuing and intelligent side he sees beyond the empirical process; and in his profound allegiance to standards and goals liberates himself from servitude to nature. By a long-continued tradition running through Platonism, Stoicism, Christianity, Roman, and English law, belief has been cherished in timeless patterns and approach to or retreat from these as constituting man's history. In the age-old notions of natural and common law, jurisprudence and the state have acknowledged the authority of a universal justice and right (beyond local adjudication in fact) as rooted in what ought to be. Similarly philosophy and religion invoke a referent in universal mind (either as consciousness-in-general or as divine sovereignty), while history itself appeals to an overall norm in the verdict of mankind or the judgment of posterity. It is this sense that the natural scene is compassed by ideal law that heartens man's hopes and helps to sustain a vast structure of freedom and rights in the life of civilization. To clarify the contrast between life viewed scientifically on the one hand, and on the other viewed philosophically as supported by noumenal sanctions, we can do no better than consider a concrete example in our own history under these two interpretations.

To understand the framing of such a historical document as the Constitution of the United States from the scientific point of view, for instance, a study is usually held necessary primarily, if not exclusively, of the social conditions from which it arose, together with the factual gains in security and prosperity anticipated from its enactment. Charles A. Beard undertook such a study in his well-known *Economic Interpretation of the Constitution of the United States,* and by framing a social hypothesis and comparing the consequences deduced from it with certain social facts in proportional correlation arrived at a 'verification' somewhat resembling that of a scientific experiment. His hypothesis presumably took its rise from the impression made on his mind by the discovery that most of the men who originated the Constitutional movement had connections with trade and shipping, money, and public securities, all adversely affected by the Articles of Confederation. So after careful inquiry into the administrative procedure by which the Constitution was put through, the class and property affiliations of those who labored for it, and the personal gains they expected from its adoption, Beard drew the conclusion that economic interests provided the main cause of the framing and passage of the American Constitution,— claiming to have 'demonstrated' that it was "the product of a group of economic interests which must have expected beneficial results (to themselves) from its adoption."[1]

Plainly such a view is at odds with popular, widely-accepted tradition. Although historians usually admit that social and economic conditions played an important part in the formation of the document cementing the federal union, not many would concede that the economic interests of the framers were chiefly responsible for its creation or constituted its essential basis. While students of the period would allow that financial repudiation in the colonies and disturbances like Shay's rebellion

[1] Charles A. Beard, *An Economic Interpretation of the Constitution of the United States* (New York, 1913) p. 17.

promoted in large measure the calling of the Convention, and
that personal interest in relief from these evils spurred those
who enacted the instrument, few would acknowledge that the
provisions of the Constitution as a whole, its meaning and
achievement, were to be understood mainly in terms of these
conditions. Beyond these things, both the philosophical and
the traditional historian would say, beyond the interest of
classes in their economic advantage or of individuals in pro-
tecting their property, stood men's allegiance to moral and
rational principles. In the Declaration of Independence these
had already been set forth as the foundation and objectives of
the new government; and the Constitution, as generally understood and as witnessed by the Preamble, was the instrument
devised to put these principles into practice. In support of
this interpretation we have not only statements by men who
drafted the documents, but a long, trusted tradition. If the
founders in the two great documents and the mass of citizens
since that time have used the conceptions of *rights, justice,
liberty,* and *self-evident truths* sincerely,—on what grounds
should recent historians like Beard deny the integrity of their
use as objectives? On what basis should a modern like Carl
Becker declare that "To ask whether the natural rights philosophy of the Declaration of Independence is true or false is
essentially a meaningless question"[2] or like Santayana describe
the same document (with its *a priori* principles) as "a salad of
illusions"?[3]

But surely Jefferson was not wrong in holding that these
conceptions gave expression to the generally held opinion of
the American people.[4] Nor were the authors of *The Federalist*
mistaken, along with the popular mind, in ascribing the founding of the new republic to "reflection and choice" rather than
to "accident and force"[5] and blind natural compulsion. Even
in their practical discussions of commerce and finance, of how

---

[2] Carl Becker, *The Declaration of Independence* (New York, 1933) p. 277.
[3] George Santayana, *The Middle Span* (New York, 1945) p. 169.
[4] Thomas Jefferson, *Works,* (ed. by Paul L. Ford, Federal ed. New York,
1904) XII pp. 307-8, 409.
[5] Alexander Hamilton, James Madison, and John Jay, *The Federalist,* No. I.

to distribute powers so as to combine liberty with stability in a strong federal union, there spoke confidence in a wisdom and virtue in man sufficient for self-government according to ideal ethical considerations. With all their regard for experience and the practical issues at hand, the authors of *The Federalist* offered a theoretical argument for ratification of the new Constitution addressed to men's deliberative powers, to their ideas of 'good faith,' 'justice,' 'liberty,' and 'sacred rights,' as well as to "one of those truths which, to a correct and unprejudiced mind, carries its own evidence along with it."[6] Would it not seem wiser for historians to accept the voice of tradition and the constitutional documents, and to admit the guidance of the founders by deliberation to ideal ends even against the preconceptions of naturalism? To maintain, on the contrary, that men's ideas are always functions of interests, determined through and through by factual causes, profoundly shifts the basis of the constitutional argument, making the language of the founders that of men either grossly deceived or insincere. Although according to the scientific view only processes verified by empirical laws control human action, to the men themselves engaged in large plans and loyal to high enterprises,— reasons and evaluative insights may be compelling in their own right and upon occasion outreach factual considerations. Assuredly this latter belief is more akin to the common assumptions of thought and speech, more saving of the historical appearances and of experiential unity.

That American tradition has borne out this belief in the *a priori* is shown by the manner in which a leader like Lincoln construed the constitutional argument at the moment of greatest crisis in our national history. Lincoln did not doubt that men could be moved by the magnetism of great ideas, like human rights, justice, equality, and that in responding to them they might rise above their creature interests. Through the light of these ideas, he held, men advance, and without their

[6] *Ibid.*, No. XXIII. Says Beard in a contrary estimate of *The Federalist's* argument for the Constitution, "Every fundamental appeal in it . . . is to some material and substantial interest." *Op cit*, p. 164.

vision peoples perish. They furnish the 'standard maxims' of free society, which though never perfectly achieved in fact serve to augment the value of life universally. It was indeed to secure Justice and the blessings of Liberty, as well as a *more perfect* Union,' as the preamble asserted, that the Constitution was established. In memorable speeches (1857 and 1858) embodying his constitutional interpretation, Lincoln rejected the notion that the founders, in declaring men equal with certain inalienable rights, affirmed their factual equality or pretended to have power to confer such a boon. "They did not mean to say that all were equal in color, size, intellect, moral development, or social capacity." Rather they meant to declare in clear language the moral truth which, in their view, the public mind implicitly accepted as its principle of guidance.

They (the authors of the Declaration) meant simply to declare the right, so that enforcement of it might follow as fast as circumstances should permit. They meant to set up a standard maxim for free society, which should be familiar to all and revered by all . . . constantly labored for, even though never perfectly attained, constantly approximated, and thereby constantly spreading and deepening its influence, and augmenting the happiness and value of life to all people of all colors everywhere.[7]

That the Constitution, both in the intention of the framers and in the people's understanding of its spirit, did look toward the achievement of universal moral right, Lincoln argues further in his debate with Douglas. But because the colonies had slavery long before the calling of the Convention, and because some of them could not be brought to join the union without it, slavery had to be allowed as a temporary evil under the Constitution; nevertheless the principles of human rights incorporated in the instrument, being in contradiction to it, implied its ultimate extinction.

I am tolerably well acquainted with the history of the country . . . I believe it (the country) has endured because the public mind did rest all the time in the belief that slavery was in course of ultimate extinction . . . The adoption of the Constitution and its attendant history led

[7] Abraham Lincoln, Speech on the Dred Scott Decision, June 26, 1857.

the people to believe so, and that such was the belief of the framers of the Constitution itself. Why did those old men, about the time of the adoption of the Constitution, decree that slavery should not go into the new Territory where it had not already gone? Why declare that within twenty years the African slave-trade, by which slaves were supplied, might be cut off by Congress? . . . I might enumerate more of these acts; but enough. What were they but a clear indication that the framers of the Constitution intended and expected the ultimate extinction of that institution? . . . We had slaves among us; we could not secure the good we did secure if we grasped for more, but, having by necessity submitted to that much, it does not destroy the *principle that is the charter of our liberties* . . . Let that charter stand as our standard.[8]

A better expression of the doctrine of human rights in the spirit of our constitutional tradition can scarcely be found than in these speeches of Lincoln. Yet here speak the categories of history against which naturalism and scientism continually protest. The spirit is invoked beyond the letter. The historical process, instead of being treated wholly by standards derived from the actual, is judged by the ideal. Reason and conscience are saluted as arbiters supreme over consequences in fact. Ideal truths though unresolvable into terms of existence, enhance its worth. "We have," says Lincoln, "to fight this battle upon principle and upon principle alone."

"But this is Platonism," cries the scientific historian in horror. Such an interpretation of history implies belief in perfects and absolutes, in moral truths that go beyond and even contrary to empirical facts of human nature; it even assumes that human intelligence can achieve a universal standpoint and act upon it,—all of which contradicts the essence of naturalism. So it does. On this view, truth is more than correspondence to fact, more than can be tested by empirical consequences; nor is reason a mere creature of interests, an anticipatory imagining, a mere tool of nature, but a power of genuine insight into moral and rational verities wider than existence. Implicitly assumptions like these long passed unchallenged among writers of American history; from its early beginnings to Bancroft,

[8] Lincoln, Reply to Douglas on Popular Sovereignty, Nebraska Bill, etc., Chicago, July 10, 1858.

Washington Irving, Fiske, Rhodes, McMaster, and Woodrow Wilson. The tacit notion was not only that ideal principles, possessing moral truth, could furnish men a motive force, standard, and objective, but (what was even more of a hazard) that in our own national history this had been the case. On the whole, tradition was in agreement with Bancroft's saying that the American colonies "in the happy morning of their existence had chosen justice for their guide."[9]

However, about the end of the last century critics (their numbers swelling with the years) began pointing out defects latent in such conceptions; how with them went all too easily the vices of eagle-screaming patriotism and romantic eulogy. Faith in the purity of the principles of popular government, it was said, led writers to invent a legend of its founding. Disregarding unpleasant facts, for them the period of the fathers tended to become a golden age, its leaders well-nigh faultless, raised on pedestals, single-minded in their devotion to eternal right and justice. As the climax of their efforts, the Constitution was brought forth, an instrument forged by pure reason and virtue, perfect in flexibility and strength, worthy of the deepest reverence, bearing as its gifts a new order of liberty and dignity for the progress of mankind.

Yet how absurd, the scientific realists countered, to portray men like gods instead of flesh and blood, as guided by ideal principles on high instead of by natural appetites and needs. Man is part of nature and history must present him accordingly. As for constitution worship,—no instrument of fallible man can ever be timelessly true, a political ark of the covenant suited to every age. Far from being a society of philosophers, the founders were partisans, each with his axe to grind. Despite much lofty eloquence, a little probing behind the scenes (into original documents) will disclose that the leaders of the Philadelphia Convention acted according to their material interests

[9] George Bancroft, *History of the United States*, Vol. I (1834). "The spirit of the colonies demanded freedom from the beginning. The United States have the precedence in the practice and defense of the equal rights of man." Quoted by G. P. Gooch, *History and Historians of the Nineteenth Century* (New York, 1913) p. 404.

and those of the groups they represented. What made possible the union under such circumstances was not any community of *a priori* principles, but a common danger *in fact* coupled with the strength of their diverse interests. In the Convention were many cross-currents of opinion, rival cliques ready to do battle with each other. But since no faction had power sufficient to suppress the rest, the upshot was a deal, a truce, a draw, an expedient, which found formal expression in the Constitution. What put a term to the strife of interests was not, on this view, the pure light of reason and conscience but considerations of self-preservation. For in that dark hour with England, Spain, and France intriguing against them, it was evident to the most obtuse that the colonies could remain independent only by uniting more strongly, and that division would be fatal. Faced with the alternative of hanging together or hanging separately, fear of the consequences obliged the contending groups to patch up their differences, and to sacrifice certain of their interests (miscalled 'rights') to save others. So a bargain was struck, a compromise effected, a makeshift devised, which proved to be a marvelous equilibrium of give and take, checks and balances, allowing no group all that it wanted, yet to each a considerable part of what it did.

Thus in historical writing the presumption that the founders sought to change the world by the power of reason and conscience was later overshadowed by other considerations. As the Constitution came to be regarded as the product of its social context, interest shifted to the local influences conditioning the men who framed it. Economic cleavages to which earlier students often paid relatively little attention, lines of separation between mechanics, small farmers, and men of affairs, divisions marking off merchants from manufacturers, landowners from traders and shippers, financial and professional from agrarian groups, were brought to the fore. More emphasis was placed too on personal rivalries, sectional and religious bias, and on the half-heartedness that all but wrecked the cause. Historians troubled less and less to inquire whether at any point devotion to principles prevailed over interest, or choice based on impartial reflection found expression in directing affairs. Indeed, the question whether men are capable of responding to abstract right and justice as opposed to natural ends like security came to be quietly ignored. Writers assumed that they already knew the answer.

But to the twentieth century was reserved the final step in the revolution of values to the new naturalism. Abstract reason lost its force for many minds, while guidance by ideal norms went the way of revealed theology. Man became 'the natural man,' a creature responding entirely to the needs, habits, impulses of his sensory and organic experience. With the theory of evolution, science (along with 'scientific history') had, as it were, come of age. Its deliverances, hitherto a scattered collection of facts and rules, suddenly fused into a new cosmic picture. Out of a kaleidoscopic jumble of bits emerged a fresh conception of the unity of nature, bound together by an unbroken web of empirical causation. Man himself, hitherto aloof and apart, took his place as a link in the chain of development. Everywhere natural forms were found to have evolved from previous forms by the working of empirical laws, with physical energies alone as the source of their unfolding. "A new epoch in the study of history," said Charles Francis Adams, "dates from the publication of the *Origin of Species*. Human history has become part of a comprehensible cosmogony."[9a] And many agreed with him. To them it appeared that history must be rewritten in the light of these revolutionary assumptions. Man needed to be divested of his former prerogatives, represented as he 'really was,' to be freed from illusions as to his guidance by ideal virtue and transcendental authority. With the recognition of the organic relation of the thinker to his thought, the historian to the past, the creature to his world, the retreat from reason was in full swing. With it went abandonment of belief in a higher court of reflection beyond the facts, together with the presumption of its possible inclusiveness, detachment, and finality. In learning of his creaturehood, the historian seemed

9a Charles Francis Adams, *Mass. Hist. Soc. Proc.*, 2nd ser. XIII, pp. 89-90.

obliged to renounce his pretension to universal, disinterested judgment which he had long shared with divinity. "He learned," as one critic put it, "that he was not God."

As has been said, the extension of the scientific conception of evolution to man altered perspectives in American history. A sociological and economic slant came to replace moral and reflective views of human nature. The rational man was superseded by the economic man; the man of duty and public spirit replaced by the socially and organically oriented one, a product of his local system, a counterpart of his age and community. Collective and impersonal factors took precedence over the personal and unique; non-ideational over ideational forces; interests as motors eclipsed intelligence, although writers were usually not prepared to designate the limits of the one or the other. Typical and outstanding in the movement, as we have said, was Charles Beard's effort to show that economic interests and not the inspiration of democratic principles were responsible for the framing and adoption of the Constitution of the United States. According to him, the Constitution was the result of a highly successful, although illegal, manœuvre by the propertied interests to set up a strong federal government to unify currency and tariffs, safeguard property, insure the payment of debts, prevent rebellion, and check radical experiments by the state legislatures. "It was," says Beard, "an economic document drawn with superb skill by men whose property interests were immediately at stake."[10] The basic law of the land thus becomes, on his interpretation, not an expression of men's sense of justice, truth, liberty, and right, but rather a weapon of the propertied class seeking controlling power. While the language and structure of the instrument were political, in his view its origin, intention, and consequences were primarily economic. According to his argument, Beard proved his hypothesis after the manner of scientific method by showing that practically all those who framed and actively furthered the Constitution had reason to

[10] *Op cit.*, p. 188.

expect substantial, material advantage to themselves from the new government,[11] whereas most of those against it had not.

Suppose (he says at the outset) that substantially all the merchants, money lenders, security holders, manufacturers, shippers, capitalists, financiers, and their professional associates are to be found on one side in support of the Constitution, and that substantially all . . . of the opposition came from the non-slaveholding farmers and debtors, would it not be pretty conclusively demonstrated that our fundamental law was . . . the product of a group of economic interests which must have expected beneficial results from its adoption . . . The data presented in the following chapters bear out the latter hypothesis.[12]

Having arrived at his hypothesis by analysis of the historical data, Beard undertook to verify it by deducing the consequences and comparing them with the facts by an approximation to the scientific method of difference. To show that "the direct immediately impelling motive . . . was the economic advantages which the beneficiaries expected would accrue to themselves first, from their action,"[13] he amassed, sifted, and classified a large body of information, not only regarding opponents, but especially regarding those who originated the movement for the Constitution, who as delegates framed it, and who urged its ratification; he then correlated their political attitudes with their economic situations. The fact that the division of attitudes toward the proposed Constitution followed the lines of men's property holdings and modes of livelihood closely, rather than any clear-cut geographical, political, or religious grouping, appeared to him to provide strong corroboration of his hypothesis. By showing in a large number of cases that *wherever certain economic interests were present, a certain attitude toward the Constitutional issue was present; whereas where these were absent the other was absent; and that the two varied concurrently,* a procedure closely resembling the scientific method of agreement and difference was invoked with great effect. In his conclusion Beard found that:

11 *Ibid.*, p. 324.
12 *Ibid.*, p. 17.
13 *Ibid.*, p. 18.

The movement for the Constitution of the United States was originated and carried through principally by four groups of personalty interests which had been adversely affected under the Articles of Confederation: money, public securities, manufactures, and trade and shipping. . . . The line of cleavage for and against the Constitution was between substantial personalty interests on the one hand and the small
farming and debtor interests on the other.[14]

In the same vein, although without the same exhaustive
presentation of evidence, Beard seeks to show that the Civil
War (which he calls the 'Second American Revolution') was
due not to a moral protest against slavery in defence of human
rights or to the question of secession, but was owing to the
shift in the balance of power from agriculture to industry in
the economy of the country. In its widest perspective *The Rise
of American Civilization* is envisaged by him as an economic
development falling into two large divisions: "the Agricultural
Era" and "the Industrial Era;" while the Civil War he declared
to be "merely the culmination of the deep-running transformation that shifted the center of gravity in American society
between the inauguration of Jackson and the election of
Lincoln."[15] In its effects no less than in its origin the war was
to him primarily an economic phenomenon,—its "supreme outcome" being "the destruction of the planting aristocracy," from
which followed "the undisputed triumph of a new combination of power" comprising capitalists, free farmers, and
industrialists.[16]

The widespread failure of previous historians to discover
the focus of American history in economic factors is due, in
Beard's opinion, partly to the inaccessibility of the evidence
(the story of our agricultural, labor, technological, and business development being largely unwritten), and partly to the
fact that politicians ("the shadow rather than the substance")[17]
have throughout our national life been permitted to hold the

[14] *Ibid.*, pp. 324-325.
[15] Charles A. Beard and Mary Beard, *The Rise of American Civilization*
(New York, 1930) I pp. 632-633.
[16] *Ibid.*, II, p. 99.
[17] *Ibid.*, I p. 632.

center of the stage. To find the causes of the Civil War we must not look to the oratory of Congress, the writings of journalists and intellectuals, to moral and religious protestations, but recognize that the agencies at work lay 'beyond the will of man,' and largely beyond his consciousness, and prevision. Instead we must turn to the business ledgers, to the government census, to all manner of social statistics.

By an inexorable process beyond the will of any man or group, the sovereignty of King Cotton and the authority of his politicians were rudely shaken, the rapidity of the operation being recorded in ledgers and carefully set forth in the census . . . When Lincoln was inaugurated, the capital invested in industries, railways, commerce, and city property exceeded in dollars and cents the value of all the farms and plantations between the Atlantic and the Pacific—a fact announcing at last the triumph of industry over agriculture.[18]

While Beard, like Buckle, turns wherever possible to social statistics as a method for history, under the weight of more facts (if perhaps less logic) he has relinquished the strict determinism of the earlier positivists. While relying on recurrent patterns and the continuity of nature, he refuses to be bound by scientific mechanism as a postulate, blaming things he cannot explain rather upon 'fate,' 'accident,' or 'the indeterminate, man.' The earlier optimism too has faded: the conviction that scientific enlightenment will succeed, where moral effort has failed, in destroying every evil. Yet withal a vague faith in progress remains: in man's continued advance in controlling nature and in reshaping the world to his dream.[19]

Unquestionably Beard's mode of argument makes a strong impression. This is particularly the case with his economic interpretation of the Constitution, in which he effectively employs methods approximating Baconian tables and correlations. Even those who strongly disagree with him may at first be unable to reply to his argument. Yet analysis of his assumptions soon reveals patent weaknesses. To begin with, there are

[18] *Ibid.*, I p. 635.
[19] Charles Beard, *Discussion of Human Affairs* (New York, 1936) pp. 110-116.

three major possibilities as regards the motivation of the men who promoted the framing and enactment of the Constitution. (1) There is the possibility that they did so for predominantly selfish reasons, for the specific purpose of reaping financial gain and economic advantage to themselves. This is Beard's hypothesis, although he frequently states it ambiguously to confuse it with (2), which is easier to maintain. (2) The possibility that they were fundamentally animated by a 'social' or nationalistic economic motivation, i.e., that their prime object was the wealth and material prosperity of the colonies as a whole, not merely their own. On this view, they favored the Constitution simply as a means to the colonists' (and their own) greater security, fortune, and affluence. (3) The third possibility is that their ends were not primarily, predominantly economic, but that they were in large measure moral and political. On this interpretation it was essentially because leading members of the Convention sought an enduring government expressive of republican principles and that would safeguard human rights, and because, having an intelligent understanding of the larger political situation, they saw the inevitability of the colonies' loss of independence and these rights without a powerful union, that they labored to promote a strong federal constitution. The weakness of the economic interpretation is of course that it fails to do justice to these moral and political factors. Yet they would seem to be clearly as relevant to the issue as the fact that Robert Morris and Fitzsimons owned public securities.

The difficulty of Beard's thesis, once we pause to examine it, is to bring the available evidence under (1) this first hypothesis, thereby negating the others. This he is never really able to do. Needless to say, the most effective way to refute his hypothesis (1) is to suggest a counter-hypothesis (3) [or even to some degree (2)] which fits the facts better. Instead of holding that the Constitution was fundamentally promoted through the economic interests of men who expected special benefits to accrue to themselves from its adoption, this alternative hypothesis would maintain that it was framed and sponsored by a group of the outstanding leaders of the country, known for their public spirit, ability, trustworthiness, and wide experience in affairs, who had the insight to realize that the preservation of the rights won in the Revolution, as well as the moral, political, and economic good of the nation as a whole, required a strong constitutional government. This hypothesis, as we have said, is the one generally accepted both by tradition and their Revolutionary contemporaries.

Even Beard does not question that the Constitutional Convention included among its members the most able men in the country, many of whom had taken a leading part in the Revolution and were well known for their republican sentiments; nor can he suggest other leaders comparable in patriotic virtue and informed intelligence to the group which included: Washington, Benjamin Franklin, Rufus King, Gouverneur Morris, Hamilton, and Madison. Men of this sort, of wide experience, broad views, and the power of analytic thought might be expected to be those who informed themselves about their country's situation in a way in which isolated small farmers, debtors, day laborers, and frontiersmen did not. On this hypothesis, a no less impressive correlation might conceivably be established between active support of the Constitution and marked administrative ability and understanding of the country's affairs, while the opposition might be shown to come chiefly from those lacking such qualifications. Though the differences of attitudes might roughly seem to parallel economic interests, the real basis of division might be, not private gain, but political competence coupled with a sense of responsibility to aid in guiding the country's affairs. The fact that a direct correspondence seems to subsist between these citizens' proved administrative ability and their support of the federal system renders it likely that public spirit and an objective grasp of the problem directed their views. That the overall situation required that the states have a strong central government if they were to preserve their hard-won independence against the intrigues of England, France, and Spain in the new world is generally agreed by authorities. The fact that the citizens best equipped to appreciate these dangers did appreciate them, and that their decision as to the proper remedy was that confirmed by a large majority of later authorities, is strong evidence in favor of their unprejudiced evaluation of the facts. Many additional lines of evidence could be cited in support of this traditional counter-hypothesis, of which we mention but a few. (1) The Preamble of the Constitution, which strikes the keynote and declares the purposes which sustain it, is a statement of moral and political objectives; while throughout the language is political and legal, *not economic*. (2) The whole structure of the Constitution is skillfully designed for the maintenance of individual liberty and embodies (prior to the first ten amendments) a long list of basic rights of person in provisions regarding *habeas corpus*, jury trial, clear definition of treason, free movements of citizens throughout the union, prohibition of bills of attainder, ex post facto legislation, and of patents of nobility. (3) It guarantees to each of the states a republican form of government, contains no mention of property qualifications in voting and shifts the basis of its representative assemblies from the medieval division *by classes* or estates (churchmen, nobles, and burghers) to the more democratic and impartial basis of numbers and locality.

Hardly less striking than such evidence is the fact that Beard himself, yielding his position, virtually accepts this counter-hypothesis when he returns in mellower mood many years later to the study of the Constitution. In his valedictory, *The Republic* (1934), he is finally willing to view the founders in the light of their political competence and the professed objectives of their work, rather than through economic self-interest. More and more he is impressed by the galaxy of talent for legislative tasks that took part in the Philadelphia Convention. Among the fifty-five men who regularly participated, he points out, were twenty-eight who had served in the Congress, seven former governors, eight signers of the Declaration of Independence; men skilled in war, diplomacy, legislation, finance, commerce, political philosophy, and practical administration. Even in his middle period, for that matter, Beard's respect for the political wisdom of the founders threatened to outweigh his earlier theme.

Among the many historical assemblies (he declared in *The Rise of American Civilization*) which have wrought revolutions in the affairs of mankind, it seems safe to say there has never been one that commanded more political talent, practical experience, and sound substance than the Philadelphia Convention of 1787.[20]

In *The Republic* Beard is brought to admit the moral grandeur of the constitutional work of the framers and to acknowledge the moral basis of government. While history is rooted in the interplay of *ideas* and *interests,* that of the United States, he now insists, has been in large measure "the story of the rise and progress of ideas;"[21] and that this has been so, is due, in his opinion, in no small part to the structure of great conceptions woven into its basic law at the outset. Accordingly he salutes with reverence the 'grand abstractions' of the Declaration, which calls men to square their conduct with its noble professions, and the 'grand purposes' of the constitutional Preamble (regarding liberty, justice, tranquillity, the general welfare, and a *more perfect* union), which by setting forth the popular aspirations and the objectives of self-government lends moral justification to support the whole constitutional system. Nor is he above tracing the ramifications by which these same ideas and those of individual rights are ingeniously incorporated into the body of its fundamental provisions. He is properly indignant at those who find moral safeguards of person and property confined to the amendments added later by the state legislators—the so-called bill of rights,—and who thereby fail to recognize the bearing of the other provisions made by the founders and the form of government as a whole upon liberty. Safeguards of human rights, he points out, are woven into its fabric with consummate skill, because the founders clearly saw the concentration of power

---

[20] *Rise of American Civilization,* I p. 310.
[21] Charles Beard, *The Republic* (New York, 1934) p. 273.

in the same hands to be the very essence of despotism, and sought by all means for a workable separation of the legislature, executive, and judiciary as the chief secret of liberty under government.

It is therefore no accident that Beard returns to Plato, the father of ideal political philosophy, for the dialogue form and title of his valedictory on the Constitution. In the end he has almost come full circle, and stands almost on the threshold of a philosophical view of government. If he never quite passed over from economic realism to moral idealism, or discarded the 'social' for a universal view of human rights, it was only perhaps because the habits of a lifetime were too difficult to break. Yet he is now prepared to admit *not only* that "without standards of justice and a mental feeling for justice widely distributed among the people, society would go to pieces (p. 84)," but that there is "moral power in many abstract ideas of rights (p. 296)" to inspire and guide us, and that there are "standards of truth and justice possessing universal validity among civilized peoples (p. 84)." Still and all there is something incongruous in Beard's attempt to play the part of Socrates, in the dialogue, meanwhile asserting that "discussing justice in the abstract is not of much use,"[22] and had modern Europeans devoted their attention to the study of *The Federalist* instead of Plato's *Republic*, they would have been better off in every way.[23] By belittling the legacy of concepts and institutions left by the parent-thinkers of all later republics, he seeks to heighten our impression of the wisdom of the hardheaded framers of our Constitution, who, instead of bothering about ideal justice, sought "to institute a *workable government*" and "refused to try by ideal standards the fruits of necessity and the frailties of human beings."[24] The correctness, however, of this last statement (as well as its consistency with some of Beard's other statements) is disputable. That the founders recognized the basis of republican government in

[22] *Op cit.*, p. 83.
[23] *Ibid.*, p. 301.
[24] *Ibid.*, p. 86.

moral standards and sought (*vide* the Declaration and the Preamble) to try their handiwork by noumenal justice and liberty is exceedingly hard to deny. But at any rate there is much more for the philosopher to agree with in the later than in the earlier Beard. For instance, he finally relinquished the scientific pretensions of history, its claim to discover the causes of things (admitting in *The Republic* "I do not know the cause of anything"),[25] as well as his early hypothesis of the economic interpretation of the Constitution. Here at last he plainly allows the presence in the historical process not merely of the weight of interests and existential forces, but in some measure the force of abstract ideas and that "*all human rights rest on the moral standards of the community.*"[26] Nevertheless he can never squarely face, much less admit with the founders, the thesis that the philosophy of rights at the basis of our government is universally true.[27] That in the end he should fail to measure up to perhaps the most critical issue of historiography, the issue of power and rights, was to be expected.

Behind all the labels historical works differ profoundly according to whether they admit power or right as the more fundamental concept. Over against the company of those 'realists' from Hobbes and Machiavelli to Bertrand Russell, who find 'power' the key-word for social science and who trace its workings from the mailed fist to the veiled 'power of the keys' and the gentle force of conditioning, there are those who find the theme of history in liberty and human liberation. To the student of rights (or the preservation of liberties) the claims of historical institutions based on moral and reflective insight express a deeper, more enduring sanction than those

[25] *Ibid.*, p. 321. Also *Theory and Practice in Historical Study: A Report of the Committee on Historiography* (Social Science Research Council, Bulletin 34, New York, 1946) p. 136 note. Van Wyck Brooks, *The Confident Years* (New York, 1952) p. 485. "Charles Beard enumerated in *The Discussion of Human Affairs* eight reasons why history could *never be* a branch of science."
[26] *Republic*, p. 39.
[27] *Ibid.*, p. 339. "We can formulate three types of propositions: a law, a hypothesis, and a fiction." "All our comprehensive ideas or theories that purport to cover universal history, including . . . American history specifically, are in the nature of fictions."

based on *de facto* conquest and force of arms. For these students there is a difference between *authority* and *power*, and an important question to be asked regarding each society is what makes law possible for it, since without recognized authority there can be no law. Conformity to law rests usually on the recognized authority of certain persons held to be backed by force sufficient to compel their subjects' obedience, or else, as in the United States, by virtue of the acceptance of the authority of a fundamental constitutional law comprising a set of basic principles together with a method derivative from them for deciding questions and distributing powers. These principles must be persuasive in their own right, invoking men's allegiance through the light of truth that is in them, rather than as blind bludgeons of main force.

That Beard should in the end try to follow a middle course, defending neither power nor rights, was to be expected. Nevertheless, although seeming to reject power as a basic concept for history, he is obliged to derive the sanction of right (and rights) from it. Thus while asserting that a society ruled by force without ethical restraints or ideal norms will inevitably go to pieces, he yet holds that ethical restraints are themselves expressions of social pressure and depend on the power of the group for their substance. Rights, for him, are essentially *claims* regarding anything asserted by anyone who chooses to against a particular community, which are respected by that community. If enough people join in upholding a claim, it *gains force* and thus becomes a right allowed by that government or society. Far from being universal and imprescriptible, rights are local and changing, extending no further than the power to back them up. "In reality," says Beard, "no one possesses any real right or rights that he or she, in conjunction with others, cannot enforce against the community or government."[28] In other words, *demands* of any sort become *rights* if, and only if, those asserting them have sufficient power to exact their acceptance by society, and the society in turn has sufficient power to enact them. No rights are unenforceable,

[28] *Ibid.*, pp. 38-39.

since unless enforced in fact they are not rights,—in which we catch an echo of the familiar emptiness of contracts without the sword of Hobbesian realism. Since for Beard rights represent neither inherent prerogatives established by nature nor normative truths grasped by reason and conscience, they remain no more than social demands, described as 'moral' because they are backed not merely by overt power but by the sentiments, habits, and practice of the community. "All our comprehensive ideas or theories [like rights] that purport to cover universal history, including American history specifically," declares Beard, "are in the nature of fictions."[29] Thus the issue of rights serves as a touchstone that divides the empirical from the philosophical view of history.

Because Beard's interpretation diverges so radically from the presuppositions of the constitutional documents, it seems worth while to compare them a little further. Taken for what it purports to be, the *Declaration* is an argument directed to the universal moral sentiment of mankind offering an *a priori* theory of rights as the justification for a new government. Its case is presented in two parts: (1) the first, containing the celebrated statement of the principles and ends of government grounding them in self-evident truths regarding human rights valid for all men and all time. *Here the right of government is not held to be established by the fact of government; on the contrary, the fact is held to be judged by the right.* This point is central. (2) The second part, pursuing the ideal justification further, lists a series of oppressive acts against the colonies imputed to the British crown, infringing the axiomatic rights laid down in the first part. On this basis,—and it is of particular significance that the list of grievances is presented not merely as *causes* (incidents leading up to and precipitating the rupture) but as *grounds* (moral and intellectual reasons warranting it)—the people of the thirteen colonies declare themselves justified in severing the bond of allegiance to the mother country and in forming a new government. The foundation principles having been already set forth in the *Declaration*, the

[29] *Ibid.*, p. 339.

Constitution offers only a brief statement of ends in the Pre-amble, appealing to Justice, Liberty, and a more *perfect* Union (not simply, be it noted, a stronger one), all capitalized as sacred absolutes, and declaring its purpose to be to give prac-tical effect through its provisions to these lofty principles. Nor are these mere verbal flourishes, but basic notions that every-where permeate the instrument supporting the dignity and responsibility of the citizens for self-government. Although the term 'rights' is not used, many of them are incorporated in the document (as was pointed out by Hamilton in No. 84 of *The Federalist*), while the construction of the whole is peculiarly designed for the protection of individual liberty.

As a practical instrument designed to put ideal principles into effect, the Constitution is mainly devoted to the organiza-tion and disposition of powers under a new system. That government is power, the framers were keenly aware; yet against its force in fact they set ideal right as ultimate sanction. Their problem was to devise a government strong enough to be respected at home and abroad, of a type to stimulate and encourage the creative powers of its citizens, yet at the same time able to hold under the dominion of public right men's love of private power often so toxic in its influence. As is well known, their answer was to combine a strong federal union with a strong division of powers. Yet the lengths to which they went to prevent the concentration of control in the same hands sprang not from a Machiavellian belief in the love of power as the ruling motive-force among men,[30] but rather from their moral disdain of tyranny springing from their belief in the nobler potentialities of human nature. In many different ways the Constitution sought to encourage men's higher motives and to hinder their lower ones; to strengthen their public spirit by affording them exercise in the ways of liberty and responsibil-ity for justice through various modes of self-government. At the same time it strove to control their love of power by divid-

[30] Long before Beard, Marx, and the economic determinists, Madison in the tenth number of *The Federalist* had considered the theory of the class struggle and the contest for economic power as a mainspring of history.

ing and arranging public offices in such a manner that each
served as a check upon the others and the individual's private
interest acted as a sentinel of public right.[31]

The view of rights implied in the constitutional documents
had its roots in a philosophical tradition reaching back to
Plato, Aristotle, and the Stoics, to Roman law and the Fathers
of the Church, to Puritanism and the radical political thought
of the seventeenth and eighteenth centuries. According to this
tradition, referred to at the beginning of the chapter, there is
a higher noumenal justice behind existing statutes, common to
all men, places, and times.[32] Appeal to this universal justice or
moral law (once called *ius naturale*) beyond the enactments
of parliaments and kings served albeit fitfully as a guiding
beacon in history, a check on flagrant abuses in behalf of the
dignity of man. Limitations upon arbitrary power were recognized in the name of reason and conscience, from whose principles governments were held to derive the true consent of the
governed. Rights, accordingly, were regarded as prescriptions
of this ideal justice pertaining to men everywhere as moral
and rational beings. Far from being mere claims of desire
backed by government force, restricted to their actualization
in fact, rights were held to express true insights into the conditions of man's being man. In the last analysis, these pre-
requisites are held to be presuppositions of experience rather
than derived from experience; and though they take time to

---

[31] *The Federalist*, No. 51.

[32] Cicero, *De Re Publica*, III, 22. "True law is right reason in agreement
with nature, world-wide in scope, unchanging, everlasting ... We may not
oppose or alter that law, we cannot abolish it, we cannot be freed from its
obligations by any legislature, and we need not look outside ourselves for an
expounder of it. This law does not differ for Rome and for Athens, for the
present and for the future ... It is and will be valid for all nations and all
times. He who disobeys it denies himself and his own nature."

Locke, *Second Treatise on Government*, Ch. II Sect. 6. "The state of nature
has a law of nature to govern it, which obliges everyone; and reason, which
is that law, teaches all mankind who will but consult it, that being all equal
and independent, no one ought to harm another in his life, health, liberty, or
possessions. For men being all the workmanship of one omnipotent and
infinitely wise Maker—all the servants of one sovereign Master ... and being
furnished with like faculties, sharing all in one community of nature, there
cannot be supposed any such subordination among us, that may authorize us
to destroy one another, as if we were made for one another's uses."

realize historically, to be in principle non-temporal and universal. They are what moral reason sees that it takes for man to be a person enjoying freedom and responsibility for a reasonable way of life in society. To government they stand as normative commitments, standard maxims (as Lincoln said) for a free society, the charter of liberties toward whose realization constitutional systems continually strive. Far from being considered as *fictions* local and changing, as the sport of power and custom, rights in our constitutional tradition are conceived as universal in reference, anterior to political power, as timelessly true,—although it takes time in the historical process to elicit their implications and for states to approximate their realization in laws (for instance, the right to labor or employment is only becoming apparent today as involved in the rights of liberty and property).

To repeat, a fundamental difference emerges between interpreters of history who maintain that ideas are wholly functions of interests and factual forces and those who allow that they may genuinely express noumenal principles outreaching the natural world. The great point at issue is whether only observable causes operating under empirical laws affect human action or whether grounds, values, insights of an ideal sort may be compelling in their own right to move human beings in affairs. To concede that even a single individual, for instance Jefferson in drafting the *Declaration,* could take a stand above or against self-interest and social profit, and could take it not merely as an exculpatory gesture or a cloak of advantage, but genuinely on principle, requires belief in more than nature.

But you forget, protests the naturalist, that Jefferson like the other founders, was but a child of the age. Rationalism was in the air, and his statements were but argumentative weapons to persuade, camouflage though perhaps unconscious of the colonists' advantage. Look deeper, he will urge, and you will see that his noble words but clothe the natural man, albeit a man with long range views, a highly socialized animal. To secure very practical benefits (not 'blessings') for themselves and their posterity was the aim of the founders' argument.

To be sure, in the documents their concern is expressed in a generous language likely to lessen hostility and to unite a divided society. Politically, they well knew, self-interest and social interest are closely allied, since the individual's good depends on the team-work of the group that shares and supports his advantage. Indeed, the self-regarding and social impulses are hardly separable in a creature for whom solidarity (to a degree) is the price of survival. Through the development of a kind of wider self-love of the group, social creatures become as it were parts of each other, so that when the interest of a member is attacked the group rises to defend him, each feeling a menace to its own existence. Socialization of motive may thus take place without loss of self-regard or self-interest, since others are felt as instrumental to oneself, no matter how wide the circle.

So naturalism claims to find in the impulse to sociality rather than in *a priori* principles the root of moral and political sanctions. The gist of the social nature of morals is simply that the individual is affected by the acts of others, and compelled to modify his behavior in consequence. Throughout, however, the individual remains the center of origin and experience. The point is well illustrated in the words of John Dewey, who as a spokesman for naturalism and an early university colleague influenced Beard. "Why be moral?" Dewey asks. Were an individual alone in the world, the issue would not arise; but since others make demands upon us, injure or aid us by their actions, the answer is the same as to the query: Why not put your hand into the fire?

The answer to the question "Why not put your hand into the fire?" is the answer of fact. If you do your hand will be burnt. The answer to the question why acknowledge the right is of the same sort. For Right is only an abstract name for the multitude of concrete demands in action which others impress upon us, of which we are obliged, if we would live, to take some account. Its authority is the exigency of their demands, the efficacy of their insistencies.[33]

[33] John Dewey, *Human Nature and Conduct* (New York, 1930) Pt. IV Sect. IV p. 326.

Thus right is established by fact, by the fact of social pressures upon us, and not by some preconceived standard of what ought to be. The old notions of reason and conscience directed to ideal goals, of man's inviolable prerogatives, give place to achieving a workable adjustment of counterclaims between oneself and others. Belief in absolute standards beyond our mundane reach involves an impossible dualism. The obligation laid on men to pattern their actions after perfect justice and right forced on them pretensions too high for human nature. Moreover, the sharp separation implied between private and public interest, between getting ahead oneself and concern with the general good, divided men against themselves and set the individual at odds with society. In our constitutional documents, on this view, the scientific historian finds no transcendental but only *natural* goods to be obtained through socialized activity. The system wrought by realists like Madison and Hamilton, they hold, did not ask men to do the impossible or expect them to sacrifice themselves on the altar of pure disinterestedness. Far from expecting them to go against their own self-interest (with resultant hypocrisy and frustration),—things were so arranged that in laboring with and for others, men achieved their own advancement. Self-regarding and other-regarding motives are used mutually to supplement each other; and gears are so meshed that interest in others' interest works to one's own interest. The old dualism between selfishness and unselfishness, the sharp separation between private and public service is thus in principle largely overcome, since in serving others we serve ourselves, and likewise discover that the best way to realize our own interest is by promoting theirs.

Nevertheless the defender of *a priori* rights is not convinced by this interpretation. All too clearly he sees that such an account of morality and of constitutional law in terms of mutual adjustment for practical ends leaves out man's pursuit of the equitable. The favorite device of those who deny fundamental principles of reason and conscience in human affairs in favor of the authority of science is to emphasize sociality.

Yet nothing is gained by blurring the distinction between public and private interests, which though related differ profoundly, nor by falsely identifying social activity with morality. For social consciousness is never free from self-love, and experience plainly shows how a man may be 'socialized' in the service of a group without at all relinquishing self-love as his supreme value. From the bourgeois in whose proprietary view his family is his shop window, an extension of himself, to the ruler whose acts (if not words) proclaim 'I am the state,' there is the same egoistic feeling. Actually only where people are able to rise above self, family, class, group or economic interest, to a sense of 'the principle of the thing,' is there real public spirit and morality. And it is this attitude, reflected in our constitutional tradition, which far from setting the individual at odds with his fellows, or submerging him in total concern with the group, lifts him to a universal point of view. Thus a great gulf separates our fellow-feeling for the existent members of our society from respect for the dignity of man, separates humanism from humanitarianism, the pragmatic settlement of rival claims from concern with justice as a nonpreferential principle.

If the founders really looked upon the union simply as a scheme for social advantage, certainly their choice of language was most unfortunate. Instead of talking like hard-headed men of affairs about production, trade, jobs, classes, and a working balance of interests, they were concerned with liberty, safeguarding rights, legislative and judicial provisions. To suppose that they failed to grasp the issues, or chose to say one thing and mean another, is unbelievably to weaken their case. However, those best acquainted with the period agree that it was not the founders' artifice but the substantial convictions of the times which framed our fundamental documents in the language of politics, ethics, law instead of the language of fact, economy, business. Here was a political system built so that men educated by their own free exertions might respond to the enlightening influence of ideas, might exercise their moral and deliberative natures. By establishing the independence of the judiciary, for instance, it was hoped to check hasty action by thought. By rejecting class and economic representation in Congress (familiar in medieval assemblies), by making constitutional amendment possible but difficult, and in many other ways, attempt was made to strengthen rational republican principles. Reason, to this way of thinking, provided both an instrument of practical action and standards of what ought to be. Through it man is endowed (if one may borrow Whitehead's analogy)[34] not simply with the craft of Ulysses but with the wisdom of Plato. His intelligence is not wholly one with the strategy of the animal, a weapon of adaptation and defence enabling the creature to survive; in addition to the cunning of the fox and the herd instinct of the pack, there is pursuit of ideal goals. Beyond the spur and lure of transient things, man has glimpses of principles and perfects in a timeless world. Justice, liberty, rights are not mere instrumental hypotheses to be used for what they are worth in factual gains, then modified or discarded, but truths unconditionally binding.

A moral and political system rooted in sociality, on the contrary, would bespeak a wholly creaturely view, lending 'rights' to the individual only on the expediency of the group and withdrawing them at pleasure. It is not too much to say that one of the great rediscoveries of our time is the insufficiency of this outlook which grants personality to men only as members of a group,—a reawakened consciousness of the individual and his rights as supreme over the claims of society. Through the universal horror roused by the political trials and purges in totalitarian states, the world in a naturalistic age has been made aware once more of the meaning of the inviolable sanctity of the human spirit and respect for its rights as beyond and distinct from the prerogatives of the community. At the spectacle of mentally ruined men scientifically destroyed by the state, at the spectacle of confessions wrung from ghosts, world opinion is aroused afresh to the meaning of the dignity of personality. Even though safety may require society upon

[34] Alfred Worth Whitehead, *The Function of Reason* (Princeton, 1929) pp. 7, 23, 29.

evidence of a man's guilt (obtained through established public procedure) to exact the death penalty of his body, yet for his punishment to be just there must be a responsible mentality there to receive it. If for this reason alone, respect for the agent as subject, respect for his freedom of mind ought to be recognized beyond all other freedoms. But today the world is confronted with a new tyranny which denies the distinctness of spirit from flesh and the proprietary right of the mind to its own attitudes and allegiances. To kill an opponent's body is not enough: by forcing him to recant, by breaking his will, it seeks also to destroy his character and the validity of his position.

Yet these terrible puppet shows, when spread before the eyes of the world, afford a lesson very different than their authors intended. Far from proving scientific materialism as a case, they only exhibit the brutality of the showmen, its masters. The world's conscience is roused anew to perceive the sanctity of the soul, and that its freedom of thought and belief ought to be respected beyond all other freedoms. Those, on the contrary, who deny them are seen to destroy the very nature of man, to exchange Reason for Force, construing his inner light as only a Grand Illusion. For the threat of free reason to the materialists is that it leads men to believe that the consciousness of the inner subject can decide the merits of human action by principles drawn from within itself and can set itself up in judgment of the world. The fact is that, reason everywhere presents itself in colors false to naturalism claiming not partiality but impartiality, not impotence but power, not attachment but detachment, an ideality beyond materiality as its substantive source. Today in the long struggle between power and rights the tide is beginning to turn once more against naturalism. For it comes to be seen that if a man cannot trust his own insights, his own intelligence as authority, both freedom and knowledge are dislocated at their source and sink in a bottomless quagmire of delusions. With their denial, political constitutions, moral codes, histories, even scientific systems, everything that is the creation of the mind and rests on norms and presuppositions beyond the sensible facts can be charged with deception. But rather than that the whole structure should come tumbling about their ears, writers have begun to retreat from the unadulterated language of compulsory forces and scientism, and in American history students again admit that the mind of the people resting its assurance on the genuineness of the principles and professed intentions laid down at the beginning has rightly understood on the whole the sustaining spirit of our constitutional system.

But before proceeding further with philosophic history, we must dispose in the next chapter of another problem connected with the scientific approach and its methodology.

CHAPTER SEVEN

Predictions
and Might Have Beens

HISTORIANS WHO FOLLOW THE PATTERNS of science incline to agree in at least one important particular. Despite professed devotion to the empirical, they do not conceive their task as purely inductive, or imagine that by merely amassing and arranging facts in parallel series, they gain adequate historical knowledge. Even though they may not say so, they know the facts do not speak nor discoveries spring from the data themselves, but that they require the invention of minds to interpret them. Because the historian rarely meets face-to-face the event he describes, he is driven to greater reliance on his power of synthetic contrivance and explanatory conjecture. Thus even Mill refers to historical method as 'inverse deduction,' declaring that in favorable instances it can show *a priori* reasons for expecting what took place, and that the events represented the most likely order consistent with the laws of human nature and natural conditions.[1]

In brief, historians under scientific influence claim to employ a hypothetical deductive treatment of their subject, collecting and analyzing a body of data under the guidance of a ruling hypothesis, and then checking it for causal relations by empirical and deductive tests. In rare cases like that of Beard dis-

[1] John Stuart Mill, *A System of Logic,* Bk. VI Ch. X Sect. 4.

cussed in the last chapter, the procedure may achieve a rather close imitation of the scientific experiment. But often, instead of painstaking analysis of a narrow field, ambitious writers prefer a wide comparative survey of periods and cultures; and by noting broad likenesses, differences, and concurrent changes among them claim to discover significant generalizations and causal laws. That such a method, familiar in Buckle or Toynbee, is more than analogical we should deny. But in any case the interpretation of hypothetical deduction calls for critical comment. Your modern 'scientific' historian does not allow the non-temporal *a priori* character of historical deduction, but interprets the inquirer's 'reasons for expecting' what occurred as essentially temporal predictions directed to present consequences. Even the evolutionary hypothesis is not to be viewed ontologically, but essentially as a tool for immediate practical problems. Such acceptance of local attachment and present orientation is held to open up great vistas of future usefulness. The historian, in construing other periods through their bearing on the practical needs of his own, more than compensates for his supposed loss in judicial detachment by increased relevance and utility. The dry bones of the past gain real resurrection. Taking as his point of departure the issues of the day, the student seeks answers illuminating present problems. Interpretation of the past becomes at once *diagnosis* of the present and *prediction* of the future, with the author in many cases plainly committed (where his social sympathies are strong) to furthering the forces on one side.

The search for causes having suffered a long and trying critique, *consequences* have lately assumed the primacy in scientific history. In a period of revolutionary movements in politics and technology, many more were found to be interested in effects, applications, social uses than in antecedents. So the focus of attention shifted from causes to the prediction of consequences, while the search for grounds or reasons underwent a still greater eclipse. Concern with the past for its own sake was discarded as antiquarian; instead history was studied more as an aid to the present. According to James Harvey

Robinson current need should furnish the principle of selection of the new scientific[2] history; while even for Croce history is "induced by the requirements of practical life."[3] No doubt the pervasive influence of the idea of evolution contributed to this emphasis. Since on Darwinian principles each creature is tested by its ability to adapt and survive, so similarly each higher institution or enterprise (like science and history) is to be estimated by its successful solution of vital problems. Yet when accepted such an interpretation revolutionizes ideas of scientific procedure, shifting the basis of proof away from logical grounds to empirical and pragmatic considerations. Practical fruitfulness, not evidential weight, becomes the central theme. Defenders of hypothetical method in a truer scientific sense, on the contrary, do not readily accept this perversion or willingly relinquish its *a priori* side. Pure scientists retain mathematics as a basis of their method, in which consequents enjoy no supremacy over antecedents and in which hypotheses are valid independent of temporal predictions or empirical checks. If hypotheses in the natural sciences are rational in a similar sense in their structure, then for them too prediction and practical fruitfulness are insufficient tests. Certainly modern science began in the heavens at the farthest reach from everyday use. At its foundation stood Copernicus, who (although the 'practical facts' seemed against him) urged his heliocentric hypothesis on the grounds, let us remember, of consistency, parsimony, probability, comprehensiveness, and the like. Nor did the fact that its empirical and pragmatic justification was long in coming deter Galileo and the competent few from accepting its truth. If we turn today to the most embracing of the sciences, astronomy, we may find the author of the theory of relativity sometimes discussing its verification in similar vein. "The experimental consequences of the general relativity theory differ only slightly from those of classical

<hr>

[2] J. H. Robinson, *The New History*, Ch. I. "The present has hitherto been the willing victim of the past; the time has now come when it should turn on the past and exploit it in the interests of advance" p. 24.

[3] Benedetto Croce, *op. cit.*, p. 17.

mechanics," he declares. "But the strength of the theory lies in its inner consistency and the simplicity of its fundamental assumptions."[4]

That the author of today's most comprehensive historical scientific hypothesis should draw attention to its parsimony and inner consistency of assumptions rather than simply to its successful outcome in passing predictive tests (the focus of popular interest) is surely not without significance. If it shows nothing else, his statement indicates that there is more to scientific method than is to be found by pragmatic empiricists. Nevertheless among those who would make history a science today there is a strong tendency to suppose that its method centers in anticipations of the future confirmed in practical life and that the backbone of historical works is to be found in hypotheses capable of predictive verification. As A. J. Ayer puts it, "Propositions about the past are rules for the prediction of those 'historical' experiences which are commonly said to verify them." "Propositions about the past are hypotheses in the same sense as the laws of natural science are hypotheses."[5] On this view, the assertion of a past event centers not in its conformity with certain ideal essences in a vanished world, but in a methodological anticipation of the present or future consequences which would substantiate it. For instance, the judgment that "Shakespeare wrote *Henry VI*" is held to amount to a predictive summary of the observations that would persuade the historian of the fact of this happening: that is, if the student examined early texts of the play he would find similarities of style, spelling, vocabulary with Shakespeare's accredited works; stigmata of forgery would be lacking; and research would probably reveal near-contemporary references which connected the poet with authorship of such a play. In brief, the historical statement would be an hypothesis whose truth rested upon a set of possible consequences confirmable by predictive tests.

[4] Albert Einstein and Leopold Infeld, *The Evolution of Physics* (New York, 1938) p. 260.

[5] Alfred J. Ayer, *Language, Truth, and Logic* (New York, 1936) p. 147.

Yet if accepted, the notion that the past does not live other than in the present and that currently observed consequences and predictions are the fulcrum of historical method profoundly alters the historian's conception of his subject. Just as science, on the same view, deserves respect not as pure knowledge, but for the new power and foresight it lends to the conquest of nature, so historical inquiry is valued not for disclosure of the past, but as a means of handling the present and shaping the future. How far this recasting of history goes to destroy both its intentional and temporal significance, we shall see later in the chapter. What comes out of a past situation, not the situation itself, is regarded as important. Knowledge is approached through and for the sake of the consequences, to which the antecedents are secondary and instrumental.

Undoubtedly the world growth of socialism and its success in employing theories of history as tools of political action has influenced students of the past to a new interest in its practical consequences and future trends. Even academic historians at the furthest remove from political revolutionaries have been awakened by such means to enthusiasm for the unsuspected possibilities of the subject as a 'scientific instrument' for shaping tomorrow through rereading the past. Yet how far they are prepared to sacrifice their trusteeship to the past, their duty to impartiality in handling the evidence, is a matter on which the academic mind (as on so much else) often remains ambiguous. Nevertheless a gulf remains between those, whom we might call political activists and revolutionaries, that is, who adopt a consciously partisan, vigorously practical outlook, and those academics or liberals, who still believe that by collating different facts and viewpoints the historian may escape a prejudicial interpretation and win relative impartiality. Both are pragmatic; but the question dividing them is whether man, conceived as a fragment of environing nature, can in recording his past really escape the bias of his place, time, and situation. To the political revolutionary there can be no escape from partisanship of perspective on a scientific cosmology. Hence the historian should frankly adopt the forceful, partisan outlook that promises most in practical goods. Nothing is more absurd in his eyes than the confused academic with his composite views, trying to face both ways by averaging out diverse lines of evidence and different slants.

That there is power in the revolutionary attitude one cannot deny. In the twentieth century no one can be blind to the results achieved by experts in writing history to make history, the mushroom growth won by movements like communism and fascism through framing from a smattering of historical facts a subtle blend of propaganda, myth, and social disaffection. By finding lessons in the past with which to arouse the dynamic emotions of the masses, they have been able to launch great social experiments. Into their vest-pocket versions of history went little laborious study of documents or pretense of impartial research. Their aim was rather to defend a preconceived hypothesis by dressing up the past in its favor, to make a case, to build a system for the future by providing ready-made historical diagnoses, a semantics of historical slogans, and a revolutionary political organization. Backed by the arts of scientific inculcation for social control, this new 'applied' history has met to a supreme degree, for the time at least, the pragmatic test. By moulding public opinion, directing mass action, overthrowing governments and setting up new ones, it has resolved in a sense the problems out of which the movements arose (though new and worse ones may have ensued) and in so far made its predictions come true. Academic historians trained in the tradition of history as 'past politics' are astonished at the transformation of the subject into the 'politics of today and tomorrow.' They are amazed to find it leaving the world of musty libraries for the surging crowds and blaring microphones of city squares. This new 'social science' has far outrun their expectations; in it preconceived dogmas and reconstruction of the past to meet future plans appear naked and undisguised; the old exacting demands on the historian not to doctor the facts and to weigh all available evidence have disappeared. To be sure, it is only in the hands of a few masters,—professional revolutionaries engaged in remaking the world,—that this variant of 'scientific method' has been fully developed. Yet even a brief consideration of examples of their skill in creating practical, predictive history shows how completely they throw their academic colleagues into the shade.

In the first volume of the official history of the Russian Revolution[6] by Stalin, Molotov, Gorky, and others, is to be found a description of the historical method which communist leaders seek to follow and which is there called 'Leninist analysis.' Lenin's most famous use of this method, although its principles are found throughout his writings, was made between the February and October Revolutions in 1917, that is, after the date of the Czar's overthrow and before the Bolsheviks rose to power. While the analysis offered by Lenin at the April Conference of the Bolshevik Party (and known as the 'April Theses') was directed at the current Russian situation, it involved a total interpretation of history. In principle its substance is simple. Lenin resolves the situation facing Russia at that time into three mutually exclusive and exhaustive alternative possibilities. By taking these alternatives as hypotheses and deriving their respective consequences, he purports to show by the method of elimination that one and only one outcome can solve the historical problem, and the inevitable failure of the others. It is of course no accident that the magic Hegelian number three dominates the structure of the argument. There are, according to Lenin, three causes accountable for the 1917 collapse of organized Russian society, just as there are three and only three classes in the society which by their action might conceivably bring about a cure. The three classes (as prescribed by Marxism) are: the feudal aristocracy, the urban bourgeoisie, and the proletarian peasants and workers; while the three causes of the country's troubles are: the military disaster induced by World War I then in

---

[6] M. Gorky, V. Molotov, J. Stalin, etc., *The History of the Civil War in the U. S. R.* (New York, 1937) Vol. I.

progress, the collapse of economic production, and the poverty of the masses.

The problem of the historian, according to Lenin, is to be able to predict which of these classes, if in control of the government, would be able to solve these three issues. His answer, predetermined from the beginning, is that the proletariat will emerge as the savior class. Nevertheless the diagnosis and arguments by which he supports his conclusions are interesting. That either of the upper classes could successfully resolve the desperate issues of the war, economic collapse, and widespread poverty, he insists, is impossible, because their self-interest is essentially in conflict with the solution of these problems. (That each class inevitably follows its own self-interest is axiomatic to the Marxist position.) But with the overthrow of the czar in the February Revolution, the failure of the feudal aristocracy which had launched the war through its greed for wealth and power was an accomplished fact. That the bourgeoisie then in control under the Provisional Government of Kerensky would be similarly unable to solve the problems, he argued, was inevitable. Since in exchange for spoils and concessions the Provisional Government had already signed treaties to continue the war, peace at its hands was out of the question. Although such a middle-class regime might try by half-measures to relieve the country's economic distress—i.e., by giving some land to the people,—nevertheless by *demanding compensation* for the land it would seek to save the capitalist system and so fail to remove the causes of unrest. Its self-interest being inevitably bound to capitalism (by its ownership of stocks, bonds, factories, and farm mortgages), any settlement by the bourgeoisie of the profound crisis in industry and agriculture would be impossible. Hence the revolution must continue until sooner or later the proletariat is swept into power. But where the others had failed could the workers and peasants succeed in finding a way out of the disaster? Lenin held that they could for one simple reason: that *their interests as a class were identical with the demands of the revolution.* Since they derived only immense suffering and no profit from the continuance of the war, hardship (not gain) from capitalism and landlordism, they, the working class would wish to take immediate steps to make peace, to confiscate the estates for the benefit of the peasants, and to restore the economy by nationalizing the banks and large enterprises. Thus, on his logic, *if* a proletarian government came to power *(as it inevitably must)*, and took drastic action in its own interests as a class *(as it inevitably would)*, the problem of the revolution would be solved.

Lenin's method in framing his hypothesis he believes to be based on a complete reading of history. According to Marxian materialism, the historical process is determined by economic laws with class as the basic phenomenon of organized society. Since each economic class pursues its own advantage and is unable to cooperate with the others, a continual struggle ensues for control of the forces of production and the expression of this mastery in government. Because governments always pursue the interest of the ruling class, those classes not in control grow dissatisfied, and to the degree that their needs are not met foment increasing trouble. According to the inevitable law of the process, as the wealth of a society becomes concentrated in the hands of a few, revolution breaks out, and if the class in power cannot solve the crisis, power passes to another class whose interests more nearly meet the needs of the time. In the Russian revolution, neither of the upper classes when their self-interest was at stake could make the economic sacrifice necessary to stem the paralysis and disaster. Therefore, said Lenin, the transfer of power to the proletariat by further revolution was inevitable, as the proletariat was the only class whose own advantage could force it "to end the war, give land to the peasants, and to save the country from economic crisis."[7]

"The chief symptom," declares Lenin, "by which Marxists determine the character of a revolution is the transfer of power from one class to another." And certainly one of the secrets of Lenin's fame was his diagnosis at a critical moment of history

[7] *Ibid.*, p. 174.

of the February uprising which overthrew the czar as a "bourgeois revolution." The outcome of the February upheaval, he asserts, was simply that Russia passed from the control of the feudal nobility to control by the capitalist landlords of the bourgeoisie. Such being the case, he predicts, the czarist overthrow which brought the new capitalist class to power represents only *a transitional phase of the revolution to a later stage.* In this later stage, control will pass from the bourgeoisie to the working class, and the proletariat will finally hold the power and resources of the country in its triumphant grasp.[8]

Having diagnosed the Russian situation according to the Marxist conception of world-history, Lenin calls upon the Bolshevik Party through its revolutionary acts and efforts to execute the transfer of political power to the workers. To this end he briefs the Party in great detail as to the tactical course to be pursued to achieve the successful overthrow of the Kerensky regime and the capture of the government. As the first step he urges the Bolsheviks to launch a propaganda campaign against all revolutionary parties supporting the Provisional Government. The flank of these less extreme radicals must be turned; they must be outflanked and outbid from the left. By isolating and attacking all moderate socialists and democrats as 'servitors of the bourgeoisie,' their influence over the masses can be completely destroyed. But once distrust of these rivals as 'compromisers' and appeasers has been instilled by a drumfire of propaganda, all radical elements, according to Lenin, will rally to the Bolsheviks as the one revolutionary party really fighting for the workers. Consequently as the next step the Party will gain a voting majority in the Soviets of Workers' and Soldiers' Deputies; and having once gained control of the Soviets, the triumph of the proletariat,—that is to say, *the triumph of the Bolshevik Party,*—will be assured. Conceivably, Lenin hinted, the transfer of authority to the Bolshe-

---

[8] Stalin, in praise of Lenin's acuteness in distinguishing the stages in what Marx regarded as permanent revolution, says that "the idea of the bourgeois-democratic revolution growing into the socialist revolution (was) propounded by Lenin as long ago as 1905." J. Stalin, *Problems of Leninism* (New York, 1934) p. 14f.

viks might come about entirely through political pressure and
ideological conquest, that is to say, "by peaceful means."[9] In
any case, once in the saddle with government power, the
Bolsheviks would set about concluding an immediate peace
with Germany, confiscating estates, nationalizing industries,
and inaugurating the transition to socialism. As all the world
knows, Lenin's program was adopted and carried through by
the Party. In the ensuing course of events the consequences
followed much as he had foreseen save that, as was to be
expected from the Marxist philosophy of unmitigated conflict,
the government power was captured by revolutionary force
and violence rather than by peaceful, electoral means. In the
end it was by a double *coup d'état* and the institution of an
iron dictatorship that the Provisional Government was driven
out and the new Soviet Government of the Bolshevik Party
was set up in Russia.

The world-wide impression made by Lenin's analysis of the
Russian Revolution and the use of the same method by other
leaders (Stalin at the next Party Congress is said to have
offered a "profound Leninist analysis" "soon confirmed by the
stormy course of events")[10] was due more than anything else
to its success as prediction. Here, people said, was history in
action that staked its confirmation not on old documents and
remains but on the outcome of contemporary events. The past
was considered in relation to present practical problems and
as means for improving man's future. Yet the nature of the
'scientific method' claimed by these revolutionaries was very
different from that hitherto employed by academic historians.
Here the hypothetical-deductive method was applied with
unmatched boldness in a frame of dogmatic theory. To begin
with, the method rested on a world-hypothesis applicable to
all places and times, an oracular recasting of the whole course
of human events. Acceptance of its scheme meant receiving
without question a set of fixed concepts, dialectical laws, and
predetermined ends unknown to orthodox science. Involved

9 *Ibid.*, p. 177.
10 *Ibid.*, pp. 308, 325.

in it, for instance, was the Hegelian triadic law of development through affirmations, negations, syntheses; the economic warfare of classes, conflict, antagonisms as everywhere the core of the social process. Far from being depressing, this notion of continual strife and upheaval is exhilarating to the Marxist, since through it alone, according to his creed, social evolution takes place. Society, in his eyes, having advanced by successive revolutionary stages from primitive agriculture through feudalism to capitalism, is now ready to pass into socialism, and stands on the brink of the final proletarian revolution, which by emancipating the working class and raising it to power will "once for all emancipate society at large from all exploitation, oppression, and class struggle."[11] In all this, as we have said, a new set of concepts: class struggle, capitalism, socialism, agencies like 'the forces of production,' propaganda, the proletariat, and 'the leader of the revolution' become central in the reading of history. The idea of 'revolution,' hitherto reserved by historians for a few rare turning-points, now emerges as a perpetual theme, just as economic outweigh political forces, and classes replace nations and individuals as actors in the drama, so revolutions supersede the old discussion of wars.

In the official *History*, Lenin appears as 'the leader of the revolution,' as the supreme brain equipped with organizing genius, deep historical knowledge, indomitable will, and the scientific vision to chart an 'unerring course' to the goal. Its account describes with reverent emotion the great moment when the 'beloved leader,' having returned from exile to head the struggle, first revealed himself to the cheering throngs in a Petrograd square; how he mounted an armoured car while "searchlights played upon him" and "confidently launched his appeal for a *world Socialist revolution* to the crowds who stood listening with bated breath." Here, says the *History*, was "the gigantic mind and will, fortified by the experience of the revolutionary struggle of the toilers of all countries and by a *scientific conception* of the tasks of the proletariat." At long

[11] Preface to the *Communist Manifesto*.

last "the leader of the revolution had assumed his post."[12]

While at many crises in history leaders, like Caesar, Luther, or Napoleon, have appeared to diagnose and take charge of critical situations, Lenin and the communists claim the distinction of alone being guided by a 'scientific' knowledge of history and its laws. Actually, however, the mixture of metaphysical dogma, economic analysis, and practical shrewdness in manipulating human nature which they seem to have possessed would not be admitted as a scientific grasp of historical laws by the free scientific world. The intuitive power of piercing to the heart of a confused situation, of crystallizing popular demand, and of organizing the forces to satisfy it, has in many ages been recognized as the peculiar gift of the political leader. Lenin's success in foretelling the course of the Russian Revolution would seem due to his faith in a dogma, ruthless pressure and propaganda in forcing a fluid political situation into channels open to capture by a trained fanatical minority rather than to any scientific knowledge of the laws of history. In short, *propaganda* and *organization* tirelessly pursued would appear the secrets: the record of how a disciplined and ruthless party machine can prevail over divided and unorganized groups by using industriously circulated catchwords, plausible lies, tricks of compulsion and psychological warfare to delude unsuspecting human nature.

In other words, the communist world-hypothesis is really no hypothesis but a metaphysical dogma accepted by those who employ it as beyond refutation. Rooted in a fixed substructure, Lenin's argument claims an inevitability in its consequences, an exhaustiveness and exclusiveness in its alternatives, unknown to science and to free scientific historians. For no academic historian could claim with certainty to exhaust the possibilities in advance, could ignore the chance of some neglected alternative or some unforeseen working-out of contingencies. Why should the Russian crisis have had three and only three possible outcomes, each dependent upon the victory of a particular class? What was to prevent the possibility of

[12] *Ibid.*, pp. 161-162. Italics mine.

some unpredictable turn of events beyond Lenin's calculations? Might not some overwhelming calamity of pestilence or foreign invasion conceivably have occurred that would have united the nation through a common danger? Or might not a new schism of classes arise—as between the peasants on the land and the city factory workers—thereby increasing their number? Or even a stasis of classes ensue, from which no government would emerge strong enough to prevent chaos and anarchy? Theoretically all manner of coalitions and cleavages can be conjured up to upset the magic triadic arrangement. Communist history, we can only conclude, is basically myth dressed up in a scientific language. For although it includes a measure of historical fact overlaid with an imaginative fable of man's destiny, its very totality of perspective puts it beyond scientific test. Basically its scheme belongs to the realm of utopian fiction where all alternatives thrive. Like other leading myths of our day, its device is simply to select a single contributory factor to human life (like economic class, race, or geography) and to magnify it into a sweeping explanation of history. By endowing the social process with a vague purposive tendency favoring its particular communist slant, and by passing off pseudo and partial knowledge as complete and trustworthy, a purportedly objective account of history is converted to the ends of make-believe and wish-fulfillment.

To claim at a stroke to bring scientific system into a field like history, hitherto devoid of laws and with few accepted generalizations, is obviously to beg the question. Yet it is always easy for power-eager minds to invent some new conception of things, and then find facts to support it. Human imagination is fertile in schemes. The very breadth of the communist 'hypotheses' together with the leeway allowed in selecting supporting facts and predictions, enables them to turn everything to account in their own favor. When one of Lenin's forecasts happened to be fulfilled, the Party claque loudly proclaimed that the course of events had exactly confirmed the Marxist theory; when they failed, as they often did, the fact was passed over in silence or excused in every

possible way short of jettisoning Party dogma. Indeed, his most
successful predictions turned largely on immediate local
manœuvres executed—not by the free working of the popular
will of the workers or the unfettered logic of history—but by
the brute force of a trained band of followers already primed
for the deed. His large scale, long range previsions (like those
of Marx) fall far short of scientific accuracy. Thus the result
of the 'Proletarian Revolution' in Russia and elsewhere has
been no new society of the free and equal. Though called
Socialism, the tyranny and terror of the police states which
follow bear little resemblance to what the communists pre-
dicted. The old slogans about the state's 'withering away' and
each man taking freely according to his needs ring today with
a grim irony. Besides failing to foresee its own future, communism failed signally to predict that of its adversaries. Contrary to its expectation, capitalism in highly industrialized
countries did not dig its own grave through economic crises,
nor did proletarian revolutions overthrow the governments.
Instead of destitution in fact, free capitalistic enterprise
brought increased prosperity to the workers. Only where
communist soothsayers are allowed privileges of ambiguity as
wide as the ancient oracles (so that no refutation is possible)
can their predictive average be rated as scientific. As a hundred
years of warring Marxist sects bears witness, their forecasts
regarding the larger future remain so equivocal in import and
timing, that usually only those persuaded in advance find a
particular interpretation scientifically convincing.

Needless to say, these exponents of history as a revolutionary
science have little respect for the cautious, tentative methods
of academic inquirers. Professorships, they are led to observe,
are rarely filled by men of action, nor are chairs of history
endowed for those bold enough to chart a revolutionary future.
The bourgeois minds of academic moderates falter before
the dynamics of Marxism. 'Humanitarian liberals' talk of action
for a better social order, but never find the evidence quite
sufficient, the circumstances quite right to initiate it. Instead
they try to face both ways. Although psychology has plainly

exposed (to the satisfaction of Marxists) how interests direct ideation and the impossibility of approaching the past without value preferences, academic minds are too timid to capitalize on such knowledge. Fearful of so-called 'propagandist history,' they refuse to read their material in the light of men's eager desires for the future. In their historical handling of the most pressing social problems, their groping tentativeness and scrupulosity render their studies tedious, futile, and ineffective. In the eyes of Marxism, their 'scientific method' is devoid of dynamic vitality—lacking the clenched fist, the creed of blood and fire. In contrast, as we have seen, communist historical writing retains its predilection for the spectacular and romantic: in its dogma of evolution by revolution, its preoccupation with crises, violent explosions, dramatic reversals, and in the stellar role assigned to the leader of the revolution.

Admittedly the 'scientific method' of the academic historians is less daring than that of the communists. Unlike Lenin, they do not boldly set up a set of exhaustive alternatives and by drawing out their purported consequences and eliminating all save one, claim to show that *it alone* can occur in the future. Nor do they assume all causes to be known in advance and merely verified in the outcome. The contrast between them turns also on the fact that Lenin's predictions emphasize events in the future and are prospective, while those of academic authors are usually retrospectively verificatory of past events. Thus Lenin's argument turns on a set of hypothetical questions asking: *If this, that, or the other thing happened, or should happen, what in each case would its outcome be?* Unlike academic historians he wastes little time in inquiring: *What might have happened if this had not happened?* Or in asking: *If men had not acted as they did, but in some other way, what would have been the result?* Oriented upon what lies ahead, imbued with belief in historical necessity, the communist leader has no fondness for 'might have beens.' While his method leads him beyond accomplished facts to forecast the future, he avoids the guessing game of lost chances, of speculating on the outcome if things had gone differently, involving arguments directly contrary to fact. Academic writers, on the contrary, are fond of 'might have beens.' Though less dogmatic in method and more hesitant in their forecasts, they too are eager to emulate science by some semblance of predictive verification. Accordingly, by 'imagining away' certain key figures or conditions in an historical action, or by arbitrarily deleting a critical event, they claim to 'prove' that without them the actual historical outcome would not have occurred, and so to have established their decisive causal weight. If Julius Caesar had not been born, there would have been (at least in the first century B. C.) no Roman Empire; if Lenin had not lived (or had not returned to Russia in 1917), there would have been no U. S. S. R. By indulging in the negative pastime of posing and answering questions contrary to fact, they seek to establish a factual case. Yet in our opinion such imaginary experiments which ask: *If what happened had not happened, how then would things be?* make a travesty of scientific prediction and the method of difference. Historical deductions which claim to derive from antecedents contrary to fact consequences similarly opposed to what actually took place are without empirical scientific sanction. Obviously there is no empirical verification of something that did not occur; while to deduce from *If p then q* the conclusion *If non-p then non-q* is logically indefensible. Yet historians continually employ such arguments, not merely as literary devices for persuasive effect, but under the impression that they have probative 'scientific' weight.

The fact is that those who would like to see history a science must claim its capacity to employ something like the method of difference.[13] The scientist who asserts that typhoid is caused by the *bacillus typhosis* is able to show that, in the absence of this specific type of bacillus, men do not contract

---

[13] Use of the hypothetical deductive process, we are arguing, is not enough. While this procedure furnishes the prime interest of the plot in most mystery and detective stories, and provides the method in deciphering inscriptions in unknown languages in cryptology, as well as that of a great deal of legal proof, the prevalence of such methods does not suffice to bring them within the domain of natural science.

the disease. Similarly the historian who holds Hitler responsible for the second world war is usually sure that, without Hitler, the war would not have occurred. Yet although he may be practically convincing, his argument from presence to absence lacks scientific proof. For he is wanting in a technique of experimental control as well as in a range of similar recurrent cases to provide positive and negative tests. Despite assertions to the contrary, his analysis fails to exhaust the possibilities. Multiple hypotheses are left standing, and even his own thesis (judged by the criteria of natural science) is impossible to prove or refute.

Nevertheless authors never tire of framing imaginary reversals of history, of supposing what the consequences would have been if environmental conditions had been different, if at some critical turning-point men had adopted a different course of action, or if there had been no great leader. It is a favorite device of those who would magnify the power of chance in history by considering the dependence of momentous events upon trifles (like the length of Cleopatra's nose or Grouchy's tardiness at Waterloo), where a slight difference in earlier fact might have led to vastly different consequences. Without such fanciful excursions, the work of even a writer like Toynbee, who claims to use scientific method[14] (in conjunction with other procedures), would markedly shrink in bulk. In his grandiose hypothesis of challenge and response—that civilizations arise and grow only where some environmental hardship rouses men to creative effort, Toynbee employs this as a line of defense. To begin with, from a synoptic analysis of all known instances of civilization he seeks to show, by considering the

---

[14] Arnold J. Toynbee, *A Study of History* (Abridgement by D. C. Somervell, New York, 1947) p. 47. Having distinguished, following Aristotle, three different methods of viewing the phenomena of human life: history, science, and fiction, and having admitted that his history makes use of all three (p. 44); *i.e.*, recording facts, elucidating laws, and employing, like art, myths and fictions, Toynbee concludes, "But it remains true that the facts of the highest order, . . . the *comparable units* of history, remain inconveniently few for the application of the scientific technique, the elucidation and formulation of laws. None the less, at our own peril, we intend to hazard the attempt, and the results of it are embodied in the remainder of this book."

alternatives open to them at the crossroads of history, that the advance of a society occurs only in correspondence to its originative response to some challenge of the internal or external environment. Like Lenin, he often seeks to divide the historical problem into exhaustive possibilities: for instance, in ancient times the people of the Afrasian Steppe, faced with the progressive desiccation of their grasslands, faced, according to Toynbee, four alternatives: they might change their habitat, change their way of life, or both or neither. In the ensuing course of events it turned out that it was neither the mere migrants, nor the half-starved nomads who remained where they were, but those who moved into the delta of the great river Nile, canalized the waters, drained the soil, and created technology and agriculture, who triumphed over the environment. "This rare double reaction" of meeting the challenge of desiccation by changing both habitat and way of life "was the dynamic act which created the Egyptiac and Sumeric civilizations."[15]

But not content with this simulation of the method of residues, Toynbee goes further and supports his thesis by a major imaginative reversal. If the Afrasian Steppe had not been desiccated, he suggests, there would have been no Egyptiac Civilization (and the same holds presumably of other great river civilizations like those of Mesopotamia and China). By imagining the opposite of the historical conditions in fact, and deriving the supposed consequences, he attempts to establish his case by a kind of indirect proof or *reductio ad absurdum*. That is, if the progressive drought had never come, the men of Egypt would have remained uncivilized. "Supposing that the challenge of desiccation had never been presented to the inhabitants of the Nile Basin . . . Would the Egyptian Civilization never have arisen? Would these people be squatting still on the edge of an untamed Lower Nile Valley as the Shilluk and Dinka are now squatting on the edge of the Bahr-al-Jabal?"[16] The implied answer is "yes," although the extraor-

15 *Ibid.*, p. 70.
16 *Ibid.*, p. 72.

dinary speculative scope of the hypothesis carries but slight conviction to the reader. Only those convinced in advance that drought by itself may be sufficient to force the origination of irrigation, agriculture, the domestication of animals, the invention of the wheel, the well-sweep, and technology, are likely to accept it. Too many variables are involved to exclude other alternatives. Good rhetoric, yes; but not good scientific argument, either inductive or deductive. It is impossible to believe that by supposing a state of affairs contrary to fact through a great arc of time, together with the non-interference of other factors, any conclusion can be deduced that is scientifically verifiable.

Of course the expansion of a hypothetical statement contrary to fact to emphasize the importance of an event is one thing (and a literary device favored by most historians); but to claim to establish causal proof with decisive or scientific weight is quite another. As an illustration of the former, harmless 'might have been,' let us take the English historian, Trevelyan's effort to suggest the tremendous consequence to civilization of the suppression of slavery in the British Empire in the nineteenth century as a case in point. In the passage he is describing Wilberforce's indomitable crusade against slavery in the British Parliament. He says: .

> If slavery and the slave trade had continued through the nineteenth century, armed with the new weapons of the Industrial Revolution and of modern science, the tropics would have become a vast slave farm for white exploitation, and the European races in their own homes would have been degraded by the diseases of slave-civilization of which the old Roman Empire had died.[17]

Here Trevelyan's main emphasis is positive: Wilberforce's leadership marked "a turning-point in the history of the world" because "in arousing the conscience of the British people," it eliminated certain possibilities. *This happened, therefore that did not happen* is the focal point. He offers no specific analysis to show that *If this had not happened, that would have hap-*

---

[17] George Macaulay Trevelyan, *History of England*, 3rd ed., (New York, 1937) p. 596.

pened (If Wilberforce had not appeared, slavery would have continued through the nineteenth century, and the tropics become a vast slave farm *etc.*), a task which would have required (like Lenin's) the exhaustive elimination of alternative possibilities. Instead Trevelyan, no believer in scientific history, is content to suggest rhetorically how near the world was to slave-civilization, but makes no pretense of proving scientifically its train of causal consequences or *the indispensability of the hero.* Indeed, a moment's reflection makes the reader aware how implausible such an attempt would be, since one can readily think of many alternative possibilities difficult to eliminate. For instance, *without Wilberforce* Parliament under economic pressure might conceivably have passed a measure on the American pattern restricting slavery to those regions in which it already existed, and abolishing the slave trade; or within a few years the issue might have been decided by war between the free and slave-holding parts of the empire, and so on *ad infinitum.*

Undeniably in everyday life men assume their power not only to deduce the consequences of alternative courses of action before choosing, but also after the event their power to cast up accounts truly in retrospection regarding *what they might have done.* In fact, a favorite American pastime is to recall with pride the wisdom shown by our forefathers in hewing their path as a nation at the successive cross-roads of history. It is commonly assumed, for instance, that the empirical consequences in succeeding centuries have justified the American colonies in their break with Great Britain; that it was 'better' for them to sever ties with the mother country and go their way, since the concrete results of an independent United States have been greater dividends in human welfare to a greater number *than would have followed had the thirteen colonies remained within the Empire.* Almost invariably we sagely applaud our statesmen's conduct of foreign wars in the nation's history, heavily discounting any possible benefit that might have ensued had they chosen some other line of action. No doubt men's sense of the worth of their past is largely kept alive through contrast with the negative. Yet judgments expressing predilection for the accomplished facts as against unfulfilled alternatives seem, like naive self-congratulation on the *status quo,* lacking in the scientific spirit. Such questions remain beyond confirmation by scientific means, since in the world of bygone facts we cannot trace the course of unfulfilled events, let alone judge their causal weight, value, or consequences.

The more critical the historian becomes, the less likely he is to rely on hypotheses contrary to fact and imaginative reversals. Though the plain man may occasionally be haunted by regrets for chances lost, the sense of 'might have beens,' the best students of the past waste little time in pursuing the putative consequences of antecedents already negated in actuality. For one thing, in *imagining away* one factor in a historical situation to see what difference its absence would have made, the 'experiment' requires the further stipulation that the other factors in the situation would have continued relatively constant,—which by adding a new load of assumptions increases the hazards of the argument. Also to be impressive such an imaginative reconstruction has to be traced through a considerable period of time; yet the further its retrospective prediction extends, the more alternative possibilities enter, and the greater the number of assumptions necessary to render the fiction plausible. Especially where human affairs are viewed in a largely deterministic framework, it is hard to show the indispensability of a *unique* leader in the causal chain or the necessity of one certain specific event. Usually the claim is made that environmental forces were already tending in that direction, so that even had this man or this act not existed nature would have produced others to parallel their performance. "The time was ripe" is a useful phrase. "If there had not been a Stalin, there would have been another like him." "If Columbus had not discovered America, if Einstein had not conceived the theory of relativity, another would have done so." Such things are easy to say without thought of empirical test. And if the factor imagined away is more massive (as when Gibbon imagines all the barbarians had been annihilated in the same hour or Toynbee supposes the non-desiccation of the Afrasian Steppe), the affront to actuality and our scientific good sense becomes, if possible, greater.

In brief, the historian, whose object is both unique and in the past, cannot, we should maintain, by erecting an hypothesis on a state of affairs already negatived in fact deduce consequences which are empirically verifiable. Yet though in our opinion his subject cannot be a science, this is not to deny him the use of hypothetical deduction in a philosophic sense through the imaginative transposition of viewpoints and their reflective substantiation. As we have seen in an earlier chapter, the supposition that we can view the world with other eyes, that a man's outlook is not organic to his body, though negatived in 'scientific fact,' is basic to communication. While I cannot in a bodily sense make the past recur, visit earlier times, circle the globe in an instant, achieve cosmic perspective, or exchange the trappings of my own period, language, and culture for another, nevertheless (although naturalistically I can do none of these things) as a historian I can perform them ideally. Indeed it is only on the logical assumption that the historian can do all this, can through ideal interchange gain varied, diverse, non-preferential, overreaching views that we grant his subject validity.

What prevents history from successfully employing predictions like science is the uniqueness of its object in the past which is beyond experimental reach. To predict scientifically is to offer valid reasons for affirming that a train of events will happen *before it happens,* but since history deals with the past its knowledge is *after the event.* Inversion of the temporal order is necessary for a scientific history, since only by translating retrospective assertions into present and prospective ones can we apply to the past a semblance of 'experiment' and predictive tests. If it is to be incorporated into the scientific scheme, history must give up its old view of the past as an irrevocably terminated, non-existent state of affairs grasped only through thought, intuition, or memory, beyond modification by behavior and beyond bodily reach. It must dispense with its notions of the past as 'over and done with,' of shadowy tableaux or petrifacts cut off from the world of action. For natural science, it may be said, admits no world divorced from contact and controls, no way of knowing ungoverned by empirical techniques. Its procedure is rooted in present observation, in apparatus men can handle, and tests backed by sensory confirmation at every step. Accordingly history, if it is to become scientific, must treat the past in instrumentally recoverable terms, through operations on present facts. Even time itself, that most intractable of objects, must be brought to yield to the new methodology.

Admittedly today in certain quarters time is regarded as an operational convention, a construction reversible in scientific theory rather than as a substantial agency or force. Even the man in the street is not wholly unacquainted with the idea of temporal reversal. Daylight saving, the setting forward or back of the hands of the clock to meet the practical needs of war and industry, serves him as illustration. In addition to harnessing the forces of nature by ingenious physical contrivances, science is continually introducing new mental devices and outlooks. One of the most telling discoveries of our age is that by altering the observer's relation to his object (or altering his scale of observation) novel perspectives may be found fertile in unsuspected possibilities. Small wonder then that students of history under scientific influence should try to 'looking-glass time,' to view the past in reverse and envisage their subject prospectively. Where the experiment is tried, historical assertions, as was said earlier, are construed as hypotheses predictive of consequences, as anticipations of experience open to empirical test. Thus that "Troy was an ancient city in Asia Minor" is held equivalent to affirming that "If archeologists dig to a certain depth near Hissarlik, Turkey, they will find the foundations of a town shown by its detritus and location to be the site of that Homeric city." In the same way any other statement about the past becomes equatable to the set of empirical tests which would persuade the historian of its happening.

But to convert statements about the past into statements about the future, we would protest, involves turning history inside out. To treat the assertion of bygone events essentially in terms of the operations confirming them and their prognostic utility is nonsense. The intentional reference of historical judgments is to terminated states of affairs, not to the activities of current research or what comes out of them. Both lay and philosophic history would deny that the meaning of an assertion is an essential function of its empirical verification, recognizing its truth as distinct from the way it comes to be known and its temporal after-effects. To construe propositions about the past *in reverse* as regards the future is as if I should say: "I put my papers in my desk" is equivalent to "If I open my desk, I shall find them there." (Actually I may find them there only because some other person who straightened up the house put them back in it.) In any event the two remarks are equivalent neither in meaning nor in consequences for many good reasons: *e.g.*, because memory and anticipation, acts done and undone, categorical and hypothetical assertions, events and their confirmations are not the same. Yet their confusion is involved in the mistake of those who make history center in predictive and pragmatic tests. They fail to see that in the temporal order past, present, and future are irreducible domains, albeit related to each other.

The whole attempt to destroy the substance of the past by converting its repose into flux, its essence into action, its realism into relativity, strikes a blow at the foundations of knowledge. To translate retrospective judgments prospectively does violence to their referential intention. Turned inside out, historical statements no longer mean what they claim to mean. And if the import of our assertions about Troy and Shakespeare is the reverse of what we intend, consciousness can no longer be relied on. For if their objective significance contradicts our inward awareness, the whole question of our knowledge of the order and direction of the world-process seems thrown open to question. If indeed the temporal order is transposable and if consciousness points the wrong way, then the meanings of the 'scientific' historian likewise must be read in reverse as infected with misplaced reference. By his course in rejecting others' views he casts doubt on his own; and in setting others right undermines confidence in his own type of procedure.

As we have seen, scientific empiricism tries to proceed entirely from present data and verified laws, and to demand that its hypotheses, if accepted, be countersigned by processes observable here and now. Past and future are treated as *anticipations* and *survivals,* as instrumental constructions. The past-in-itself is denied as a categorical presupposition, while the future becomes an imaginative projection of contemporary need. Even the 'potential' and the 'ideal' are construed hypothetically as contingent future goals of present interests. In short, past and future tend to become mere calculatory devices, believed in only because their ideas yield practical dividends today.

Nevertheless the methodological view of history remains caviar to the general. On such an intellectual tightrope only the most sophisticated can hope to preserve his equilibrium. Even the expert cannot retain his balance for long despite shiftings of weight and ground. Say what you will, historians like ordinary men believe in the truth of history and the reality of the past in a substantive sense, other than instrumental. They are convinced that events in the past occurred in a single, definite way independent of subsequent hypotheses regarding them. And any view which denies this by treating the past as essentially a function of current modes of manipulation must in the end be discarded for violating this fundamental conviction. Take belief in evolution, for instance. Here is a notion methodologically developed as a scientific hypothesis which in naturalistic circles has come to be accepted as substantive fact. Although the empiricist himself may deny this, the structure of his thought clearly reveals that he employs evolutionary language not merely as a useful device for anticipating eventualities, but because he believes that nature involves a gen-

uine underlying stream of progressive development. To be
sure, he is agile in shifting his ground; to the charge that
evolution has become his substantial cosmology, he replies
that "It is only an hypothesis;" yet if you try then to treat it
as a methodological fiction, he protests its reality because "the
process has been empirically verified." Unwittingly he is
caught in his own trap, in the conflicting pragmatism and
realism of his views of history. If, as he claims, 'evolution' is
a mere calculatory device or convenient fiction, he can make
time unroll either forward or backward, and perform any feat
of historical inversion. Nevertheless always behind the scientific conception of evolution as a calculatory convention, the
dynamic urgency of the organism employing this device and
engaged in a living economy is presupposed. Tacitly one way
time underlies hypothetical reversible time for the instrumental empiricist. Chronology remains a tool forged by living
observers, whose experience itself involves tension, direction,
durational stretch. The invention of reversible time has its
source in creatures whose temporal becoming points toward
fruition in a prospective order. In short, their method of scientific hypothesis is anchored in the acceptance of living beings
whose endurance in time presupposes a realized past related
to an unrealized future in an irreversible, non-hypothetical
sense.

The treatment of human history, we have urged in this
chapter, cannot be compressed into scientific method. To use
such procedure the inquirer must have a recurrent process to
work with or one under empirical control to be able to produce
similar cases at will, to predict and reverse their order. Yet
this the historian cannot do. His simulation of scientific hypotheses is largely pretense: both when he feigns negatively to
check *what might have happened* (if what actually happened
had not happened), and when he claims positively to predict
the consequences in the future through discovering a law. For
history deals with individuals, unique beings (even though
they may be complex wholes like societies) in their actual
particularity, and asserts categorically their specific existence

in a given temporal locus,—instead of like the scientific hypothesis tentatively putting forward a universal sequence of essences which can be verified many times. In other words, history maintains that *certain things happened;* and not that: *if you frame a certain hypothesis and perform certain operations you can get certain evidence for believing that they did.*

CHAPTER EIGHT

Philosophical History

_____

HISTORICAL PRESENTATION REMAINS largely under the sway of one or the other of two tendencies. On one side there is the personal, heroic approach which emphasizes the acts of great men or critically placed individuals; on the other there is the impersonal collective approach concerned with massive social movements and their underlying forces. When Bertrand Russell says that he believes that "if a hundred men of the seventeenth century had been killed in infancy the modern world would not exist,"[1] he gives voice to the first attitude, whereas those who find the focus of history in the developing processes and institutions of social life (including the whole spectrum of social scientists and Marxists) are exponents of the second. Yet in addition to these two major tendencies there is, as we have tried to show, a third, often overlooked, which takes as its controlling conception neither the influence of a few individuals nor the action of empirical forces, but the persuasive enlightenment of certain ideas. Frequently, it goes without saying, historical works combine these different impulses in varying degrees; yet where the third, the influence of ideas is shown to be fundamental in human affairs, permeating men's thoughts, constitutions, arts, cultures, religions, and driving them forward, we have what may be called the philosophic view, to which we turn in this chapter.

Undoubtedly so broad a term is misleading. To most people

[1] Bertrand Russell, _The Scientific Outlook_ (New York, 1931) p. 34,

it suggests either the rationalists of the eighteenth century: Voltaire, Montesquieu, even Kant; or else in the nineteenth century the schools called Hegelian of the right or the left. Yet historical writing may be philosophical, as we understand it, without committing itself either to the specific creed of the Enlightenment or to the dogmas of a dialectical idealism or materialism. To be sure, all these movements may be called 'philosophical' in the sense of finding a larger meaning in events, in discerning beneath their flow an intelligible frame, and in denying existence as an unfathomable mystery. For to rationalism even in its aberrant forms, things have reasons, and though seemingly senseless accidents may appear through lack of knowledge, and though factually the historian must stop short where his empirical evidence fails, reflectively he cannot halt but is obliged to account for events through some scheme of things entire and plausibly interwoven relations. Your philosophical historian, though he may not write universal history, consciously or unconsciously has recourse to general ideas in explanation, and in his orientation toward the whole finds patterns that prevent the world-process from being meaningless and chaotic. His concern is with understanding the relevance and significance of affairs rather than with exhaustive exhumation of facts in the search for causal relations. He does not hesitate to suppose that he may be able to trace the bearing of actions upon each other without full knowledge or verification of their causes. Through grasping the relevance of events, in his eyes, the historian's reflective insight may outreach his empirical knowledge, albeit both remain only probable. Even though it is impossible to gain certification in a scientific sense of 'the causes' of a war, the rise of a hero, or the decline of an empire, nevertheless we may win fairly intelligible comprehension of the reasons that account for it. Admittedly the historical inquirer, lacking as he does the methods of repeatability and control, cannot isolate factors to determine their relative weight. He has no real way of showing that: if this had not happened, that would not have either, or of generalizing decisively that one type of event invariably accompanies and alters with another. Such being the case, on the philosophic view the historian would do better to accept the explanation that appears most reasonable upon the evidence: that is, not simply correspondent to the empirical facts, but that fits together the different relevant considerations regarding persons, actions, values, and laws so that they make sense by their internal and external consistency,—rather than withstand some pretended ordeal of prediction, experiment or pseudo-scientific test.

Admittedly in the rationalism of the eighteenth century are to be found many elements of what is here termed philosophic history. On the assumption of its greatest writers men are capable of responding to reason and ideal good, and not merely to organic drives and the solicitation of the senses. They can be influenced by considerations of justice as well as by force; while in the pages of the past with all their blood and lust for power is revealed an inextinguishable striving for truth and freedom. In Rousseau and Voltaire, for instance, the actual in the name of reason is forever found wanting as against the ideal. In Voltaire's attack upon the church, the love of truth and right finds negative expression as hatred of superstition, persecution, and fanaticism; while in Rousseau the whole social and political life of the old regime is indicted in the name of universal principles of what ought to be. As guiding ideas for the study of the past Voltaire stresses both looking at things in the large (to avoid sinking under the weight of minutiae) and concern with laws, arts, manners (rather than with military campaigns and the lives of kings and generals) as of chief importance to history. This last idea besides expressing his rationalistic spirit gave voice to his love for the whole range of cultural values and general enlightenment. "A canal-sluice, a picture by Poussin, a fine tragedy, a truth established," he says in his correspondence of 1735, "are all of them things a thousand times more precious than the whole mass of annals of the court, and than all the narratives of campaigns." In Montesquieu the tendency to emphasize social institutions in history and to relate them to particular material conditions is carried yet further. At first glance his historical method might seem to be wholly of an empirical, scientific variety. But in looking more closely at the *Spirit of the Laws* we discover that in relating historical 'facts' to their underlying conditions Montesquieu also recognizes the action of what he calls 'principles' (of honor in monarchies, of virtue in republics, of fear in despotic states) which arise through the interplay of varying physical circumstances with an unvarying core of human reason. Thus history, in his view, is the expression both of material causes and of moral grounds; and man guides his social life, albeit most imperfectly, by the light of his reason which is a spark from the primal reason which governs the world.[2]

No doubt the thinkers of the Enlightenment overrated the power of human reason to save mankind. Even the pessimistic Montesquieu probably exaggerated the contribution of intelligence to the creation of human laws in finding their root in reason as diffracted by physical and social circumstance. And though the biting logic of Rousseau and Voltaire went far to undermine the old regime, their arguments were constructively less successful in helping to build a new order. Nevertheless, although they were better in exposing the frauds and errors that crowd historical experience than in providing relevant patterns to reconstruct the world, yet they shared Aristotle's insight that while "the things which are ... by human enactment are not everywhere the same ... there is only one justice which is everywhere by nature the best."[3] Because they were the heirs of the great philosophical, legal, religious tradition of the 'law of nature,' the historical process did not unfold for them wholly in terms of conquest and factual forces of individual and social might. Timeless though explored in time, there are principles of truth and right which serve as abiding

[2] Montesquieu, *Spirit of the Laws* (trans. by Thos. Nugent, New York, 1949) p. 1. "There is, then, a prime reason; and laws are the relations subsisting between it and different beings, and the relations of these to one another." p. 6. "Law in general is human reason, inasmuch as it governs all the inhabitants of the earth."

[3] *Nichomachean Ethics*, 1135a.

standards of the historical process they outreach. However
man's knowledge of them varies with circumstance, and however his realization falls short, human societies advance in so
far as they bring their institutions in accord with them. Without some reference in history to standards beyond history, the
human struggle lacks a compass, a bedrock of hope.

For that matter, the conception of a natural law of reason,
universal and immutable, prevailed in Western social and
political thought from Roman through Medieval and Modern
times until the nineteenth century. Then as Darwinian evolution became the reigning climate of opinion, it came to seem
as if irrational mutability and organic process had permanently
gained possession of the field. But such was not to be the case.
After confronting two world wars in a generation, mankind
turned in horror from a philosophy of history based on organic
patterns of the Darwinian struggle back to the conception of
a universal law of reason. Those scientific moderns who had
long dismissed rational sanctions in favor of social expediency
and the collective authority of the state and society, found to
their surprise that neither of these provided a firm safeguard
for human dignity. Reason and natural law (the ideal moral
law of the Stoics), long a whipping-boy, were suddenly revived
in political respect.

In founding the association of the United Nations at the
end of World War II, world leaders sought to build an international structure for peaceful history on the assumption of an
identity of moral reason among men and the sanction of an
overarching right. The objectives, stated in the Preamble of
the Charter[4] were to realize peace and justice, to *protect*

---

[4] The Charter, adopted at San Francisco in 1945, sets forth the aims of the
United Nations (which now claims a membership of sixty nations) as follows:
"We, the peoples of the United Nations, determined to save succeeding
generations from the scourge of war, which twice in our lifetime has brought
untold sorrow to mankind, and to reaffirm faith in fundamental human rights,
in the dignity and worth of the human person, in the equal rights of men and
women and of nations large and small, and to establish conditions under which
justice and respect for the obligations arising from treaties and other sources
of international law can be maintained, and to promote social progress and
better standards of life in larger freedom, . . . have resolved to combine our
efforts to accomplish these aims."

human rights, and to promote social progress and better standards of life. To these ends, different organs were instituted
including an economic and social council, an international
court of justice, and a parliamentary structure of two cham-
bers: the one, in accordance with the presumed hierarchical
realities of the world power situation concentrating enforcement largely in the hands of the so-called 'big powers,' and
the other, a popular assembly of nations, allowing all members
an equal voice. While representation and membership is
throughout by national groups, the dignity of the individual is
strongly supported in the Charter (human rights are referred
to in no less than seven places), as well as in the Universal
Declaration of Human Rights later adopted by the general
assembly. This latter document affirms not only that "all human
beings are born free and equal in dignity and rights," and
"endowed with reason and conscience" so that they "should
act towards one another in a spirit of brotherhood," but
declares that recognition of these "equal and inalienable
rights" "is the foundation of freedom, justice, and peace in the
world."[5] Handicapped, however, by the veto held under the
Charter by the five 'big powers' in the upper chamber and by
the lack of its own military arm as a means of enforcement,
the political fortunes of the United Nations so far appear disappointing and dubious. Nevertheless the very continued existence of such an organization as a world forum may in time
lead to the development of a strong sense of a world-commu-
nity, even if not to a world-state. Certainly never before has
mankind made such a concerted effort to adopt a rational and
philosophical interpretation of history, or mobilized in such
great numbers and strength for the purpose of supporting, in
the name of reason and conscience, recognition of universal
dignity and human rights.

Perhaps the relation of their ordering conceptions to *time*
marks the most striking contrast between the rationalists of
the eighteenth and nineteenth centuries. Whereas among
thinkers of the Enlightenment, timeless, unchanging principles

5 *Universal Declaration of Human Rights,* Article I and Preamble.

and the canons of consistent inference still ruled the structure of things, in the nineteenth century through the dialectic of Hegel and Marx, the identification of reason with nature in an existential sense ("the real is the rational and the rational is the real") progressed so far that logic came to be taken as the temporal force of evolutionary development. Under the influence of this process philosophy, principles like everything else were held subject to incessant flux. They too come and go, melt, change into their negatives, while a mysterious new *Logos* according to which "nothing is itself but everything is becoming its opposite" transforms history into dialectic. So the course of events comes to be read as the unfolding of a grand design of an unconscious reason, tending (according as one is an Hegelian of the right or the left) to the realization of a pantheistic world spirit or to a materialism involving the socialization of the productive forces of the environment.

Strangely enough many fateful events in the recent past appear in large part accountable to the influence on men's minds of this false Hegelian 'logic' according to which everything is held in transition, lacking any essential nature of its own, a bundle of incipient contradictions. Harmless as such abstract verbiage may sound, the dynamic blend of Hegelian dialectic and Darwinism has provided the greatest ideological threat of our time. Whether in the hands of fascist-minded idealists or of Marxian materialists, all processes according to the dialectical version of history, operate through perpetual strife and negation. Every idea, creed, institution, nation, society, culture is held to be in principle at war with itself, and carries within it the seeds of its own destruction. Sooner or later each by the dialectic of its nature develops a negative, antithetical element engaged in mortal strife with the parent idea or institution. Although at a given stage the contradiction may be resolved and the adversaries reconciled through the negation and absorption of one by the other, at a further stage warfare breaks out once more and history enters a new phase of the struggle. What is worse this process of evolution by revolution is represented not simply as the temporal order of natural development but as the essential order of reason and value in the world. Not only biological evolution, social and historical movements, but the valid operations of logical thought, are held to advance only by successive clashes, antitheses to some higher unity from which there breaks forth a new tension. Nevertheless by the dialectic of conflict the course of logic and human affairs is held to be progressing towards a grand climax. To Hegelians of the right the goal is frankly some form of the triumph of statism ("the divine idea as it exists on earth,") while to the dialectical materialists of the left the triumph of unconscious reason in history will be marked by the arrival of a socialized society and proletarian dictatorship.

To a genuinely philosophical outlook as we understand it, this dialectical view of history (masking unreason as reason) fails to make sense. While its errors must admittedly be traced to names in philosophy, its worst aberrations do not extend beyond the last century. To Hegel and those who came under his influence may be charged the strange obfuscation by which dialectic, hitherto regarded as the method of abstract reasoning by consistent inference, was suddenly transformed into a magic triadic process by which previously accepted principles were denied and a strange conglomeration of incompatibles set up as the new logic of the changing world and the sinews of the whole cosmic process. By mystical transmutation, opposites are said to be fused, inconsistencies and contrarieties melt into one another to form syntheses in which yeas are nays, blacks are whites, lies truths, war peace, and slavery liberty. A counterfeit *Logos* is enthroned by the followers of Hegel and Marx as the great generative and redemptive principle of the world. "Internal contradictions" are declared to be "inherent in all things" and the struggle of their opposites the very essence of advance.[6] Stretched to include

6 "Internal contradictions are inherent in all things . . . and the struggle between these opposites . . . constitutes the internal content of the process of development." *History of the Communist Party of the Soviet Union* (New York, 1940, Little Lenin Library) Vol. XXV Ch. IV p. 11. (Section written by J. Stalin.)

both reason and nature, essences and existences, the normative and the factual, such 'dialectic' is presented as the creative urge and dynamic content of the historical process. Mistaking the fluidity of factual change for the valid structure of reason, and identifying the antagonism of natural forces with a logic of progress is the root of the absurdity. Needless to say free scientific minds recognize no such embracing 'dialectic' superseding the positive laws of physics, biological evolution, and logic as hitherto known, or constituting, as Lenin held "the science of the general laws of motion both of the external world and of human thinking."[7] The fact is that men do not advance in sound understanding of the world by embracing contradictions, but by rejecting and excluding them, declaring them frankly for what they are: stumbling-blocks rather than mainsprings of progress. Contrary to the prescriptions of the dialectic method, men do not arrive at their goals by seeking their opposites: they do not find peace by promoting strife, gain democracy through dictatorship, or liberty by oppression. In refusing to admit timeless, unchanging principles beyond the facts, and in making becoming the final word, dialectic betrays history to mystagogy and pseudo-science.

Nevertheless the dialectical view of history, when presented with skill, may cause all but the most clear-sighted to waver. To cling to belief in fixed principles, it asserts, in the face of continuous change, is to be blind to the nature of things. To stick fast in unchanging ideas while the world moves on, to deny that they, unlike everything else, are subject to alteration, is a mark of perverse stupidity. For intelligence is simply the aptitude to change, experiment, and adjust, the power to recognize that the notions suited to one time and situation are outmoded in another. To be, on the other hand, inflexible in belief, undeviating in one's habits of thought, is to be a die-hard, say these advocates of flux, a reactionary, an enemy of progress. Men who refuse to compromise and adapt by trying what the opposite may be worth—far from being reasonable—are intransigent, beyond reach of persuasion, who understand

[7] V. I. Lenin, *Collected Works* (New York, 1929-1932) Vol. XVIII p. 23.

only the arbitrament of force. Too often, it is objected, historians of inelastic mind belittle as opportunists the outstanding practical men of the past who were compliant to the needs of their time, to lavish praise instead on some odd, obstinate fellow who stood four-square for an ideal. Yet what, your dialectical thinker may ask, is the sense of exalting as heroes those eccentrics who burn to die for a formula and who refuse to come to practical terms with the facts for survival? To 'die for freedom' may be a tribute to the ideal, yet, since flesh is mortal, seems a decidedly Pyrrhic victory. Once the exponents of this ideal are dead, who has freedom? Historians who extol the inflexible martyr or saint, the steadfast patriot or seer, fail to grasp that the life of reason centers in adaptation to material circumstances. What wonder if (as is coming to be the case today) such authors and their heroes are in the long run discarded, thrown on the scrapheap of history; clinging to their timeless abstractions, which they refuse to revamp to meet the needs of the age, they pass to oblivion. They and their ideas having ceased to exist, refutation is complete of their 'unchanging principles.'

Yet in this outlook a deeper rationalism sees the surrender of reason to the unconscious forces of nature. In adjuring men to shape their thought and action to fit the changing tendencies of their time, to practice a wider social conformity, such thinkers are falsely supposing that right is established by fact. They call upon us to obey the powers that be, without realizing that calling these powers 'nature' and 'science' does not make them less offensive. Today, for instance, the student of history is being widely asked to accept the authority of dialectic and social science. His acquiescence is demanded when 'experts' assure him that most histories are prejudicial works ruled by unconscious preconceptions, that perceptions of value are expressions of social conditioning, and that so-called freedom of choice is but an illusory glow arising from physical determinations. Shall he believe them? If he does, he renounces trust in his own inner light for reliance upon an extraneous authority. At once he is beyond his depth. How shall he know, in relin-

quishing confidence in his own judgment, to which of the
rival claimants to surrender, or which of the competing sciences offers the safest guide? Such are the hazards of losing
one's way, where the condition of accepting a new master is
to renounce the touchstone in oneself.

A genuine philosophical history, on the contrary, does not
lose faith in individual consciousness, or fail to perceive that
the mark of intelligence is not its mere staying-power, adap-
tiveness or factual survival, but a grasp of values, significances,
overall scope. However one tries to phrase it, a sign of the
reflective spirit is its unabashed reach. Philosophical, as
opposed to popular and scientific histories, are distinguished
by their effort to grasp a larger meaning, a fullness, a grandeur
in things. Even in dealing with a very restricted subject matter,
their horizons seem wider, their vision deeper. To be sure,
the scientific historian surrounds his subject with a vast scheme
of natural laws. Often his enthusiasm runs high as he praises
the ways of nature and the adaptive ingenuities of men. Nevertheless throughout his work a certain chill pervades the air.
Nothing can disguise the bleakness of a view, which denies
the larger import of events, and in which the episode of humanity, its marches and counter-marches, has ultimately no more
significance than the story of some vanished monster in the
weather of the flux. Perhaps the lay chronicler with his hun-
dreds of disconnected tales is wiser. Though in reading him
we know no more at the end than at the beginning of the
encompassing nature of things, at least we had no expectation
of doing so. In his pages, man not being viewed as wholly a
part and precipitate of nature does not have his importance
questioned, his dignity traduced.

Much the same shortcomings that appear in scientific writers pervade dialectical histories. Here too all seems engaged
to cosmic instability. Races come and go; societies, cultures,
empires arise and disappear. Nevertheless amid the strife and
flux a few a while endure; breasting the waves of fate, eluding
ambuscades, changing when change they must, they somehow
avoid extinction. On these that so persist, dialectic like science

sets its seal of approbation. For these are nature's heirs, victors in the fight, winners of the prize, continuers of the struggle. Vanished races, extinct cultures, ideas too high for earth, of what account are they in comparison? Wanting in force to exist, too weak to last, too feeble to prevail, history has passed them by. Even though they served as stepping-stones in the evolutionary process, the moral is plain: they failed of survival, the final test of nature. Only those creatures, institutions, ideas that are able to outlast the assaults of change have in the sense that counts value and validity. This lesson conned from science has left its mark strongly on writers of dialectical history. As a result every sort of achievement has its importance gauged by its success in retaining its hold on existence. In general, things are judged by their after-effects; the present is extolled as the heir to the past and the test of it; while the march of events appears as a series of experiments in which through sifting and discard mistakes are eliminated and practice improved. Since on these assumptions *what is worth while lives on,* while what is lacking utility is discarded, history tends to be interpreted as social evolutionary progress.

However, more truly philosophical historians, surveying the same facts, read them differently. In their eyes, what lends worth to existence is not mere existence, but man's striving for values, his ideal motives. The founding of commonwealths, schools, religions, codes of law, the creation of arts and sciences all bear witness to such impulsion. In them the urge toward freedom of spirit, toward the right, the sacred, the beautiful, and the true has led men to rear instruments for their cultivation. And it is in the expression of these impulses, rather than in the power to outlast rivals and success in earthly continuance, that a reflective mind finds the milestones of man's journey. Lost causes, ideas too high for earth, heroic ventures at the price of survival are not deemed lacking significance. In the pages of history the example of Greece shows plainly that survival is not the measure of advance, that wealth, power, and conquest do not always bear off the prize. Such things may be bought at a price that robs them of worth.

Viewed as a struggle for existence, the story of empires: Egypt, Greece, Rome, Spain, France in the new world, seem always to end in defeat. Only the kernel of values, the cultural achievements, the victories of devotion and spirit won by the way save us from mounting depression at the spectacle of the wasted energies and vanished glories of the past. Indeed, it is only when the past is viewed in a philosophic light as man's efforts to add greater value to existence rather than to preserve his existence that the study of history comes to illumine and not overwhelm the student's mind. Proof, if proof were needed, that men's hearts are not always centered on survival is their readiness in every age to risk their lives against heavy odds in allegiance to larger enthusiasms. In almost every society there are those not lacking 'the divine folly of honor' or who follow a gleam beyond bounds of the possible. Inextinguishable curiosity, love of adventure, impulses to creation, sympathy, desire for improvement are motives no less real than the lust for power and the spoils of empire. Because man strives for the unattainable, earthly goods seem never fully to satisfy the craving of the human spirit. Existence, with the things that minister to it, loses its savor in a world conceived without some hint of the supernal or the transcendent. And because of this men's highest veneration is reserved not for the warriors and administrators who enlarged the boundaries of states or filled the granaries and cradles of the world, but for the memory of those who spent themselves in selfless devotion to some less worldly goal. It was they that showed their fellow mortals what the secret of the good life was: that it lay, in the words of Thucydides, not in possessions and length of years, but in a brave heart and a free spirit.

Such high-flown rhetoric may be all very well, replies the naturalist; but how can a student scrupulous of facts find in the brutal, blundering march of events such ideal meanings? Blunt power historians, successors of Machiavelli, would seem far closer to the actual than such rationalism with its anemic values and principles. To this your philosophic student must again reply that the greatest historians convey a sense of vaster issues, profounder principles at stake in events. Their theme is larger than men's mere struggle for power or conflict with natural forces, and involves in some mysterious way the over-mastering of right. Because this lends them a depth beyond other histories, the works of Thucydides, Tacitus or Parkman, for instance, outrank Gibbon in this respect. There is a quality in them akin to that of tragedy in art. Not that they bespeak a mere melancholia of their authors at the spectacle of the decline of noble societies or states; nor a sense of unrelieved fatality at man's helplessness in the toils of forces he is unable to oppose or control. But in such works, as in art that is truly tragic, it seems impossible to view that which governs life simply as blank power, the wanton tricks of circumstance indifferent to good and evil. On the contrary, the succession of actions is regarded as possessed of a cumulative, retributive effect, as part of a larger moral process. There appears in them a depth of meaning beyond the episodes themselves, a sense of larger forces engaged, a vision of human facts which is not wholly blind chance beyond the governance of man's will, but in which can be dimly discerned through the elements crowding the field some reason in it all, some hint of over-arching justice and cosmic order.

Perhaps among American historians Francis Parkman has been most successful in expressing what we should call the philosophical outlook in history. Though confined in his task to a limited field, his genius suffused it with far wider perspective. Indeed, his very choice of a subject: the old French and Indian wars involving the long struggle of France and England for control of North America, betrayed his philosophic turn of mind. It was he who first discerned the importance of those half-forgotten guerilla conflicts, and who saw how scattered contests in the wilderness stamped the patterns and forged the sinews of later American life. Judged by the numbers and booty involved, the clashes were often trifling: mere petty skirmishes at lonely outposts between handfuls of obscure settlers. Yet in them Parkman saw portents for the future. In these actions a new breed of men was being hammered into shape and tried in the fire of adversity. In the hazards of frontier life they grew immensely in self-reliance and resourcefulness. It was Parkman's achievement to uncover the pathway in American history blazed by these forgotten pioneers in their long treks through the wilderness, their journeys down unknown rivers, their scouting forays, bushfights, and ambuscades. Merely to have brought to light the outline of the action would have been great service, but Parkman did more. Coupled with his imaginative genius to present events with 'the vivacity of an eye-witness,' he had the power to grasp their tendency and significance, the ability to make plain, as he said, how "on the obscure strife where men died by tens or scores hung questions of deep import for posterity."[8]

Here is history written from an overall view, but in which events are not used merely to illustrate theorems (as might be the case with a Hegel or Voltaire), but have a tridimensionality, a substance, and concreteness that makes them emerge from the evidence as the natural course of affairs. While capitalized abstractions like 'Feudalism' or 'Democracy' are occasionally used in asides, they never interfere with the sense of reality. Parkman is able to hold the balance between imagination and reflection, between the life lived in flesh and blood and men's glimpses of larger unfolding conceptions. In his pages, Champlain, Marquette, LaSalle, Frontenac, Montcalm, French leaders around whom the story turns, are strongly marked as individual characters. At the same time, they embody the wider spirit of France: its love of knight-errantry and bold exploration, its tireless zeal for the Church, and temper of absolute monarchy. In contrast only a few Englishmen (like Wolfe, the conqueror of Quebec) are etched with similar vivacity. Not only were the English lacking the trappings of feudalism, but somehow for Parkman the greater rational transparency of their cause deprived them of the fire and romantic color of their adversaries. Yet in their life as pioneers, subduing the wilderness, practicing local self-gov-

---

[8] Francis Parkman, *Pioneers of France in the New World* (Boston, 1874) p. vii.

ernment, building agriculture, industry, and trade, hung issues
crucial to mankind in the long view of history.

> In their toils, their sufferings, their conflicts, momentous questions were
> at stake, and issues vital to the future world,—the prevalence of races,
> the triumph of principles, health or disease, a blessing or a curse.[9]

In the disclosure of the play of the forces of liberty on a
vast new stage we find the deepest chord of Parkman's work.
"A boundless vision grows upon us." In the foreground we see
the hard-pressed colonists engaged in an unremitting struggle
with the untamed country, with savages, and each other. In
the background looms the shadow of feudal France, warlike
and Catholic, falling athwart the outposts of a more commercial England with a freer Protestant tradition. Throughout the
ensuing action, two ways of life, two modes of thinking confront each other. Behind the outposts of France, Parkman
sees the unfolding of a grand design—the ambition of an absolute monarch eager to grasp a new world. Louis XIV and his
glittering court pass in these pages before our eyes; we learn
the colonial plan of his ministers—their policies of monopoly
and exclusion. In New France government, commerce, and
religion are placed under heavy restrictions; land grants, trading rights, appointments are reserved for the favored few. To
the Roman Church is assigned the mission of winning the new
world to the cross, while Huguenots are forbidden to emigrate
thither. In all this we see the patterns of feudalism being trans-
planted to fresh, free horizons. Here again appear the sharp
class divisions of *les trois états:* a clique of proud nobles
devoted to war and their large seignories; sons of the Church
fired with intrepid zeal and the power of the keys; while
below throngs a vassal peasantry bound to a hard life on the
soil or to bushranging in the wilderness. Throughout the heavy
hand of authority and privilege enters to dull the spirit of
enterprise.

Over against the outposts of feudal France stand the colonies of freer, industrial England. At first glance these British

[9] *Ibid.,* p. vii.

settlements seem lacking all elements of success: mere acci-
dental associations of an ill-assorted multitude. Here, instead
of the favorites of the court, flocks many a black sheep, stiff-
necked reformer, and fugitive from the laws of the mother
country. Without unity of plan, each toils for himself, free of
the feudal hierarchy. Farmers, planters, woodsmen, traders
labor unceasingly each to win a fortune in commerce or agriculture. To Parkman this busy multitude intent on its own
affairs (though wanting the knightly devotion to war, the
mystic devotion of martyrs, the pageantry of a courtly tradition) offers its own lessons of self-reliance and industry. Clear-
ing the wilderness, tilling the soil, fashioning necessities with
their bare hands, these men gained in stature. They drank in
freedom with the air they breathed, and in their hearts grew a
love of liberty, strong, tumultuous, full of promise for the future.
On the surface the struggle that ensued between the colonists
of France and England might seem but "the strife of a united
and concentrated few against a divided and discordant many."
Yet beneath flowed an irresistible tide which marked it as "the
strife of the past against the future, of the old against the new,
. . . of barren absolutism against *liberty*, crude, incoherent, and
chaotic, yet full of prolific vitality."[10] In Parkman's eyes the
contest for the new world involved more than a conflict
between specific men and powers; here "adverse principles
contended for the mastery." "Feudalism stood arrayed against
Democracy; Popery against Protestantism; the sword against
the ploughshare."[11]

Ability to combine many levels of insight, to unite breadth
with depth, expanse with penetrating detail marks the philosophical historian. Because Parkman has this gift, he is able,
while writing with the vividness of actual life, to suggest the
bearing of deeper influences and ideal principles at work. At
the same time he does not chill us with the scientific abstraction of a Buckle, oppress us with the sententiousness of a
Prescott, or wither us with the skeptical rationalism of a Vol-

[10] Francis Parkman, *Montcalm and Wolfe* (Boston, 1882) Vol. I p. 35.
[11] Parkman, *Conspiracy of Pontiac* (Boston, 1907) Vol. I p. 46.

taire. While the issue of liberty everywhere underlies his thought, he abstains from interpolating preachment in his narrative. To him the moral judgment of history is a spirit to be extracted from the pattern of events, not to be imposed from the outside. And that no heroism, no sacrifice or devotion however noble can atone for the evils of despotism may be said to be the substantial conclusion of his work.

Even those critics who would discount Parkman's version of the struggle as too strongly colored by Protestant and patriotic sentiments nevertheless usually admit the necessity of moral appraisal in philosophic history. While scientific writers may try to present human affairs in wholly factual terms, to the philosophic student man is more than the product of nature. In the last analysis men shape their course themselves; even their institutions reflect to a degree their preference of choice, their imputable, creative activity. So with Parkman. As a historian he is not satisfied to rest his case on the record of factual causes and non-ideational influences. France's loss of her colonies in the new world is not to be explained, in his eyes, simply by a chain of natural necessities, but involved rational grounds and moral reasons. He set himself against those who attributed the outcome to the weight of superior manpower and consequent superior might. "It has been argued," says Parkman, "that the success of the English colonies and the failure of the French was not due to the difference of religious and political systems, but simply to *numerical preponderance*." "But this preponderance itself," he answers with a wealth of evidence, "grew out of a difference of system." Nor was the success of the English colonists owing wholly to their imported social institutions any more than to material causes. Rather it was due to the fact that so many of them had come to the new world *"seeking the realization of an idea,"* specifically *"the enlargement of popular liberties."*[12] Because they used their new life as a training-school in habits of independence, ingenuity, responsibility and forethought, they found themselves as the years went by more and more fitted for self-

[12] Parkman, *Old Regime in Canada*, (Boston, 1874) p. 397. Italics mine.

government and the enjoyment of ordered political freedom. Of course different incentives may alert men's better side and awaken higher motives in history. Individuals toiling for themselves may, through the necessity of mutual aid, kindle to nobler, more generous enthusiasms. Or the shock of evil deeds, the spectacle of blind forces of destruction may open their eyes to worthier goals. But even in the simple beginnings of the struggle for human rights, for the liberation of men's powers, through the building of churches, courts, and schools, the improvement of technology and arts, the pursuit of values is traceable. For the urge to breathe a freer air, to draw nearer to the sacred, the true, and the good impels men to rear institutions for their cultivation.

According to philosophical history there are two chief ways in which the ideal scheme of things operates to influence the human spirit. There is the positive way of great ideas (often expounded by great men) as the magnet of attraction, and the negative way of nemesis, the lesson of suffering. In Parkman the notion of liberty and the enlargement of human liberties provides the positive goal, while the fate of the Indian furnishes the clearest expression of nemesis. Sometimes Parkman's apparent coolness in describing massacres, the wildest barbarities, and in telling the whole terrible story of the white man's treatment of the Indian has been censured for lack of moral warmth. Yet it was his love of truth which compelled his Stoic calmness, not lack of moral appraisal. He felt acutely the difficulties of tracing the mingled currents of wisdom and folly, good and evil in his subject. He knew all too well how men struggling in wild country, gnawed by hunger, beaten by the elements, hunted by enemies, grow reckless of the blood of others. While not wholly excusing the invading white man, Parkman sees a kind of inevitability in the outcome. In the struggle for North America, in his opinion, the Indian through his intractable, unchanging character brought upon himself his tragic extinction. The only alternative to the disappearance of the Indian, in Parkman's considered judgment, was the abandonment to barbarism of the Western world.[13] Parkman had too deep a respect for the indomitable spirit of the Indian to wish to sentimentalize him. Instead he made it his task to show the stark yet magnificent tragedy, the nemesis that underlay the Indian's fate. The Indian character, he says, is hewn of rock. Unlike those races who can adapt to change of circumstance, theirs is a granite nature, a form which cannot change without destroying the substance, the genius of the race itself. In this fixed and rigid quality lay the Indian's ruin. "He will not," says Parkman, "learn the arts of civilization and he and his forest must perish together."[14]

Needless to say, the presence of nemesis in an historical work marks its philosophical character. For nemesis is the *via negativa* of the idea by way of a nexus of disaster and self-destruction. Its keynote is that man as a nation or an individual may bring ruin upon himself, may partly by the history of his own free acts induce a process involving a kind of shadowy retributive justice as a natural reaction. It is this interplay of freedom and fatality, by which men reap their sowing and actions earn their bitter fruit, which is the source of this tragic effect. Only in the most gifted hands can historical writing rise above the burden of detail and subplots to a level something like tragic art; only in the hands of a Thucydides or a Parkman can nemesis be brought to culminate in catharsis, a liberating insight of the spectator granting him in the midst of history a new vision of the ideal.

However buffeted by misfortune, where nemesis is active, man is not bereft of dignity, reduced to an ignoble puppet. He is not simply 'an accident in an accident,' but has moral imputability; and there is recognition of something moral and teleological in the nature of things. In some measure the world permits him to take advantage of its structure; and reason is not betrayed to unreason and utter inconsequence. In nemesis, freedom and determination, the normative and empirical,

---

[13] *Conspiracy of Pontiac*, Vol. II p. 170. "Their (the Indians') intractable, unchanging character leaves no other alternative than their gradual extinction, or the abandonment of the western world to eternal barbarism."

[14] *Ibid.*, Vol. I p. 44.

moral and factual processes are combined. While in exercising liberty of choice men are often overruled, and seldom achieve all that they intend, nevertheless great happenings are not imputed to absurd and trivial causes, nor noble enterprises destroyed by senseless chance. Accident is an element, yet beyond this a willful obtuseness in the human heart leads it to fall short of high action. That despite a measure of freedom, men none the less bring ruin upon themselves is the source of the tragic effect. Through jealous bickering Athens and Sparta unloosed the train of catastrophes that finally destroyed them both. Through his arrant schemes Louis XIV brought cumulative disaster upon his people; while the North American Indian by his unbending pride compassed the virtual destruction of his race.

Although to many the Indian may seem more the victim of circumstances than guilty of *hubris,* to Parkman it remains his stubborn pride, his indomitable spirit of untamed liberty that at once awakens admiration and provides the source of the tragedy. As to the chances that the white conquerors in turn through some defect of character may in future suffer similar nemesis, Parkman does not say. That, of course, lay outside his story. But at the close of *Montcalm and Wolfe* he issues a warning. It is the ancient counsel that the greatest foes are within one's own household. With nations as with individuals the most dangerous enemy lies within themselves. To continue strong, America must "shun the excess and perversion of the principles that made her great." She must *regulate her freedom,* preserving the republic against the power of demagogues and mobs, resisting 'the race for gold,' 'the fever of prosperity,' and especially by directing her mental resources to worthier goals, resist the 'game of party politics' and escape that subtlest of materialisms the worship of 'material progress.'[15] "It remains," says Parkman in a noble conclusion, "for her to prove, if she can, that the rule of the masses is consistent with the highest growth of the individual; that democracy can give to the world a civilization as mature and pregnant, ideas as

[15] *Montcalm and Wolfe,* II, pp. 413-414.

energetic and vitalizing, and types of manhood as lofty and strong as any of the systems it boasts to supplant."

In the end what makes history tragic is not the fault of nature but the moral failure in man. However much he casts the blame on the circumstances, the flaw is in himself. Be it some defect of character in a hero or in a nation, some flaw of pride, ambition, hastiness or blind passion that destroys all sense of proportion, the ensuing fatality is overwhelming. Acting freely, men set in motion a chain of forces that, like an avalanche, carries them to their doom. In philosophical, unlike scientific, histories, the laws invoked are not wholly empirical and amoral; rather in them as in great tragedies there is an interweaving of human freedom with moral and metaphysical nexus. The tragic evil of history, as we have said, does not center in inescapable misfortunes, the niggardliness and harsh necessities of nature. Its heart is rather in man himself. That despite his power to steer his course and to master his situation in some measure freely, he none the less brings havoc upon himself is the root of the matter. Yet even where the penalty seems vastly in excess of the offense, a sense of justice in the sweep of destiny before which flesh is grass, tinges our horror with moral awe. However terrible his lot, the fact that man is accountable for his acts lends him heroic and tragic grandeur.

To the philosophical historian, the nature of things appears not wholly indifferent to value, not equally favorable to good and evil. Some intimations of this sort may be discerned in that the bad seems always at war with itself, as tending by its inner disruption to destroy itself, and so in the long run to yield place to the good. For "the morally bad," says Kant in a famous passage, "has one peculiarity, ... it is in contradiction with itself, and counteracts its own natural effect, and thus makes room for the moral principle of good, although advance in that direction may be slow."[16] On this ground, Kant holds that we must believe that slavery will tend in the course of history to disappear and that the amoral relations of states

---

[16] Immanuel Kant, Perpetual Peace (trans. by M. Campbell Smith, London, 1917) Appendix I p. 180.

marked by armed conflict will gradually give way to an international federation of states founded upon civil justice or law.[17]

Yet if we look beyond a few supreme victories of reason and
virtue that glow down the ages, the thesis that history favors
the good seems sadly lacking in documentation. The mere fact
that Rome destroyed Carthage, that the Mohammedans were
routed at Tours, that Europe with the aid of America stopped
Hitler, or that the British colonists defeated the French and
Indians in North America cannot of itself be taken as proof of
the triumph of virtue. We can no more say that the historical
process positively and directly favors the good than we can
judge those good who are favored. Like other values, goodness
operates as a *ground* rather than as a simple *cause* in history.
The most that can be said positively is that in some cases we
can see that the moral ideas and way of life of a victorious
people are those for which more reason, more consistent and
comprehensive principles of operation, can be assigned than
those of their opponents. And in such cases, because we judge
the victorious side of higher worth, we mark the event as an
advance for man's better side in history. Usually, however, all
that can be urged is that evil tends to its own destruction (as
well as that of others), and that in this sense nemesis by eliminating the bad tends indirectly, as Kant held, to advance the
good. Somewhere in the background hovers a kind of retributive logic, suggesting in history as in art though more nebu-
lously, some trace of a moral and rational order. In a sense
men tend to reap their sowing, actions to beget like outcomes,
making through all the chequered confusion for some repay-
ment in kind. At the same time it would be inept to expect to
find good men rewarded in the substantial things of this
world, just as it would be unfitting, if not impossible, to find
evil doers requited in full measure with earthly misery and
disgrace. On such terms conscience would be robbed of nobility. In any case the scale of the process seems too vast, the

[17] *Ibid.*, p. 177. *Cf.* Carl J. Friedrich's translation, *Kant's Moral and Political
Writings* (New York, 1949) especially Kant's 'Idea of Universal History,'
Seventh Principle, p. 123.

course of nature too rough-and-ready. Probably William of Orange endured more pain and anxiety than were ever felt by Louis XIV. Napoleon could hardly pay in a lifetime for the manifold suffering he caused. A Talleyrand or a Metternich scarcely got their deserts. Perhaps their allotted spans were too short to contain it. For what is worst in evil deeds of this sort is that even when they return on the heads of the doers, they drag guiltless thousands to destruction. In our own day as so often in previous centuries the world stands aghast at the havoc wrought by ruthless men blindly threatening to topple the pillars of civilization. Now as then we have seen tyrannous schemes destroyed by the rising spirit of liberty. Admittedly the nemesis traceable in history is far from the clear-cut poetic justice of literature, the squared accounts of the law, or the *dies irae* of religion. Searching for justice in the historical process is like seeking an almost invisible bow in the heavens, nebulous, incomplete, yet an earnest to those who find it of an eternal beyond the temporal order.

Strangely enough although Kant stands in the front rank of those who grasp the moral *a priori* in human life and trace man's gains to rational freedom, he is not without responsibility for errors of later philosophic history. Within his thought lurk certain seeds from which germinated the Hegelian dialectical interpretation: such as emphasis upon the state, a partial exaltation of strife, and of unconscious teleology. Despite an inclination to Platonism, Kant remained entangled in the notion that unconscious nature imposes a plan, by which events evil in themselves become in their larger relations a means to the good, and statism (albeit world-statism) becomes the goal of history. While he recognized that men must employ certain transcendental ideas as directives in the historical process, Kant unlike the true Platonist maintained that their significance is methodological not ontological, and that in so far as they are pressed beyond their regulative function and mistaken for concepts of real things, they are chimeras and transcendental illusions. To this, however, freedom is the great exception. "This," says Kant, "is the only one of all the Ideas of pure

Reason whose object is a thing of fact, and to be reckoned under the *scibilia* (*i.e.*, things that can be known.)"[18] Men become aware of the reality of freedom in the consciousness of moral obligation. "I ought, therefore I can" implies freedom, by which human beings rise above the course of nature and penetrate the noumenal world. Within these circumscribed limits Kant became the great defender of ethical rationalism. Autonomy or intelligent freedom in which the subject acts essentially in accordance with those principles whose rationale he grasps and which he legislates upon himself as a member of a kingdom of ends, is the heart of Kant's ethics. No one saw more clearly than he that *right* conduct was action guided by a maxim of universal law and that obedience to a self-imposed impartial standard (and not Toynbee's mimesis of a hero or the leadership principle) was the road to political liberty and moral grandeur.

Yet at some point Kant falls into confusion and turns aside from the conscious autonomy of the *homo noumenon* as the line of moral progress in history to emphasize a process of unconscious natural teleology. He seems not to grasp that wherever men make political contracts, build temples, carve statues, write books, discover laws, build machines to release their fellows from toil and necessitous living, they are responding to the idea of freedom as ontologically real, and that their institutions of worship, learning, art, science, technology, law, and exchange express an insight into a noumenal world as genuinely there as the American continent prior to the adventuring prow of Columbus. Influenced by his phenomenalism, Kant at some point lost his hold on the light of practical reason and the archetypes, although he still grasped the logic of

---

[18] Kant's *Kritik of Judgment* (trans. by J. H. Bernard, London, 1892) p. 406. *Cf.* pp. 413-414. The idea of freedom, he says there "is the only concept of the supersensible which ... proves its objective reality in nature ... We have therefore in us a principle capable of determining the idea of the supersensible within us, and thus also that of the supersensible without, for knowledge, although only in a practical point of view ... Consequently the concept of freedom (as fundamental concept of all unconditional practical laws) can extend Reason beyond those bounds, within which every natural (theoretical) concept must remain hopelessly limited."

nemesis as the self-destruction of evil through its own inconsistency.

Instead of man's moral consciousness and his responsiveness to the Ideas, Kant saw nature imposing a plan, with the human race advancing in history on the shoulders of an unconscious teleology. Despite moral landmarks like Luther's *Ich kann nicht anders* and the principles of the French Revolution, Kant seemed to feel that ethical motive and conscious reason were too weak to explain the facts of human progress. Certainly the human race has had no conscious plan of its own to execute on the great stage of history. Yet viewed in perspective, its ascent from barbarism, the creation of technologies and civilizations conveyed an impression of a pattern with design and direction. Should we not say that in mankind's development there lurked an unconscious fitness of structure not unlike that of a coral reef island fashioned unknowingly by the billions of polyps composing it? In the end Kant's disinclination to trust the transcendental function of reason as ontologically valid leads to a serious contradiction between his ethics and his philosophy of history. For if neither a human nor a divine plan can be proved, yet there apparently is, we are led to assume, an unconscious scheme or purposiveness of nature. This is the design hidden from her own sightless eyes by which antagonism, conflict, greed, and strife become the great source of man's advance and the 'whetstone of virtue.' Thus unwittingly Kant sponsors the doctrine, later responsible for so much suffering, of the bad (or amoral) as the essential means to the good, of strife as the author of harmony, and the generation of opposites from each other. Hard as it is to believe, it was not Hegel or Marx or some militaristic prophet of the Darwinian struggle, but Kant who declared:

All culture and art which adorn mankind, the most beautiful social order, are the fruits of asociability . . . Without these essentially unlovely qualities of asociability, from which springs the resistance which anyone must encounter in his egoistic pretensions, all talents would have remained hidden germs. If man lived an Arcadian shepherd's existence of harmony, modesty, and mutuality, man, goodnatured like the sheep he

is herding, would not invest his existence with greater value than that
his animals have . . . Thanks are due to nature for his quarrelsomeness,
his enviously competitive vanity, and for his insatiable desire to possess
or to rule, for without them all the excellent natural faculties of mankind
would forever remain undeveloped.[19]

Thus the chief cause of man's historical development Kant
finds in his self-regarding appetites, his predatory, asocial
impulses. In such passages we have a clear precursor of the
amoralism of Hegel and his successors who held that passions
are the levers of history. What makes the doctrine the more
difficult in Kant, as we have said, is its conflict with his ethics,
in which moral values were achieved essentially through
deliberate, disinterested intent, whereas in the historical
process the worth is in the consequences of action, often
gained by motives quite the opposite. The same act (of strife,
greed, war) which from the standpoint of individual ethics is
held to be evil or wrong, is from a wider historical perspective
held to be good or at least productive of human progress in
nature's scheme. Genuine philosophical rationalism seems to
have fled and in its place we have an unconscious teleology
in which the whole of history is regarded as the unravelling
of nature's plan for establishing a perfect political order
through man's unsocial sociality—through the careful counter-
poise of his opposing impulses: on the one hand his desire for
conflict, and on the other his impulse toward collective security
under a civil constitution. The final purpose of history, which
Kant holds himself privileged to detect, is the establishment
of a world commonwealth for peace, an international federation of nations under law. Indeed, all wars, according to him,
are the expression of nature's unconscious efforts toward peace
and to form new political bodies. And even though past history has been dominated by strife, the same forces that drove
men to relinquish the lawless liberty they enjoyed in the state
of nature in favor of the greater peace and security of the
national state must eventually drive the nations to seek pro-

[19] *Kant's Moral and Political Writings* (Idea of Universal History) (ed. by
Carl J. Friedrich, New York, 1949) pp. 120-123.

tection in the establishment of a world federation under law.[20] Here Kant seems to turn away from Rousseau to a kind of pantheism and to be representing history as advancing by nature's unconscious design rather than through man's grasp of rational principles and ideas and their application to facts.

Although Kant declares that a world state is possible because it ought to exist[21] and in so far subsumes history under the moral law, nonetheless in shifting his center of gravity in his historical essays from the consideration of practical reason and the ideas of freedom and right to the realization of an actual institution (the world state) by the blind forces of nature, he breaks with the Platonic tradition and turns men's minds away from their duty to their amoral hopes of achieving tranquility and security through the operation of natural teleology. The new problem becomes one of enjoying the stimulating fruitfulness of human conflicts while preventing their destructiveness by establishing a union of nations armed with force and law. But in favor, on the contrary, of interpreting history as the pursuit of liberty and ideal values rather than the fulfillment of a specific earthly plan, in favor of a philosophy which maintains a system of general ideas as against one promoting the adoption of some concrete political structure, it may be said that the first is able to survive the *débâcle* of many mundane schemes: that devotion to 'brave translunary things' can withstand disillusionment with many a projected world government, world church or world economy, the failure of many a blue-print and time-table said to employ the secret designs

[20] *Ibid.*, "Idea of Universal History," Props. IV-VIII.

[21] *Immanuel Kants Werke* (ed. by Ernst Cassirer, Berlin, 1914) Vol. VI, p. 398 "I for my part rely on the theory which issues from the principle of right determining what the relation of men and states ought to be, and which obliges the gods of this earth to follow the maxim of conducting their wars always in such a way as to bring about a universal commonwealth of all peoples, which is assumed possible (*in praxi*) because it ought to exist. . . . I rely on the nature of things which drives us toward a goal contrary to our inclinations. Since in human nature there is still reverence for right and duty, I cannot and will not regard it as so sunk in evil that the moral-practical reason will not finally triumph after many unsuccessful attempts. . . . Thus it remains true in international relations that what is valid on rational grounds in theory is also valid in practice." (From the essay "Concerning the Common Saying: That may be True in Theory but is not Valid in Practice.")

of nature or history. Awakened through disenchantment men may find that the true object of their love, the energizing source of their allegiance was not the created idol with clay feet but the creative principles beyond this world serving as standards and goals. In giving aid and comfort to the doctrine of natural teleology Kant unintentionally sowed the seeds of that later pantheistic amoralism, that vindication of whatever is as right, that dialectical upside-down way of thinking, by which strife and egoism were glorified as blessings in disguise, as making for world unity and progress, which through Hegel's followers has led to so many disastrous consequences in our century.

The truly philosophical historian, on the contrary, who grasps the tragic sense of history is far from allowing that man's jealous striving and lust for power are the essential road to social harmony and global order. Even should a world government result from such a means, he sees that it might well prove not a blessing but a curse, might bring despotism instead of freedom to mankind. For him the roots of hope are to be found in means consistent with ends, in widespread integrity of motive and action, in the existence of good will and popular virtue. It is not through conquest but by forging increasingly liberal institutions that men stand the best chance of advancing in liberty. Neither the egoism of conquerors nor the blind operations of nature is the key to progress in history. The fact that Alexander scattered the sparks of Greek culture across the world and Caesar planted the pillars of empire does not convert their thirst for power into a boon for mankind. The resources of nations are not strengthened by squandering their blood and treasure; nor is their humanity increased by training in the techniques of butchery. Men do not gain truth by deception, honesty by trickery, the spirit of generous deeds from the example of egoism. The logic of human advance is not that of doing by undoing. The forward movement of the classic world, in so far as it existed, occurred in spite of, not because of, such things; it is to be sought in the deposit of sound laws and traditions, in the noble teachings of the Stoics, the moral vigor of the

Christians, in the energetic spirit of many artists, philosophers, administrators, and in the simple virtues of the common man.

To say that in the nature of things wisdom comes through suffering does not mean that man advances to love by hate, peace by strife, morality by immorality, and a perpetual course of contradictions. Though evil may be an occasion for moral choice it is not itself good. Nor does this merely restate the platitude that by making mistakes we learn to avoid them, and so prosper. Rather the tragic insight is that only by standing ready to sacrifice their natural inclinations and creature happiness do men rise above themselves to the highest achievement. So it is that natural suffering (but not moral failure) often mark the finest moments of history, its hours of greatest enlightenment and advance. Men transcend themselves and lay life and fortune on the altar of the idea. Under conditions of trial and crisis they winnow the worth from the dross, the important from the unimportant, and rise to a perception of values gained in no other way. Marathon and Salamis, the Dutch against Philip of Spain, the Philadelphia Convention, the British in the Blitzkrieg, and many more such moments might be mentioned. Again, many lives honored as the highest type in history were sustained by the clear-eyed perception that virtue may be the sole reward of virtue. While side by side with the statesmen, saints, and sages whose names shine in the record stand countless other heroes, nameless, forgotten, unsung. In many fields of endeavor we salute the worth of such men and do honor to this general attitude in such phrases as 'justice for its own sake,' 'truth for truth's sake,' 'duty for duty's sake,' *etc.*, phrases stressing devotion to some ideal essence beyond natural perquisites and extrinsic gains. Those capable of maintaining such an attitude may count the world well lost in the service (from the standpoint of naturalism) of some impractical, visionary perfection. Nor can one deny that it is this sense of worth transcendent to existence that haunts the deepest religions making them recommend unworldliness and renunciation as the way; that it is the heart of that heroic spirit by which men stake their lives in witness of a cause; that it helps to sustain the pioneer and explorer at their lonely outposts through hardship and neglect, and consoles the artist and inventor through years of thankless toil. There is a sense that man's deepest personal interest is not simply in his own creature interests, but in values like liberty, justice, and truth; he feels his dignity to consist in loyalty to them for their own sakes rather than for his own sake as measured by tangible returns. Today even the post-war existentialist, bitterly disillusioned with causes, still denies the self-enclosed humanism which takes man as the end. Rather it is by projecting himself, losing himself outside himself, by pursuing transcendent goals, that man is able to exist.

CHAPTER NINE

Nemesis and Catharsis
in Two Recent Examples

IF WE ARE RIGHT, the deeper strain in the writing of philosophic history is to be looked for not among the followers of Kant and Hegel but rather among those influenced by the Platonic tradition. In this first group, to be sure, we have the doctrine of a teleological process operating through nature as unconscious reason, an evolutionary development tending toward the realization of a particular institution like the state or a world federation, while in the latter we catch glimpses of the working of nemesis and tragic catharsis in history, the destruction of evil through its own logic, and man's asymptotic advance in the time process toward eternal values or transcendental ideas. This second kind of historical insight, though less concerned with predictions of specific events in the future, holds fast to reason as the 'beckoning light' which has its source both in human consciousness and beyond the rim of the world. To illustrate this profounder view of history we can find no better recent exponent than Whitehead. In his *Adventures of Ideas*, and to a lesser degree in his other works, we have historical inquiry which fastens no predetermined outcome on events, flatters us with no dream world of an earthly Utopia, yet maintains an *a priori* basis of history in cognitive principles. To Whitehead as to Voltaire history, as distinct from the barren sequence of events, is in a sense the history of the human mind, its movement of affairs through conscious effort and psychic action. Yet the attempt to disengage the story of arts, laws, manners from the confusion of happenings is not enough for Whitehead, his theme is the adventures of exploration and discovery in human life brought by increasing knowledge of great conceptions like liberty and justice, "the effect," as he puts it, "of certain ideas in promoting the slow drift of mankind toward civilization."[1]

Like Plato and the eighteenth century rationalists, Whitehead is convinced that the force of these notions which attract and impel mankind onward is no mere emotional projection or merely a matter of human creation. The ideas reveal antecedent patterns in the universe, a terrain of 'eternal objects,' values, essences, principles, which even when unknown to us are as truly there as were spiral nebulae and atomic energies before the physical discoveries of the twentieth century. At the same time Whitehead does not deny that, in abstraction from actual minds, the eternal objects remain "static, frozen, lifeless," and that "they obtain life and motion by their entertainment in a living intelligence."[2] So long as our consciousness is unaware of them they operate only negatively in the background; that is, while beyond our knowledge, they do not enter as positive agents into the redirection of human events. Thus, although the laws of mechanics operated long before the invention of machinery, and although the principles of numerical proportions and equality subsisted before men devised majority rule in elections, nevertheless both of them through the ingenious discoveries of human thought entered practically into history at definite dates in new ways. The ideas through being grasped by men's reason acquire application, effectiveness, agency in the human scene. They are brought down to earth, so to speak, incorporated in inventions and social institutions, and open up fresh paths of unprecedented fruitfulness.

Thus Whitehead plainly allows that for their positive action

[1] Alfred North Whitehead, *Adventures of Ideas* (New York, 1936), p. vii.
[2] *Ibid.*, p. 188.

in full force the ideas require to have the gaze of conscious intelligence fixed upon them and their acceptance by practical reason. As a member of the distinguished company who look upon history as the development of the consciousness of freedom,[3] he shows by implication how empty a thing is so-called natural freedom apart from the normative idea of freedom as a right fermenting in the mind of man. Becoming explicit first in Plato's speculative notion of the potential grandeur of the human soul, the idea passed by successive stages from high generality in human thought to diverse concrete applications through the classic to the modern world. Acting as a principle of criticism, it nerved the attack on slavery for two millennia and as a vision of hope inspired great modern reforms and revolutions. First glimpsed, according to Whitehead, through the intuition of genius, the conception of the *freedom* of the *soul* as liberated through the *ideas* became gradually after many vicissitudes clarified, diffused, and incorporated into practical life, spurring the development of civilization. Spreading beyond the confines of the classic philosophic schools the notion of the soul's grandeur and the dignity of man penetrated Roman jurisprudence; and in Rome fused with the similar moral intuitions of the Hebrew prophets, from which it fired the enthusiasm of early Christianity. Slowly as the implications of the idea of free spirit were revealed, it became embodied in successively wider programs of reform. Men awakened to a noble discontent and strove to bridge the gap between their hopes and actualities. A new temper of criticism goaded them to refashion their lives to a transcendental goal: to seek to succor the oppressed, to enlighten the ignorant, and to end the compulsory degradation of mankind. Through its driving force the humanitarian gospel won its way to the seats of power and overthrew traditional authorities. Nevertheless after its first great success in the early church and empire, the idea of freedom seemed to slacken its pace. Losing its drive to all ap-

[3] *Ibid.*, p. 29. While in modern times this list includes such names as Hegel, Cousin, Michelet, Lord Acton, Croce, etc., to Whitehead the whole history of human thought is, as he once said, a series of footnotes to Plato.

pearances, it became entombed in secular and ecclesiastical hierarchies or took flight in scholastic theory. Yet despite blunders and temporary recession, the idea had not lost its hold upon the hearts of men. With the Enlightenment and Reformation came a reawakening. Fresh questioning, challenge, widespread movements of attack raised freedom as a standard, exposing the inconsistencies of church and state. They unmasked the contradictions of a society in which a church preaching poverty amassed great wealth, in which rulers ostensibly guarding the public good pursued their private profligacy, in which commonwealths prating of virtue legalized chattel slavery, and a Christendom professing the sacredness of life allowed the poor to die of starvation. "Great ideas enter into reality with evil associates and with disgusting alliances" says Whitehead. "But the greatness remains, nerving the race in its slow ascent."[4] Through more than two millennia we can trace how the driving force of certain great conceptions has helped men to liberate their powers, to realize their rights, and to introduce new forms of legal, political, religious, and social coordination.

In viewing history as the gains won by men in rational freedom, Whitehead diverges sharply from the materialist version which treats man's life as wholly a product and function of his natural setting. His approach is closer to traditional rationalism and far removed from the mole-like burrowing of the unconscious reason of dialectical philosophies. For him reason progresses by way of excluding not by embracing contradictions, by pursuing 'eternal objects,' transcendental ideas, whose light beckons beyond the verge. While not dialectical, his usage of reason is distinguished by his enlargement of the term beyond the strict limits of verbal articulation to include, besides abstract logical operations, not only the practical reason of morals, the presuppositions and methods of the sciences, but the synthetic vision of metaphysical speculation. In its lower sense, reason has appeared as a 'dodge to live,' which reaching back in the evolutionary past millions of years to the first 'faint

[4] *Ibid.*, p. 22.

sporadic flashes of intelligence' furnished a means of ascent and survival. But in addition to this pragmatic intelligence which aids continuance and renders vital interests effective, there is a second metaphysical kind of reason. Its operation seems limited to the past few thousand years, to the period of the earth's civilization; and with it appears man's godlike power to survey, to understand, to judge, to seek ontology and final causes. At first we see it in the sporadic intuitions of the prophets, in the divination of the seers who inspired the ancient East in its religious philosophies. But it remained for the Greeks (by their discovery of mathematics and logic) to transform speculation from fitful bursts of inspiration into a systematic method of progress and discovery. To them we owe what Whitehead calls "the self-discipline of the originative element in history."[5] Its secret is to combine order with novelty, systematic procedure with objective test, and to adventure beyond set bounds. This method, in his eyes, is what transforms the inward life of man and is the source of the advance of civilization. In the past century and a half by combining theoretical thought with practical skill we have made great progress in technology. Yet for further light on the path of advance we need not merely the strategy of Ulysses on how to outwit and survive but the urge toward perfection of the wisdom of Plato. In history this impulse of the human spirit to press beyond accomplished gains and to outreach its grasp appears as the pursuit of freedom, adventure, the ideal, and unattainable. Always a transcendent goal beyond mere creature satisfactions is necessary to save civilization from degeneration into lazy indulgence in obvious gratifications. "Apart from some transcendent aim," says Whitehead, "the civilized life either wallows in pleasure or relapses

[5] Alfred North Whitehead, *The Function of Reason* (Princeton, 1929). Introductory summary, pp. 52-53. "Speculation expresses the transcendence of any particular method. The Greek secret is how to be bounded by method even in its transcendence." Its logic of discovery applied through centuries of experience provides a set of criteria for testing the content of belief (p. 53): conformity to intuitive experience, clarity of propositional content, internal and external consistency, possession of a logical scheme having widespread conformity to experience and no discordance with it, and coherence in its categorical notions and methodological consequences.

slowly into a barren repetition."[6] Lack of such an aim strongly marked in cultural life was a reason for the decline of the Roman Empire and also for that of the civilizations of the Near East.

At its highest level in history reason rises above organic gratifications and extraneous tasks, serving only itself and comprehending facts as illustrations of the principles of its own nature.[7] It carries within it a profound metaphysical sense of order in the universe (akin to the principle of its own inner order) and by imparting this sense of order to institutions, enables men to reach beyond the confusion of events to some measure of serenity and concord. Through art, science, jurisprudence, religion, and morals, classic civilization diffused this sense of order which sprang from the serious opinion of the times. For instance, nemesis, the 'messenger of justice' of Greek tragedy, expressed both men's insight into the moral order, its expression rising from an undercurrent in the chorus to religious exaltation, a mystic sense of the *harmonia mundi,* and also the sense of the inexorable 'order of nature' later the nerve of scientific thought.[8] How the Empire spread abroad the sense of order through the rule of Roman law and how the Church (through its organization and scholastic theology) continued the process through succeeding centuries despite the discord of the times, need not detain us here.

The nature of history as manifest in civilization is finally expressed by Whitehead under the figure of tragedy. Reason, as we have seen, is the creative element in the process: being in its short range function preeminently practical and engaged through its various methodologies in transforming existence into better and better existence; while on the other hand, as a speculative urge its long range concern is not simply with *existence* but understanding the universe. The fruits of man's comprehension as embodied in his art, science, law, morality, religion, and civilization express the harmony attained by his

[6] *Adventures of Ideas,* p. 108.
[7] *Function of Reason,* pp. 29-31.
[8] Whitehead, *Science and the Modern World* (New York, 1929) p. 15.

soul through disclosing and uniting with diverse patterns of order in the cosmos. Civilization, in so far as it achieves such harmony of the soul with its surroundings, is marked, according to Whitehead, by the definitive qualities of *truth, beauty, adventure, art,* and *peace;* qualities which preeminently connote the energizing force of the Ideas in history. As for *peace,* Whitehead's final word chosen by him to express the culminating temper of them all, it is, he says *"the understanding of tragedy,"* that "harmony of harmonies which calms destructive turbulence and completes civilization."[9] At this point one is irresistibly reminded of the passage in the *Laws* in which Plato speaks of the fairest life in the ideal commonwealth as 'the truth of tragedy.'

Best of strangers, we also according to our ability are tragic poets, and our tragedy is the best and noblest; for our whole state is an imitation of the best and noblest life, which we affirm to be the very truth of tragedy.[10]

To Whitehead, sharing the intuitions of Plato, the deepest insight into the significance of the history of civilization is in terms of the catharsis of tragedy. For him the development of civilization means learning through suffering, it means being weaned from ourselves through a sense of being more than ourselves, a sense of being part of a harmony as both participant and spectator, as being in and above a battle, aware of liberation and reconciliation despite the fury of the struggle through glimpsing spirit as eternally triumphant over the complex tangles of the world.

No student of human affairs, least of all the philosophical, can fail to give a central place to the facts of suffering, privation, loss in the interpretation of history. If he reads life naturalistically as a struggle for power and existence, he may report them as gross, inexplicable evils which man combats by his know-how and technology, and let it go at that. Or profounder thinkers like Kant may look upon them as trials of the soul, the whetstone of virtue, or like Hegel as only rela-

9 *Adventures of Ideas,* pp. 367-368.
10 Plato, *Laws,* 817 a-b. (Jowett trans.)

tively evil, as stepping-stones to the better, themselves lesser goods. Thus the hardships of earlier generations and the tribulations of great men find their place in an evolutionary process of development in which man rises to fulfill his destiny. But Whitehead, less optimistic than those who find the realization of history in some particular institution like the state or a type of social economy, or who view evil simply as a negative moment of lesser good, sees an essentially tragic universe. In his eyes, not merely change, flux, transition, but the very essence of creative advance involves decay, loss, displacement. In history every individual actuality is superseded, since the very condition of its self-attainment is that it should surpass, outreach, overtop itself. To his way of thinking the union of the classic and Christian traditions expresses the notion of that peace at the heart of endless agitation which marks the catharsis of the tragic process.

Peace (says Whitehead) is hard to define and difficult to speak of. It is not a hope for the future nor is it an interest in present details. It is a broadening of feeling due to the emergence of some deep metaphysical insight, unverbalized and yet momentous in its coordination of values . . . Peace carries with it a surpassing of personality . . . It is a sense that fineness of achievement is as it were a key unlocking treasures that the narrow nature of things would keep remote.[11]

In the last analysis the understanding of history achieved by civilization is the understanding of tragedy. Its outlook reaches beyond mundane hope for the future. It recognizes that suffering, decline, displacement are of the nature of creative advance. Yet in the passing of so much beauty and heroism, in the midst of loss, evil, and frustration, there is for the historian an intuition of permanence, of the eternal beyond the fading fact. The survival power of the ideal marks the difference between tragic evil and gross evil; and the vigor of civilization is preserved by the widespread sense that high aims are worthwhile, a deep reliance that fine action is treasured in the nature of things. History is the intertwining of a moral and a physical

[11] *Adventures of Ideas*, p. 367.

process. Regarded as a natural evolution Whitehead finds in it small grounds for optimism. Considered as a physical system, the world, he says, presents us with a finite process steadily running down, in which the evolutionary formulae reveal no tendency contrary to ultimate decay.[12] It is only within his psychic experience that man finds traces of a counter-tendency upward toward fitness, order, ideal ends. And it is this leading of reason and speculative imagination, however vacillating and dim, which has provided the touch of infinity goading the races onward toward a transcendent world.

> Faith in reason is the trust that the ultimate natures of things lie together in a harmony which excludes mere arbitrariness. It is the faith that at the base of things we shall not find mere arbitrary mystery . . . To experience this faith is to know that in being ourselves we are more than ourselves: to know that our experience, dim and fragmentary as it is, yet sounds the utmost depths of reality.[13]

Thus history for Whitehead is profoundly metaphysical; and it is through the force and grandeur of the ideas exemplified in different cultural fields driving forward human life that we must understand man's long voyage home, his journey toward the source of all harmony.[14]

Another recent writer, more historically learned but less philosophical than Whitehead, who has employed tragic nemesis and catharsis as a theme of history is Arnold Toynbee. For both history expresses the development of a many-sided freedom and has its core in a deep moral process and metaphysical idea. Steeped in the classic and Christian traditions, they share alike a sense of cosmic order at once immanent and transcendent. In Toynbee, however, the wisdom that comes through suffering which is the measure of advance is more permeated with a theological interpretation, so that men's liberation or catharsis is less clearly the outcome of a logical

---

[12] *Function of Reason*, p. 72.

[13] *Science and the Modern World*, p. 27.

[14] *Adventures of Ideas*, pp. 21-22. "We find . . . this whole bundle of more special notions, legal, political, ethical, religious, driving forward human life, and deriving a force of grandeur from their various exemplifications of the mystery of the human soul in its journey toward the source of all harmony."

requital and more often a cloudy gift of grace. In him appears a historian of the heavenly city, who is not afraid to use the term 'providence of God' or to speak of Western man as transcending his history in making it, dying to live, fulfilling himself by surpassing himself in striving to bring unity to the world. To put civilization back on religious foundations, according to Toynbee, is the gigantic task facing our time, because religion finally provides the bedrock and essential function of the human race.

Unlike Whitehead, Toynbee finds in cosmic myths,[15] the ancient folk tales of the race rather than in the speculative vision of philosophers and prophets, the best insights as to the 'divine plan' of history. In contrast to Whitehead's view of man's ascent as a story of crimes, blunders, profanation, in which the grandeur of great notions like freedom and justice diffused in ever widening circles penetrates practical human institutions, Toynbee finds the secret of the process in the mythology of primordial images expressing the racial unconscious, whose meaning (though never fully permeable by the light of reason) has been in the possession of the masses from the earliest times. In the fables of Yang and Yin, in the fall of Adam and Eve, in Greek tragedy, in the Faustian legend, or the ever-recurring one of Virgin, Father, and child, we have folk wisdom expressing the mystery of existence as essentially a spiritual creation. The meaning of life, says the primordial insight, is a spiritual challenge; creation is the outcome of a great encounter, in which supernatural persons are involved and suffering is the lot of the human protagonist. Nevertheless, through the ordeal of striving and suffering comes the triumphant birth of a new order, the production of some glorious fruit. By expressing this insight in the form of a story, the myth evades the contradictions, says Toynbee, that arise when mean-

[15] Arnold J. Toynbee, *Civilization on Trial* (New York, 1948) p. 11. *A Study of History* (abridgement by D. C. Somervell, New York, 1947) p. 60 ff; p. 570. "A survey of the great myths in which the wisdom of the human race is enshrined suggests the possibility that man achieves civilization, not as a result of superior biological endowment or geographical environment, but as a response to a challenge in a situation of special difficulty which rouses him to make a hitherto unprecedented effort." Thus the problem "is really spiritual."

ings are stated in logical terms. For the question how the perfect is related to the imperfect (since the imperfect can be logically neither within nor without the perfect) appears insoluble. Yet in mythical guise, the challenge put to God by the Devil can be represented as placing only a part of the whole (the human part) in jeopardy, while its very evil by giving God an opportunity for further creation ultimately serves the purposes of good. This story set forth in symbolic form, according to Toynbee, is the story of the genesis of human cultures; it is the story of man's wrestle with cosmic powers, a long struggle in which through returning to their challenge free, strong, unprecedented replies man achieves the rise and growth of civilizations. However, human progress through the pattern of 'challenge and response' (first discerned through myth) is not too encouraging. Societies pay heavily for their errors, and of the twenty-one experiments in civilization known in history, nemesis of some sort has overtaken all save our own.[16] Yet through all the trials by suffering an ascending order of spiritual growth can be discerned, a process of 'etherealization,' in which the field of action shifts slowly from the external to the internal environment, from a lower to a higher sphere. In falling civilizations give rise to others, and in the wisdom gained through loss lies advance through the furtherance of a higher purpose beyond their own. Dimly we trace a "divine plan" in which "the learning that comes through suffering caused by the failures of civilization may be the sovereign means of progress."[17]

[16] *Civilization on Trial*, p. 38. Like Spengler, Toynbee rejects the nineteenth century evolutionary notion of history as 'progressive development' as well as its traditional division into 'Antiquity-Middle Ages-Renaissance-Modern Times.' On his broader scheme history embraces a collection of societies in contiguity and succession including: the Western, the Byzantine, the Russian Orthodox, the Persian, the Arabic, the Hindu, the Far Eastern, the Chinese, Japanese-Korean, Syrian, East Indian, Hellenic, Minoan, Sumerian, Hittite, Babylonian, Egyptian, Andean, Mexican, Yucatan, and Mayan. Three factors mark the transition from an old to a new society where there is a parental relation: a universal state, a church as a means of transition, and a barbarian heroic age. (*Study*, p. 14.)

[17] *Civilization on Trial*, p. 15. "While civilizations rise and fall, and in falling give rise to others, some purposeful enterprise, higher than theirs, may all the time be making headway, and, in a divine plan, the learning that comes

Long before this, however, a critical reader pondering Toynbee's 'mythological clue,' for which he acknowledges his indebtedness to the psychoanalyst, Carl Jung,[18] may be led to ask whether it has really sufficient strength to bear the weight of his historical edifice. The field of comparative mythology, it is generally agreed, remains a battle-ground of rival schools: psychiatric, linguistic, philosophic, anthropological, that disagree among themselves in theory. As Cassirer[19] points out, the interpretation of myth has proved a magic mirror, in which each school sees only its own face, reflection of the likeness of what it wants to see. Elusive and equivocal as a dream, the meaning of myth behind its disguises has been construed in the likeness of everything. Whether these early legends represent mere linguistic confusions, the vegetative cycle, the movements of the sun and moon, the wishes of man's sexual life, or (as Toynbee would have them) the burden of cosmic religious truths, they remain mysteries wrapped in dramatic image yielding no definitive test or decisive answer. That as a historian he should choose these ancient folk tales as his central clue to the meaning of history plainly shows that (unlike Whitehead) he places his trust in the primordial unconscious and tribal tradition as authorities rather than in the light of reflection. Moreover, as myths involve the actions of heroes and supermen, advances in history, according to Toynbee, spring from the leadership of inspired personalities rather than from the guidance of ideas. Here he diverges from the Platonic tradition, expressing his belief that civilizations arise as the creation of a few masterful spirits through the disposition of the masses to mimic their example and follow in their steps. In borrowing from Bergson the doctrine of *mimesis* and ascribing to a few mystic personalities and the leadership principle the progress of mankind, his philosophic grasp of history falls short of Kant at his best, and of Parkman or Whitehead, for

through suffering caused by the failures of civilizations may be the sovereign means of progress."

[18] *Ibid.*, p. 11.

[19] Ernst Cassirer, *The Myth of the State* (New Haven, 1946) p. 6.

whom the course of guidance is to be found ultimately in the ideas. Although allowing the clarification of a creative principle at first by a gifted few, these men, avoiding the sharp distinction between leaders and followers, recognize the power of great notions in their own right to arouse initiative and enthusiasm in the human breast, and to extend their influence in ever widening circles. Here is no cleavage between the originative few and the unoriginative many. For them social progress results when notions like liberty, justice, and right permeate the minds of the people and spur them to respond to their meaning. The process is not simply of mimicry of persons or social drill in the steps of a master, who might fail or betray his followers, but the illuminating splendor of great ideas.

Toynbee's analysis of the forms of nemesis which have overtaken previous civilizations gains special interest (and reveals obvious promptings) from the formidable problems which confront the world today. In each great decline in the past he finds always the same story: a society's failure in crisis to convert a searing ordeal into a challenging opportunity. In considering the power relations of the peoples involved in such failures, Toynbee has recourse to analysis of class. Usually a society involves three elements: a ruling group, an 'internal proletariat' and a barbarian or 'external proletariat.' In facing critical situations Toynbee holds that responsibility for a breakdown rests with the ruling minority, its failure to provide dynamic leadership to the rank and file. Just as the rulers deserve the credit for the growth of a civilization, so theirs is the discredit for its collapse. For a civilization arises from the energy of a creative minority, whose originality in meeting the problems of the age and inducing the masses to follow its bidding, forges a new way of life marked by some distinctive excellence in art, religion, agriculture or technological advance. Yet once having arrived, the leaders of a successful civilization are almost inevitably tempted to *hubris*. Gradually the creative minority is transformed into a *dominant* minority which, having ceased to lead, tries to drive instead and becomes oppressive. "Nothing fails like success." When the ruling class turns from creative activity to the pursuit of power and privilege, tensions appear, strife multiplies both within and without, and the civilization having lost its unifying spirit expires. In all this the action of *hubris* takes different forms. In some cases the intoxication of military success may spur the rulers to undertake perpetual wars of conquest until the nemesis of destruction finally overtakes the destroyers. Or again the rulers may succumb through 'resting on their oars,' by trying to maintain the *status quo* by force, fatuously imagining that their achievements are too good to be improved on. Idolization of some institution of church or state, of science or technology, which they regard as their special creation, present instances of this fatality. Wherever, as is the case today, the moral flaw of idolatry is widespread,—that is, a blind worship directed to the creature and his creations (man and machines) instead of to the Creator,—men stand under the shadow of nemesis to their civilization.

The great challenge facing our world today is that posed by industrialism. The impending crisis, having passed beyond physical problems to an acute moral phase, is at once political and economic. The issues confronting us, according to Toynbee, are world government and socialism. In regard to the first, it is easy to see how the industrial revolution unified the world technologically by its miracles of production and shrinkage of space, yet how it left it politically and morally at loose ends. Nevertheless that the world in consequence will be unified politically in the near future (through peace or war), Toynbee holds almost "as a foregone conclusion."[20] The destructiveness of atomic weapons and increasing global interdependence have forced world-government upon us as an inescapable choice. Like Kant he looks to the coming of world-political union as the fulfillment of a cosmic purpose;[21] like him he sees men driven

20 *Ibid.*, p. 127.
21 *Ibid.*, p. 23. Kant, *Idea of Universal History*, Prop. VIII. "The history of the human species as a whole may be regarded as the unraveling of a hidden plan of nature for accomplishing a perfect state of civil constitution for society."

to peace in an international body based on law as the sole alternative to their mutual annihilation. Yet he is less cautious than Kant, more confident of man's boasted power to play God by compassing his total destruction, more, shall we say, of an unwilling idolator of technology. For where Toynbee sees a world-union as the sole option to man's complete annihilation, as "the choice of life or death, not only for ourselves but for the whole human race," the canny sage of Königsberg (writing to be sure a hundred and fifty years earlier), while recognizing union as the sole safeguard of peace, did not doubt that despite the mounting destruction of wars there would always be enough men left to keep the old game going.[22]

But in addition to the international political issue, there is, according to Toynbee, the internal, predominantly economic problem introduced by technology, the so-called challenge of socialism.[23] Between them through their industrialism, modern England by urbanizing the peasantry and modern America by industrializing them, have helped to awaken the slumbering masses of the world. With their awakening, democracy has entered a new, economic phase, opening men's eyes to the inequalities of distribution and bringing to a head the old question, why the fruits of corporate labor should be so largely enjoyed by the few? Perhaps in the ages of productive scarcity before the industrial revolution such confinement of economic privileges to a minority was a necessity that alone made possible the continuance of civilization. However, technological progress in the last century and a half, according to Toynbee, has rendered this argument invalid. Today the want and underprivilege of millions, far from being unavoidable, has become an intolerable injustice. "In a society that has discovered the 'know-how' of Amalthea's cornucopia, the always ugly inequality of the distribution of this world's goods in ceasing to be a practical necessity, has become a moral enormity."[24] In consequence, our Western civilization with its

[22] Kant, *Perpetual Peace*, Appendix I, p. 181,
[23] *Civilization on Trial*, p. 26f.
[24] *Ibid.*, p. 27.

superior concentration of industrial wealth has come to play the mythical role of Mephistopheles to all the other needy extant civilizations,[25] while within itself a similar ugly economic disparity among classes (marking the need to share the corporate wealth with the many) hangs like an ominous cloud as the second great moral challenge of our day.

But let us pause to examine Toynbee's eschatological interweaving of Christian dogma with Marxian class analysis, his diagnosis of the crisis of our age in line with currents of world propaganda. Are men indeed faced with an inescapable choice between universal peace in world union and universal annihilation? Is it true that the masses of men progress only through following a leader (or the creative minority of a church or a party), that is, by having faith in salvation by a savior? Has technology finally solved the problem of poverty, so that the want that remains in the world is due simply to the moral injustice of the few expropriating from the many? Is profit-making really robbery? An affirmative answer to these questions seems to underlie Toynbee's theory. Nevertheless if Toynbee's analysis of the world crisis is correct, if we indeed stand on the brink of a death struggle launched through the titanic growth of technology, the destructiveness of modern weapons, and the clamor of the masses for the world's wealth, it would seem that we can only be saved by a miracle, a miracle of total proportions. This miracle would require a savior whose powers extended beyond the regeneration of men's souls to establishing a heavenly kingdom upon earth that included politics and technology. Since men require to surrender to a master, a plan of total salvation would seem to imply a kind of spiritual totalitarianism. That is, not only would the claims of lesser groups be subordinated to those of a global political union and global economy, but the component individuals would joyfully confer direction of themselves upon some leader, regarded as the apotheosis of the whole and entrusted with the guidance of world society.

Yet oddly enough, although this redemptive scheme of sur-

25 *Study of History,* p. 73.

rendering controls to a privileged soul or creative few (with its suggestions of the absolutism of the higher authority) appears as the frame of Toynbee's history, this is not the solution of the present world-crisis which he looks to or favors. For his own age this English don advocates no absolute *élite* of party or church, no savior genius, or extreme measures as a world-panacea. The rooted traditions of limited government, constitutional law, free enterprise, civil and religious liberties are too deep within him. Even in the midst of his portentous picture of the 'last days' threatening civilization, he expresses the hope that the dire alternatives in mortal conflict may somehow be resolved through a compromise or middle way. Nevertheless, if his diagnosis is correct, the gulf would appear too wide to be bridged, the impending avalanche too overwhelming to be halted by any such half-way scheme or *via media*. His premises and conclusion seem at odds. If the enormity of the world situation is as he describes,—the headlong rush of social forces, the rivalry of nations, the schism of classes, the race for arms,—the chance of moderation prevailing at the last minute and civilization finding peace and good will through a middle way seems well nigh impossible. Thus Toynbee's hope of salvation which is "in politics, a golden mean" between "the unrestricted sovereignty of parochial states and the unrelieved despotism of a centralized world-government; in economics ... something ... neither unrestricted private enterprise nor unmitigated socialism"[26] appears more of a vague wish to pour oil on troubled waters than the expression of a clear idea.

In brief, this new fusion of spiritualism with materialism, so resonant with echoes, is hardly convincing. Behind an elaborate superstructure there remains on the one hand much of the Marxian class struggle, emphasis on social forces and the dictatorial principle, coupled on the other with belief in a divine plan in which wisdom comes through suffering and guidance by saints, the whole topped by the delusion that this incongruous mixture provides a middle-of-the-road way out. To Toynbee, unlike the materialists to be sure, historical prog-

26 *Ibid.*, p. 27.

ress springs from the great souls, the mystics, or religious geniuses who inspire the masses rather than from the secular supermen who read the dialectic of matter and dictate the economy. Nevertheless in exalting as all but infallible the authority of the leader and in bidding the rest but imitate his example, Toynbee resembles the totalitarians. However much may be said to the contrary, his belief that civilizations are saved by a creative few or the rise of some savior, rather than by the people themselves or the power of truth to move them directly, is not democratic. Whether it is a truly religious interpretation of history, as he believes, is another question. If the historical process be regarded simply as building an 'oecumenical house of many mansions' under the bidding of masters, it may be so; yet it is less religious if the infinite dignity of each human soul requires its direct responsibility to the divine, superseding dependence on intermediary spokesmen and authorities. One must challenge the sharp separation made by Toynbee between leaders and followers and his denial of creative power to all but the gifted few. For most men, he seems to think imitation suffices, following in the steps of a master, without the labor of intelligence, initiative or response to the weight of ideas. In stressing the force of rare personalities he tacitly rejects the power of great principles themselves to act on the minds of the people, to permeate and transform their lives. Like Kant, though for somewhat different reasons, Toynbee sees history tending toward a world political union, which he welcomes not so much for its own sake but as a great means to the realization of the primacy of religion,— "for religion after all is the serious business of the human race."[27] "In the fullness of time," he declares "when the oecumenical house of many mansions stands firmly on its own foundations, and the temporary Western technological scaffolding falls away, . . . it will become manifest that the foundations are firm at last because they have been carried down to

[27] Ibid., p. 94. "In studying history as a whole (we should) . . . relegate economic and political history to a subordinate place and give religious history the primacy, for religion after all is the serious business of the human race."

the bedrock of religion."[28] Thus the heavenly city, the goal of the process which Toynbee discerns appears apparently as the kingly rule of a divine personality over a universal church and world-government rather than as the sovereignty of transcendental reason with its archetypal ideas.

The deepest philosophers of history, as it seems to us, keep their eyes on the ideal goal, not mistaking a universal church for religion, not unduly exalting world-government or idolizing technology. That Mr. Toynbee, despite his intentions, sometimes tends to the contrary mistaking the institution for the spirit, is matter for serious criticism. Having protested against man-made gods and the idolization of the machine, for instance, he seems at times himself to yield to this very deception. While formally saluting the saviors of religion as the saviors of the world, his living faith appears anchored in the miraculous powers of technology. Not only does he find that industrialism and fear of its product, the atomic bomb, has wrought a unification of mankind which religion failed to achieve, but that machine production has solved the riddle of scarcity and launched the world on an economy of plenty. With man having achieved the mechanical know-how, the underprivilege of populations, in his opinion, is no longer necessary.

Here Toynbee's touching faith in the limitless powers of technology, his confidence that there is enough to go around and to spare in a world whose population (increasing at an unprecedented rate) has grown by at least a third in a century, is profoundly disturbing. To assume, against the warnings of experts, that the law of entropy will somehow not hold for our planet, but through the prodigies wrought by science its resources can be consumed at an indefinitely accelerated rate while supporting a continually rising population, may well be a fatal delusion. At any rate his remarks on the subject, assuming the inexhaustibility of supplies, too often suggest the arts of the orator, the easy indulgence in verbal generosity, day dreams, and moral censure, rather than careful considera-

[28] *Ibid.*, p. 91.

tion of evidence. Regard for such things as population statistics, the location and limited amounts of oil, minerals, fertile soil, and other natural resources, the differences in customs and human abilities, the special requirements of machine production, and the basic incentives necessary to rouse men to sustained large-scale output, these things will deter many from accepting his easy solution. To represent, as Toynbee does, the economic need of the world as a problem already solved by technology, and to blame continuing poverty on a minority group, by implication depicted as robbing and starving the majority, is not only a misrepresentation of the facts, but a false conversion of them into a moral issue, thereby sowing distrust, multiplying hates, and poisoning human relations in a way that may lead to incalculable enormities.

To repeat, Toynbee's conviction that the solution of an economy of plenty has been found and that only the moral problem of distribution remains, rests on an unquestioning faith in the inexhaustibility of natural resources and the limitless powers of technology. These postulates many thinking men would deny just as they would deny that the machine age (though admittedly enlarging our social responsibilities) has changed the moral issue of property relations in principle. Despite his insight into man's false presumption to supplant the divine by idolizing himself and his works, Toynbee himself half-succumbs to the same temptation. For his faith that science and industrial skill can create world-wide plenty despite the limits set by nature, and that an impending world-government will insure an equable distribution of goods to all, virtually makes man his own god, since the state and technology, his works, become the supreme arbiters of his destiny.

But a distinction should here be drawn between works the content of which is a survey of the facts of universal history, and those rather stressing simply a universal outlook on history. The second may be less a product of carpentry than the first. Unquestionably an attempt like Toynbee's to cover all known civilizations, analyzing their species and affiliations, is an amazing feat. Amazing too is his skill in holding the balance between material and secular factors, class struggles, heroes and masses, and a religious interpretation. Unlike Gibbon, to him a universal church is not a barbarous force destructive of civilization, but a midwife bringing to birth the new from the old society.[29] In a wider sense civilizations, as we have said, are seen as stepping-stones to an 'oecumenical house of many mansions' resembling St. Augustine's city of God. Again we must admire the ingenuity with which Toynbee escapes the deadliness of natural determinism through his pattern of 'challenge and response,' even though this is weakened by his accompanying aristocratic principle and analogy of the helpless sheep in charge of the shepherd. To escape the action of nemesis, to negotiate a new turn in the life of society or to meet some unprecedented challenge, mystics, supermen are necessary.[30] They provide the energizing force for advance, and bestir the rank and file to enroll as their followers. Imitation, tractability to a leader, faith in a savior, is the chief, if not the only way, in which the uncreative masses are led into paths of social progress. Here Toynbee, accepting Bergson as his mentor, diverges from the Platonic tradition, to declare his belief in historic advance through mimicry by the many of the few, by the lesser of the great, and the leadership principle. Moreover, it is obvious how this hierarchic division fits in with his broad conception of institutions as means of progress: his anticipation of a world-government, world-economy and technology guided and fructified from the top, the whole vaguely patterned after the image of the universal church and the docile sheep in the care of the shepherd.

In a more philosophic history like Whitehead's, comprehensive vision obtained through reflection is preferred to the effort to cover inductively the chief events in leading societies. Instead of trying to label exhaustively the chief facts of past existence, here there is search for the principles of universal order linking microcosm to macrocosm, the individual to the universe as idea. Unlike Toynbee on this outlook there is no

[29] Toynbee, *Christianity and Civilization* (Wallingford, Pa., 1947).
[30] *Study of History*, p. 212 ff.

great gulf fixed between the few and the many, no imitation
without creation, no faith without understanding attributed
to the rank and file. On the contrary, the power of a few to
awaken the many is, on this view, owing not to the mere magic
of personality but to the sense that these personalities embody
great ideas. Perhaps there will always be a conflict between
ideas and heroes in the pages of history: question whether
the figures of Caesar and Christ or notions of justice and liberty are greater sources of progress and truth. Religion inclines
to the former, philosophy to the latter; for the philosophic
insight is that, although the spirit of justice and liberty may
operate in and advance a society without great personalities,
the movers and shakers in so far as they make for historical
progress do so through their ability to release in mankind the
energizing vision of great ideas. To the philosophic spirit,
reason, logos, the conceptual and normative sparks in awareness have unannullable status in history. Ideas cannot be considered as wholly the product of things not ideas, since without
the presupposition of a train of ideas in which to describe
them things cannot be conceived as the product of anything
at all. Trains of events are not history unless significant, and
not significant unless reflected in mental experience. What is
not idea depends on idea (the intelligible, the normative, the
mental), not simply as an invariable accompaniment but as an
essential ingredient of the process. However, this does not
mean that the course of affairs is always actually known by
human minds, which would seem to deny the possibility of
discovery; rather that what can be a part of history must be
in principle intelligible, a potential content of ideas. Nor, on
the other hand, is the simple sequence of events reflected in
mental pictures the gist of the matter. News reels are not
history: flashes of troops marching, bombs exploding, ships
launching, and politicians shaking hands, are a mere montage
of associations. The mill-race of human affairs must somehow
be brought to a focus, its miscellany yield a relevancy and
meaningful pattern with an ordering in which actions are
rooted in each other, in which a unique occurrence may some-

times illustrate a generality, and in which there are basic conditions that underlie and support the rest.

Philosophically regarded, there is a frame of values incompressible to facts in the historical process, which operate as norms in human life. The true, the good, the noble and the sacred appear interwoven in the texture of things so that they tend to fuse in institutions, men, ideas, in a Platonic sense as many aspects of the one, blending in harmony with each other. Even though no mundane purpose can be set for history, nonetheless the process suggests a structure founded on certain standards and goals, embodying forces of attraction, nemesis and catharsis in human life. Through nemesis men often pay for their misdeeds; they are caught in a chain reaction of a retributive process by which greed, oppression, treachery bring punishment through the disharmony of their own nature. For injustice raises the cry for justice, blood cries for blood to cancel the score and square accounts. So the havoc sweeps on like an ancestral curse, awakening men on rare occasions to learn from their misdeeds so as to sense the presence of a moral process and the overruling action of spiritual powers. Again there is the affirmation of values shown in the inner fortitude of the common man, his integrity, and loyalty to defend those qualities that mark the deepest relations of his life; and there is allegiance to the traditions of generations and to the teachings of great ideas manifest in all sorts of legal, political, ethical, and religious notions that point the way.

Liberation in the course of history comes to man in many ways; it comes not only in the struggle to gain freedom *from* but freedom *for:* in the struggle against oppression which nerves the sinews of revolutions, in rebellion against ignorance and toil, and on the other hand in the striving to release men's powers, to gain fulfillment and self-realization. But in addition to the desire to be master in one's house and master of oneself, there is a deeper call for liberation. Usually this comes unsought, for human nature does not easily renounce self-preference or transcend the search for creature happiness. Nevertheless there is liberation in the tragic patterns of life, and sometimes through this means as no other men rise above themselves, escape their petty round, and illumined by suffering separate the gold from tinsel, worth from dross, and catch in the perishing a glimpse of the imperishable. To the eye of the philosopher, the relation of the microcosm to the macrocosm is latent in every breast, for as consciousness is a seamless web, a river composed of many drops, even the humblest may respond to the liberation that comes with the resurrection of the ideal moments of history. Nor can the awareness of catharsis be lacking in a historical work of genuine philosophical temper, since in it we have the magnetic power of the ideal issuing in a quality of mind characteristic of high civilizations.

CHAPTER TEN

Values and Standards
of Reference

WHEREVER MEN SEEK TO ORGANIZE their thought and knowledge about the world, they appeal to some standard of reference. Just as there can be no measuring without a yard-stick, so there can be no judgment without a basis of comparison, no criticism without a criterion, no valuing without a norm. Whether the field be science, politics or history, the same condition holds. Moreover, the nature of the referent determines in large part not only the selection and arrangement of the subject matter but the conclusions reached. Ambiguity as to the standard may rob a man's statements of significance. A modern liberal historian, for instance, who cannot decide whether liberty means essentially freedom of choice or social control is like a chemist who does not know whether he is using the centigrade or fahrenheit scale.

Though historians' views are often vague and shifting, they tend on the whole to crystallize round some dominant criterion or referent. These standards seem fewer in number than the general cosmological schemes distinguished in recent historiography. For while the so-called 'frames' of reference indicate the different metaphysical patterns used (such as the theological, materialistic or scientific conceptions of things), the 'standards' of reference refer mainly to sanctions or criteria.

These latter we suggest are chiefly three: depending upon whether the historian consults his desires, his senses or his concepts,—whether in his analysis he keeps his appraising eye turned toward his interests, the given facts or the light of regulative ideas. At the outset we must concede that it is usually impossible to classify histories under one or the other of these labels entirely to the exclusion of the others. All historians worthy of the name exhibit devotion to facts; many are biased by personal interest, and not a few (especially those who accept the notion of development or progress) judge the actual by comparison with the ideal. They appraise, for instance, the social, economic or political institutions of the past by reference to some model or paradigm found nowhere fully realized in fact. Nevertheless we can hardly fail to recognize a difference of emphasis between the historian whose work subtly applauds his country and his class, the annalist absorbed in data, and the author who, like Whitehead, claims that "the understanding of actuality requires a reference to ideality" and makes this the foundation of his position.[1]

To begin with, there is the writer who makes the satisfaction of desires consciously or unconsciously his supreme referent. We have always a natural tendency to take the world as revolving around ourselves, and in recounting the past it is easy without being aware of it to paint the picture as favoring our group or personal interest. Egoism of this sort is by no means lacking in social scope, since a man's self-interest tends to be as wide as the circle on which he depends. In history this takes the form of focusing attention as much as possible upon one's own countrymen and their past, of praising cultures like one's own, while dispraising those dissimilar, thereby creating a background to increase one's stature. Not only historians in the narrow sense but economic, political, and scientific writers may weave their work on patterns of self-interest by skillful arrangement of the materials, by emphasis, disparagement, and eulogy. Nor is it always plain how far the authors themselves are aware of their ulterior motives, that

---

[1] *Science and the Modern World* (New York, 1929) p. 228.

they are making a case, building a system in which events are construed not on the basis of the logical structure of evidence but of their inclinations. Such writing covers wide differences of range and degree. Sometimes it appears as naively partisan history unconscious of self-preference; again it may be a full-fledged ideological work in which bias is made a conscious technique and ideas deliberately forged as tools, weapons, icons. Such is outright propagandist history, in which the interpretation of the past constitutes a calculated bid for power.

At the lower, innocuous end of the scale may perhaps be placed Macaulay's defense of the Whig party, Protestantism, and the rise of the middle class in England; or Taine's justification, under the cloak of a scientific analogy, of the conservative reaction from the French revolution; or a work like Mommsen's, from which it was said (perhaps unjustly) that one could learn more about European liberalism in the 1850's than about the whole history of the Roman republic. At the other end might be placed the radically propagandist histories inspired by Marxism or by such writers as Nietzsche, de Gobineau or Houston Chamberlain. Ingenious minds disaffected with the present and eager for radical change have found it easy to write books purporting to show that some familiar social phenomenon like race, class or culture is endowed with quasi-magical force directing man's history. In them imperialism appears as a guiding principle: in a world in which nothing stands still, to expand or perish is the immutable law of survival. Hence an acute competition of groups (united by blood or economic need) is preached as the thread of manifest destiny. These strange distorted versions of human events, magnifying a single contributory factor like race or class into a sweeping explanation of things, have lent Nazism and Marxism in our time their terrible dynamism and fanatic fervor.

To the outsider the distortions of such history are plain to see, as well as the circularity by which their partisans believe what they want to believe and fit their evidence to their conclusions. Nevertheless it is hard to resist such temptations.

Nothing is so natural as for each of us to assume his own party or group as the real center of things and in the long run their arbiter. Nothing is more difficult than to avoid taking as the unspoken premise of one's thought: "My side is right because it is mine; and my view the correct one for the same reason." We have continually to cope with the tendency to believe our standards are best because they are ours, and to judge others accordingly. But assuming things so does not make them so. The more men's versions of history are made to express the desires of those who propound them, the more surely they are to be confronted with conflicting versions, the product of rival groups with opposing desires. What one affirms, the other denies; and each rides roughshod over the others' claims to right and preeminence. Again, facts have a way of revenging themselves on those who manipulate them; sooner or later extravagant pretensions are refuted by the evidence, by the harsh unfolding of the actualities of existence.

On the other hand, there are those who prefer facts to the self-centeredness of interests as a referent. They try like Ranke or Niebuhr to 'stick to the facts,' seeming to agree with Aristotle that it is the facts of life that are the test of truth in practical matters as possessing the supreme authority. On their view, the aim of the historian must be to let the original documents, the letters and archives speak rather than partisan or patriotic feeling. Only by following the evidence of the senses, by respecting the hard residue left to observation and empirical test, can we obtain trustworthy knowledge. Even though history deals with human beings, it is inhuman, impersonal in its treatment of records and remains by rigorous methods of inquiry. Like the scientist, the honest student of the past must rid himself of likes and dislikes, theories, and romantic dreams when he seeks to know events. He must be content to collect, arrange, restate the gist of his historical findings, following wherever the conclusions lead. This is the spirit in which Ranke, a leader of this school, conceived his task. In the preface to his *Histories of the Roman and German Peoples*, his first work, his purpose was expressed as "simply to relate the facts as they actually occurred;" to which he added later confirmation in his autobiography, saying: "I resolved to avoid in my works all imagination and invention, and to restrict myself severely to facts."[2] From the standpoint of objective knowledge to allow the historian, who comes after the events, to read the evidence as he pleases in the light of his sympathetic preferences seems both silly and false. Only by excluding himself from his data, by respecting the rights of his subject matter, can the inquirer gain truth from his documents unclouded by subjective bias.

But whether he can even so, the critic may wonder. For today it is becoming obvious that we can never catch pure facts apart from perspective. Certainly the historian cannot divest himself or the witnesses on whom he relies of all emotional partiality, as though he were studying chemicals in a test tube or balls on an inclined plane. Indeed, we are beginning to suspect today that, since facts always occur in a scheme of interpretation for inquiry, the rolling balls and streaming electrons may not be wholly separated either. Yet to a far greater extent than in science, it is generally agreed, the historian's compilation of facts reflects the social background and preferences of the compiler. Not only is he, like the scientist, part of the physical world, but in a far more intimate way he is part of a particular society. Thus, while the scientist can successfully practice a certain disengagement, in studying life without being lifeless, matter without being immaterial, mind without the intrusion of his own mentality, the historian in his study of human institutions and events seems unable to divest himself of his own human peculiarities or to bracket them in any strictly commensurate way. Nevertheless even though the historian can never view facts apart from perspective, he can distinguish the two and greatly widen the latter; while those are the best histories, we might say, which comprise the largest view and approach actuality most nearly by approximating to a total perspective. As the scientist distinguishes mass from

[2] Leopold von Ranke, *Sämmtliche Werke* (Leipzig, 1890) Vols. 53-54. "Zur eigenen Lebensgeschichte," p. 61.

weight by considering bodies under different conditions, at various distances from the earth or even as located where forces upon them cancel each other, similarly the student of law or history by balancing conflicting partialities against each other seeks to arrive at truth and impartiality. By taking cross-readings from different angles, as it were, by consulting many witnesses and standpoints the actualities of the past may be learned despite biased interpretations.

Lastly, we come to the historians who subordinate their facts and inclinations to an ideal referent. These are the writers who appraise the historical process by means of archetypes drawn from beyond the empirical world. Instead of viewing the past simply as the reflection of man's creature interests and the natural conditions from which he arose, they appeal to another scale. Whether the subject be law, politics, biography, economic or cultural events, the historian, on this view, rates and ranks objects as better or worse, as differing in respect of some quality or degree, in the order of their approach to some ideal pattern. Even in appraising science as truer than mythology, Greek art as more beautiful than Roman, democracy as better than tyranny, he is invoking standards of truth, beauty, goodness nowhere found in fact. Similarly in assuming the modern industrial order an advance over feudal society, or jury trial as more equitable than ordeal by fire, he is employing regulative notions of justice and progress. Conceptual perfects are firmly imbedded wherever there is criticism, analysis, appraisal; and the historian most clearly aware of this may be called normative, since he is one who knows, like Whitehead, that the understanding of actuality requires a reference to ideality, and makes this the basis of his position.

But what possible sense is there, a critic may ask, in the historian's appealing to norms in presenting past actuality? What justification is there for estimating the given by the not given, the actual by the ideal? Since we have in our minds no clear picture of perfection, it is nonsense to say that historians constantly rely on it. We really do not know what it is. Wherever men try to describe in detail the contents of their ideal norm, they fail ignominiously. Forced to face the question, they have usually to admit that they cannot tell what the ideal society, the faultless leader, the best economy or absolute justice is like. Or if they boldly attempt to give a blueprint of the perfect state, citizen or social system, the disagreements in their versions which are obviously projections of themselves, only excite derision in others. It is an old story that the gods were for the Ethiopians black and snub-nosed, but for the Thracians red-haired with blue eyes. Just as heaven and the gods elude description so do the specifications of perfect justice, the perfect hero, state, economy or code of laws.

To all this the normative historian replies that standards are not pictures. Rather they are like the pure white which we never see, but by reference to which we criticize all the muddy whites of this world; they are like the geometer's figures which nobody is able to draw, but which must be kept in mind for progress in the subject; they are like the pure gas, the perfect vacuum or conductor, the constant measuring-rod, the friction-less, perpetually moving machine, so essential as archetypes to science yet not part of the actual world. While the qualities of some of these latter can be more closely related to measure-ment than those of the perfect state or hero, each is a regulative notion, an ideal limit beyond sensible fulfillment in its field. In every sphere the notion of a standard appears as the idea of the thing carried to its utmost reach of integral unity and completeness. Even if men never know the sensory content of the ideal (it being non-sensuous), they continually rank things by means of it to the degree that they embody its coher-ence and comprehensiveness; and reject them to the degree that they betray disharmony and narrow exclusiveness. Thus tyranny is rated by Plato the worst of states because it is government by the passion of one man, unbalanced, at war with himself, disregarding the welfare of the totality. It is the worst because most confined and incoherent. Everywhere is unreason, the narrow restrictions of force, dissonance and con-flict. In contrast, the pattern of the best is the body politic ruled for the general good by those men most enlightened by ideas, using methods of reason and harmony. Without claiming sensory fulfillment of the archetypes in the actual course of affairs, the father of the theory sketched in a masterly manner the forms of the state and the implications of constitutional history.

Needless to say, it is among those who accept man's capacity to reflect, to initiate, to choose, to sense justice and injustice, and respond to ideational directives that we find the students of history whom we have called normative. From ancient writers like Plutarch to recent ones like Croce, Toynbee, and Whitehead, this stream of thought has persisted and deepened. Instead of reading history simply as universal warfare, the struggle for power or as the play of natural forces, it has emphasized liberation of the ideal aspirations of man. Somewhere, in Walt Whitman's phrase "amid the measureless grossness and slag... nestles the seed Perfection." From this standpoint ideas are not only criteria of history but forces in history, since man's lot becomes history in so far as it is lifted above the compulsions set by nature and starred with achievement through mental effort. It is not simply material conditions but the way people respond to them that determines the character of a culture or epoch. Men's attitudes are decided by their basic beliefs as to what is worth while in large part, by their courage and ingenuity in grasping situations. On these convictions depend whether they rise to meet opportunity or collapse before the obstacles facing them. The driving urge of bold ideas is necessary for men to forge fresh techniques, create new arts, sail far seas of thought, carve empires, and launch large adventures in action. To do such things requires a sense of the importance of issues sufficient to make men put forth great efforts. The 'little explanations' of the factualists are not enough, pressing through chains of unilateral causes (economic, geographic, social), but denying significance to the totality. Only the conviction that the threads form part of an ideal meaning of the world seems sufficient to provide men with the buoyant temper and coordinated outlook necessary for the highest achievement.

There are many versions of history involving the significance of larger relations, especially as the story of liberty. For instance, there is the romantic primitivism which conceives the natural man as the freest of men until enchained by priests, property, governments, and the fetters of civilization. Again history is viewed as the freedom of self-realization gained through release of man's various powers: his emancipation through technological ingenuity from physical handicaps and economic wants, the liberty of conscience which impels him on occasion to obey a higher law within himself even against the established order, and his cultural enlightenment through ideas. In its highest expression this growing consciousness of freedom is not simply 'the understanding of necessity,' not the deterministic freedom of the Hegelians and Marxists, but the power of creative choice resident in consciousness as a first cause to act as it sees fit in the light of reflection. History, instead of being the record of the rise and fall of empires, races, classes, becomes the slow explication of an ideal world in legal, religious, political, economic, cultural, and personal gains. Rights are painfully elicited from the matrix of thought and custom, and the continuing creative effort maintained of securing them in practical concreteness. If, as Croce holds, "liberty is the eternal creator of history," its "explanatory principle" and "moral ideal," then indeed one may say that "ideas in history qualify or mould generations and not vice versa."[3] Instead of ideas being mere human creations, the historical process takes its character from its goals. In short, liberation comes not through mere victory of factual claims over counter-claims, but through creative discovery of the meaning of the world. Thus human history may be viewed on the one hand as man's slow liberation from force and oppression and on the other as the infinite adventure of the soul in eliciting its presuppositions and objectives. Yet whether freedom or some other idea be set as the goal, or even if no word can be found for it, those who discern objective meaning to history

[3] Croce, *Op. cit.*, p. 59, p. 91.

discern a rationale, an ordering principle, if not a specific purpose, in the process.

What is not always appreciated is the difference between those who appraise human affairs using some transcendental notion and those who accept an earthly dream of social salvation as their referent. To understand things, say the Platonists, you must grasp them not simply in their space-time sequence but in their presuppositions and implications. These implications belong to a world of ideal limits (maxima, unsurpassables) which, though attracting us through our sense of rightness and fitness, are not always in accordance with our wishes. Unlike desires, they can never be empirically realized in the full sense. Instead they are limits, *ne plus ultra's*, which though approached indefinitely can never be gained by a step-by-step process; as the number '1' can never be reached by enumerating the series of proper fractions, so values like 'liberty' or 'justice' remain unattainable in human history, although societies come nearer and nearer to their realization. Desires, on the other hand, are often completely attained or have to do with what there is some chance of compassing. Thus the difference between, for instance, the world-state and freedom as a goal is that between an earthly object of desire and a transcendental value of reflection.

✿   ✿   ✿   ✿   ✿   ✿

So in the end, having rejected the humanist and naturalistic outlooks, we return to the judgment of history as that of a great high court before which men and nations pass in review. Without wishing to push the analogy too far, we must nonetheless admit that the judicial role appears to fit the historian's activity better than that of the scientist checking hypotheses, the politician promoting his party's cause, or the artist fashioning a work of art. At the same time, in our opinion, one may espouse a judicial view without accepting in Hegel's sense the dictum that history is the judgment of the world or without regarding it as the secular equivalent of the day of judgment with which religion closes men's accounts. A truly philosophical history, unlike that of the Hegelians, does not equate the 'is' with 'what ought to be,' or accept whatever is as right under a cloak of relativism that reduces distinctions between the best and the worst altogether to a matter of degree. Unlike them, it is far from placing the full accomplishment of the verdict in the actualities of the historical process—or in the works of historians—, and certainly far from construing affairs as a stream of becoming in which nothing is itself but only the existent consequences. Taken at its minimal terms, the judicial outlook on the contrary expresses simply the normative urge of reason and conscience seeking some power of total vision above the heat of strife. Its mood is speculative, a search for enlightenment and moral understanding, for a vantage-ground on history yet beyond history, for a truth overreaching statement of facts, though at the same time remaining aware of the gulf that separates man's outlook from the finality of divinity.

Various attitudes have been noted which deny the historian's right to mount any such lofty tribunal to evaluate the past. Such pretensions, says the naturalist, contradict nature, belying as they do the writer's situational confinement and animal bias. History is what you make of it, says the pragmatist, extolling the advantages of orientation toward the future, and discarding the pretense of disinterestedness for a frankly practical slant. Others urge the wisdom of avoiding value judgments, and with them the old high verdicts of appraisal. It is as senseless as boxing a statue, say some, to condemn a Caesar or a Borgia for his acts. So far as the dead are concerned, the historian's sententious moral verdicts are a waste of breath. What harm does it do Aaron Burr to condemn him? Does Washington benefit by all the praise of succeeding generations? No burning eulogies can warm the men at Valley Forge. Their deeds, being done, cannot be affected by us. Why not admit with the positivists that the historian's business is not with such matters, that value judgments regarding the past are not really judgments at all, but emotional ejaculations, expressions of our likes or dislikes, adding nothing to knowledge? Valuations are said to involve nothing but the tendency to project our feelings in action. To be sure, where the present and future are at stake, taking sides may contribute to success; interjections of praise or dispraise may help to turn the tide of fortune. But since in regard to the past such pronouncements lose their force, they should be dispensed with. Endless disagreement among scholars as to the worth of characters like Hamilton or Robespierre, as to the balance of good or ill in events like the Reformation or the triumph of the Bolsheviks in the Russian Revolution, plainly suggest, it is contended, that the verdicts of historians, far from reflecting the even-handed justice of a court, express a basically emotional partiality.

Usually, as suggested, one of two opposite courses is recommended by those who accept an emotional theory of values. On the one hand, there are those who advise aiming at strict neutrality. By excluding feeling attitudes as far as possible, and by exposing the way in which valuations are built up, the historian may hope to counteract their influence and achieve a nearer approach to objectivity. On the other hand, in partisan history, or that which is emotionally committed, the neutrality of carefully counterpoised views is more or less frankly discarded in the interests of action. But in the first case, as is often noted, the writing tends to acquire a dead, colorless quality from its eclectic, middling view, which while escaping party strife loses vigor and vitality. Partisan and propaganda history, on the contrary, despite distortion lays hold of something important not found in neutral writers. Though the past admitted by the propagandists may be largely a product of their own construction, a fabrication of desire, a bid for power, at least there is more to it than the humdrum inconsequence of fact. Historical studies woven on a pattern of national self-praise, myths of progress, fascism or socialism illustrate the latter. The trick of altering men's minds by recasting accounts of the past becomes part of the social control of reality. History is subverted to the service of many masters. By weaving into the web of the past a design stretching into the future, men are summoned to seize the red thread of their destiny. Here inspiration finds a foothold and the old disjointed spectacle of flux is clothed with new vistas of meaning: with some variant of paradise lost and paradise regained. Of course to the neutralists or sober students of facts, the partisans appear as the great corruptors of history, betrayers of the dead, who pretend to find in some romantic nostrum the secret of human affairs implanted from the beginning. They are the false prophets, the demagogues, the arch-deceivers who gull men into believing that success is won in this world by following their propagandist prescriptions. By them old faiths are shattered, the real becomes unreal, and their followers walk tranced through life pursuing a dream. Yet despite their manifold defects, such partisan histories see the falsity of trying to exclude values from the method and content of knowledge. That their self-centeredness sins against the objectivity of truth cannot be denied; nevertheless they do not make the mistake of disclaiming judgments regarding the worth and importance of events as essential to historical inquiry.

At bottom, however, both partisans and neutrals suffer from the same defect. To both values are images of desire, wishful projections, devoid of objectivity in their own right or transcendental quality. They fail to see that almost nothing can be said without some tacit judgment of worth, some intentional reference to a norm which (beyond mere relation to ourselves) is granted validity. Even the most cynical propagandist writing historical copy to put over a scheme must claim truth for his statements and objectivity for his values on their own account in order to be effective. While defaming his adversary he must garb his own side in virtue, assuming himself as being no mere spokesman of his likes and dislikes, but of metaphysical truth. Certainly he cannot in the same breath condemn his opponent and admit that neither of them is any more right than the other. Such contradiction would destroy both the strength of his own conviction and his power of persuading his fellows. Inevitably he assumes that the forces of the universe and not merely human passionate strategy are on his side. Just as facts cannot be divorced from some interpretation, so it seems impossible to divorce history from the imputation of values as objective. This is not to deny that there is an autobiographical aspect to the historian's judgments. "It appears to me" is understood to precede them. Nonetheless the reference to one self is not the whole of their nature. There is a sense of significance beyond our feelings, of discovering something distinct and other than human experience. If consciousness means what it claims to mean, not everything of worth in the world is traceable to an origin with man, reference to man, or application to man's use. The view which makes man the measure of all things falsifies our attitudes in valuation. Significance involves discovery, disclosure of inherent character, order, and degree that cannot be resolved into the expression of human desires and creation.

In narrowing values to the appreciative experiences of those who have them, humanistic historians make the mistake of denying their universality and absoluteness. They do this obviously on grounds of the variety and incongruity of human opinions. Since men have praised or dispraised practically everything upon occasion, it would appear that 'nothing is but experience makes it so,' and therefore that anything and everything may under particular circumstances be called worthy, good, useful, genuine or the opposite. Accordingly humanism falls back upon localism, relativism, and the explanation of values through their natural context. Every expression of man, in its view, is altogether a function of his natural constitution and environment; and since these are local and partial, none of his valuations can be inclusive and impartial.

If, for instance, as a student of recent history you condemn fascism or communism as unjust, and declare that democratic governments where they have existed in the twentieth century have been more equitable,—a consistent humanist would be obliged to deny that your remarks were any more absolutely right or universally true than those of a convinced fascist or communist who declared the opposite. Like those of your opponents, he would be obliged to say, your statement reflects your individual and social interests and your effort to use ideas as weapons in the struggle of rival groups. You are no exception. Like other human beings you are a natural product of your period, country, class, organic drives, and cultural conditioning. As a function of these, your remarks are essentially provincial, causal, relative in their significance. Even when you appeal to science and the scientific method to decide the issue, you inevitably appeal to science in its democratic, rather than fascist or communist, version as your preferred criterion. What you judge the 'optimum conditions' and scientifically recommended course is determined by your particular 'democratic' background as referent. Once more 'my side is right because it is mine' operates as an inescapable assumption. Belief in the possibility of an overall, impartial standpoint, such as might belong to a disembodied spectator or transcendent oversoul, has been discarded along with supernaturalism. Hence we should not delude ourselves into believing that any of our pronouncements escape their localism or have an unqualified or inclusive import.

Unlike the humanist, however, the believer in the objectivity of values would maintain that our axiological perceptions, our judgments of worth, do in part transcend their local perspective and grasp something absolute. This he would maintain on the ground of its being the sole alternative to denying that such judgments mean what they claim to mean altogether. For unless our judgments of comparative appraisal can indeed span different contexts and lay hold of certain constant relations between them, the bulk of our historical and scientific estimates, not to mention the moral and aesthetic, would seem without credible significance. Admittedly, owing to the mutual exclusiveness of our organisms and our situational confinement, it may be hard to find an empirical object to which precisely the same valuation attaches everywhere for all. Nevertheless it seems impossible not to assume the subsistence of certain constant relations between different groups, contexts, and perspectives. Because of this constancy we can compare, and with education come to appreciate, widely separated fields of values. We can feel the worth, for instance, and with reflection tend toward agreement in rating things as diverse as ancient, medieval, and modern painting and sculpture; we can place high in the scale of achievement Greek dramas and philosophic works written more than two thousand years ago; we can trace and evaluate the development from the blood feud through the trial by ordeal to our modern courts of justice, and so on. In short, it is only because there are invariable relations through variable contents, which hold for different people of different times, that pertinent estimates can be made across gulfs of culture, language, race, age, and distance. Historians, scientists, no less than students of arts, morals, and religion constantly make this admission: that, although perspectives and canons vary from age to age, group to group, nevertheless because they alter proportionately according to certain principles of translation, estimates made by an observer in one period under certain conditions can be translated into those of another. If we allow a certain generality to our statements, certain common features can be found in men's conceptions of the valuable in any given field. For instance, in the most varied moral codes good faith, loyalty, and service (though diversely expressed) are accorded worth. Again there is a common core in notions of justice extending from the *lex talionis* to modern judicial concepts, involving the idea of the equality in apportionment of something among persons; and so on.

In brief, in support of absolutism and the objectivity of values, as against relativism, we may repeat two arguments: one negative, the other positive, which have recurred in this essay. The negative argument is simply that universal relativism cannot be asserted without contradiction. The relativist is sceptical of everything save the adequacy of his own premises. His assertion of the universal relativity of values he holds to have value (truth and use) in a non-relative sense. In declaring all values to be merely local and variable, he assumes his own theory of relativism to have an inclusive, invariable worth. For him his statement is not merely about value but has value. Yet he contradicts himself both in assuming his transcendental competence to prove all values everywhere relative, and in claiming the indefeasible standard of value to be the negation of such a standard. In declaring absolutely no absolutes, he reaffirms them in his denial.

Secondly and positively, we shall argue that unless the genuineness of values, transcendence, and constant relations be granted, knowledge is impossible. For knowledge presupposes our ability to rise above our natural context and to make reliable cross-cultural appraisals. By a few examples let us illustrate the point. Our best accredited works of science and history abound in such assertions as the following: "Roman morals decayed in the first century A.D." "Prayer is on a higher level than magic for prayer is a recognition of superhuman powers which must be petitioned, not coerced." "Certain dinosaurs were the most terrible devourers of flesh the world has ever seen." "The class B (blue) stars have an atmospheric temperature ranging from 80,000 to 100,000 degrees Fahrenheit." Now nothing is more obvious than that the authors of these statements had not directly experienced for the most part the conditions to which they referred. No twentieth century writer has lived in prehistoric times, observed dinosaurs eat, viewed the world with the eyes of an ancient Roman, let alone felt a temperature of 80,000 degrees. But how can we correlate these different viewpoints if, as naturalism holds, each man is strictly limited to his situational locus and perspective? Unless our comparative surveys can indeed embrace different frames of reference without direct acquaintance, and can pass from one to another according to some constant connection, our most fundamental beliefs in history, no less than in art, science, and morals, would seem worthless as knowledge. For most of our knowledge is got by comparing different states of affairs, by occupying a plurality of frames, and moving from one to the other in such a way as to retain the invariant relation of their perspectives. To grant that any one should be able reliably to compare his own results got under his own

conditions with those of other persons got under other conditions of time, place, etc., is plainly to embrace a transcendental
outlook, in principle universal since no limit can be set to the
capacity for such inclusion. Yet only acceptance of the validity
of these assumptions which contradict relativism makes possible trustworthy comparison of the characters of different
systems, phenomena, and points of view. In brief, although
admittedly our experiences of values involve a relationship
between ourselves and the environment by which as the latter
varies our experience varies, nevertheless the variability need
not destroy the news they convey—any more than playing a
tune on different instruments in different keys need destroy
recognition of it. As in recent scientific cosmology, relativity
(despite its misleading name) invokes formulae of translation
which besides connecting local systems hold for all frames of
reference, so judgments of values, though differing for men in
different historical contexts, retain their invariancy of pattern
in an absolute matrix.

In the matter of values the normative historian is continually engaged in a search for conciliation and the elimination
of contradictions. His interpretation of history, one might say,
is the contrary of that which finds in discord, division, and
the antagonism of opposites the marks of creative advance.
For him system is a regulative idea. Historical inquiry, like
other branches of knowledge, rests upon certain foundations.
The competent historian has a body of notions, defined and
undefined, which he takes for granted, rules of procedure, a
general conception of things. Nor is this a mere device for
literary unity. The patterns and relations which organize the
disposition of facts are held to be as real as the facts themselves. Both in regard to the nature of his subject matter and
his method of treating it, the student of the past assumes that
there are certain things which must be taken for granted and
other things derivative from them. Starting with the admission
of certain characters as belonging to the persons, laws, and factors of the environment, he must present their combinations and
unfolding in a way to satisfy the understanding of the reader.

Given specific people in specific circumstances, the action and events of their lives must follow in accordance with their nature and surroundings. Individuals must act in character, and peoples (so long as they preserve their cultural identity) must be shown to express a distinctive temper and mode of life. To be sure, the pattern must not be as closely knit as in the drama or novel, else the reader will feel that the story is too pat, too good to be true, and have a sense of being put upon by the author. Nevertheless to interpret the past to the present convincingly, the historian must be able to show that changes in human life took place as explications of fundamental factors and tendencies to meet new conditions, and not as breaches of continuity and coherence. As in other fields history employs relevance, sufficiency, convergence and consistency as criteria. Generally students of the past agree that an account, the evidence for which is in conflict with itself or with the best established probabilities of nature and human nature, lacks credibility. Tales of genii, of dragons, of heroes slaying thousands in hand-to-hand combat tend to be rejected. On the other hand, the wider the range of evidence intelligibly coordinated by a historical hypothesis the more likely it is held to be true. In the history of science, the test of alleged actualities by means of harmony and inclusiveness has been notably successful. In the case of competing hypotheses (incapable in their early stages of decisive experimental check) such as the Copernican against the Ptolemaic, the Einsteinian against the Newtonian, biogenesis against abiogenesis, the presumption of superior truth was allowed to the one with the simpler assumptions in rendering coherently intelligible a wider range of facts. Similar use is made of these criteria, though with greater difficulty, in estimating the comparative adequacy of rival versions of human history. By means of them the professional student may be able to rank the work of authors like Bancroft, Fiske, McMaster, Beard and others in American history or of Gibbon, Mommsen, Ferrero in that of Rome. On this basis Charles Beard eventually passed judgment upon himself, recognizing that his later interpretation of the framing of the American constitution made more sense and was consilient with a wider area of evidence from human experience than his earlier economic one. Indeed, it may be said that the materialistic interpretation of history, even in its watered-down versions, by its irreconcilability with the meaning which man has up to now attached to his past (to his cultural heritage, his moral and spiritual life, his understanding of himself), turns his values upside down making nonsense of his world.

The same criteria of consilience and comprehensiveness may be used in judging social states of affairs as in judging personalities in history. Yet often the process is so familiar as to escape notice altogether. For instance, it is a commonplace that an economy in which outgo exceeds intake, consumption outruns production, cannot be continued indefinitely; and that as deficit and unbalance grows the lower the value of the economy. In not dissimilar fashion, harmony and inclusiveness may be applied in judging historical leaders: the best being held to be the one whose life shows the widest scope and integrity. Congruence of thought, word, and deed, on the one hand, combined with breadth and depth of understanding of the world around him, on the other, serve as means of rating. Thus the historian who ranks Gandhi above Hitler as a leader makes a statement involving gradation of personal worth. Judged by consistency, Gandhi's character is held superior in integration, more of a piece in promises and performance, less schizophrenic, freer from double-dealing, favoritism, and making exceptions. Similarly rated for inclusiveness, Gandhi's outlook appears to have entailed a wider perspective on life as a two-way street, a deeper comprehension of the need to practice reciprocity and universality. Also through these men some evaluation may be made of the movements they represented, rating one below the other on the ground that Nazism contained more contradictions and implications that could not be universalized. Certainly a view of men as brothers based on non-violence and truth-force (satyagraha) has greater possibilities of inclusive harmony than one based on history as a struggle of races. In the latter, as in communism, the view of history as warfare teems with exclusiveness and disruptive force.

Faced with the operation of systems with rival postulates, the normative historian will seek to rank that higher which offers more rationality in its government and way of life. He will judge as better that which takes a large rather than a small view of human nature, admitting man's guidance, albeit imperfectly, by reason and conscience as against his blanket control by environmental necessity. Where man is made wholly the product (albeit an interacting product) of matter and social forces, he is robbed of his dignity. The sanction of the individual as a free personality is gone. If the rules of historical morality are but group prejudice and economic reflexes, anything is permissible. Democratic notions like free elections, majority rule, the protection of civil rights become empty forms to cover social determinism and dictatorship.

Needless to say those who deny objectivity to values reject consistency and universality as criteria. Instead they fall back on man's projective tendency. Human nature, they hold, has an inveterate impulse to mistake the subjective for the objective qualities of the surrounding scene. Nowhere is the danger greater than in history of mistaking our way of looking at things for the things looked at, our partialities of view for traits of the objects viewed. But at the same time these thinkers are forced to admit that we have no way of knowing the outside save through the inside, no access to the extra-mental world save through our mental deliverances. The problem of avoiding error therefore for them consists in being able to refer our experiences to the proper source, in knowing where to draw the line. To solve the problem, those who deny the objectivity of values seek in measurability the mark distinguishing the two. Thus, to say that the climate of southern India is 'insufferably hot' is held to be a mere subjective opinion or evaluation, whereas it is a scientific statement publicly confirmable to say that the average temperature of Madras from March to December is such and such in degrees. Similarly the historian who asserts that 'Gandhi was a better man than Hitler' is held to make a statement utterly different in principle from the assertion that 'Gandhi weighed less than Hitler' or that his stature was less in height. That the spatio-temporal aspects of our perceptions (regarding length, mass, velocity) can give us information regarding the world around us is held evident because they can be aligned with a universal system of number and measurement; whereas our evaluative perceptions (being, it is said, expressions of our likes and dislikes) tell us chiefly what goes on within ourselves—beyond extraneous, quantitative check. Accordingly, the metrical becomes the dividing line between the subjective and objective, private and public, deception and knowledge.

But against this bifurcation of experience into the measurable and the evaluative, and the restriction of knowledge to the former, the normative historian protests. For one thing he objects because our experience appears all of a piece. It seems impossible to believe that its continuity is a deception, and that half our conscious deliverances point the wrong way, telling us merely of subjective reactions within ourselves and little or nothing of the nature of the surrounding world. Valuation, he would point out, is omnipresent in experience. And since all alleged knowledge (not excepting the scientific) is essentially evaluative, if valuation is illusory, knowledge everywhere is undermined. For in all our experience we take our sense of meaning, worth, significance as no mere autobiographical act of feeling our feelings, perceiving our percepts, but as genuine insights into the import of things in the objective world. Thus we continually discriminate our deliverances into those which are relevant and irrelevant, useful and useless, important and unimportant, adequate and inadequate, sense and nonsense. Yet none of these value distinctions are listed in books of natural science as constitutive elements of the physical world. Rather science assumes them without scientific proof, tacitly recognizing that it cannot include the props it rests on, and that acceptance of a framework of values as authentic presuppositions is the condition of natural knowledge.

In the second place, the normative historian would urge that evaluations no less than quantitative perceptual judgments can be tested for truth in principle: that the assertion of Gandhi's moral superiority to Hitler may be as objective as a comparison of their weights. Whether we say that a man or an institution is 'better,' 'worthier' or merely 'larger' than another, what is asserted is primarily an estimate involving relation to a standard and system,—in neither case merely to an immediate datum or sensum on the face of it. Far from being directly presented in perception, truth (like other values) is indirectly revealed through comparative inference. While scientific measurements, to be sure, employ quantitative enumeration, judgments of 'better' and 'worse' arrange objects according to an order of their scope and integrity which, without saying how much, recognize qualitative differences of degree. The important point of resemblance between them (overriding the fact that one uses enumerative measurement and the other does not) is that both involve coherence and universality, the criteria of logical system, as their ultimate yardstick. Since both rest on the notion of system and comprehensive consistency, objective conclusions would seem possible of attainment in one as in the other.

It is hardly deniable that there are judgments of value upon which a majority of historians would agree,—although admittedly consensus is greater where there is generality of statement rather than in detailed application. In the precepts of human rights and the golden rule, for instance, we have expressions of definitive principles of moral value. Both, moreover, appeal to harmony, consistency, and inclusiveness for their justification. Thus the morally good life is assumed as that which involves carrying through a universal and consistent standpoint in dealing with one's fellows. The old maxim of treating others like oneself and vice versa provides a rule of action making for harmony. That slavery is wrong, that man has rights, are coming to be recognized—not as generalizations—but as presuppositions of history; so that the nearer societies approach these norms the higher their status in value. If man is capable of being guided by the light of reflection, to treat him as a non-rational being by denying him the possibility of self-guidance, is a contradiction of his nature. At the same time 'bills of rights' in requiring (even within a limited group) the treatment of 'this' man as 'any' man, admitting the equivalence of their claims to legal status, voice, and vote, imposes a transcendent demand upon the natural partisanship of human nature. Yet man becomes most himself by going beyond himself; advances in dignity and worth by surmounting the limits of his factual exclusiveness and partiality. Behind the many formulations of political rights, and indissolubly related, stands the so-called golden rule, which however honored in the breach, has appeared as the normative principle of personal morality around the world in leading cultures.[4]

The upshot of our argument is then that fair treatment of his subject requires of the historian an overall view. In confronting the dual claims of historical integrity and proportionality, in striving to regard his material both in its uniqueness and in subordination to a wider appraisal of events, the student of the past invokes a cosmic scale. For him parity of consideration,—to be as just and humane to one people as to another, and without belittling the action of his characters to relate them to a larger sequence,—seems a duty not to be gainsaid.

[4] *Confucianism.* "Is there one word which may serve as a rule of practice for all one's life?" "The Master said, 'Is not Reciprocity such a word? What you do not want done to yourself, do not do to others.'" *Analects of Confucius,* 15:23.

Hinduism. "Let no man do to another that which would be repugnant to himself. This is the sum of righteousness." "In refusing and bestowing ... a man obtains the proper rule by regarding the case as like his own." *Mahabharata,* 13:55 71; *vide* E. Westermarck, *Ethical Relativity* (New York, 1932) p. 92.

Judaism. "Thou shalt love thy neighbor as thyself." *Leviticus,* 19:18.

Christianity. "All things whatsoever ye would that men should do to you, do ye even so to them; for this is the law and the prophets." *Matthew,* 7:11.

Islam. "No one of you is a believer until he loves for his brother what he loves for himself." *The Forty-Two Traditions of An-Nawawi.*

Buddhism. "In five ways should a man minister to his friends: by generosity, courtesy, and benevolence, by treating them as he treats himself, and by being as good as his word." *Dialogues of the Buddha* (Sacred Books of the Buddhists, London, 1921) Iv. 182.

Plato. (Prayer.) "May I being of sound mind do to others as I would that they should do to me." *Laws,* XI, 913.

The past too has its rights; the dead like the living require to have their versions of events presented in good faith, assuming as far as possible that they grasped the genuine mainsprings of their actions, and forbearing to override their views in the light of later hypotheses. At the same time, as we have said, the historian who comes after has the added task of judging men and events in a wider perspective, of assigning their relative importance in a more comprehensive scheme. This latter involves a framework beyond the view of the participants, in which the historian without neglecting the authority of their accounts must nevertheless assign them place. In this sense history is always philosophical and comparative, viewing each particular situation in relation to a multitude of others that follow and precede it, setting it against a scale of values and a total conception of things.

In sum, our argument has rejected history as written in purely existential terms, presenting man as wholly a part and product of nature. For any such account by man of himself and his origin from a vast panorama of geologic changes, evolutionary biology, microphysical and astronomical events, which he has never seen, involves a transcendent metaphysical sweep contradictory to its purportedly empirical authority. There is no question but that the naturalist's tale offers a magnificent cosmic story. The only trouble is the conflict between its method and its findings, its theory of what we know and what we are, the gulf between man as a beast and as a god. How could this microscopic bit of dust, this feeble carnivore driven by clamorous needs, empirically encompass the macrocosm? Surely this frail creature of an hour could no more reabsorb the creative process than a fish could swim through all the seven seas or drink the ocean dry. This radical inconsistency at the basis of naturalism accounts for the tendency among those who have reflected most upon the subject to adopt a transcendental view. For the historian, whether he wishes to or not, claims pretensions not unlike those of divinity: power to review the past forward or backward, to survey the globe, and to grasp through the comprehensiveness of mind an order of purpose and grounds beyond mere efficient causality. At bottom he cannot but allow that man in his range of meanings and personal life reaches out to a genuine value world incompressible to natural existence. Moreover, in his inquiry the historian often puts his trust not in the purported genetic sequence but in the analytic order or that of logical dependence. Instead of always following the course of temporal duration, he often reverses it, passing by causal regress from later events to the earlier, or again (as when he finds economic dependent on geographic factors or democracy incompatible with dictatorship) he treats history as a logical structure. While all three orders mingle in his study, it is nonetheless evident that the non-historical underlies and supports the historical pattern, since it is finally upon the order of evidence that his acceptance of the causal succession and temporal sequence rests.

INDEX